About the Author

Jason R. Rich (www.JasonRich.com) is the best-selling author of more than 55 books covering a wide range of topics. Some of his recently published books include: *How to Do Everything: MacBook Air* (McGraw-Hill Professional, 2012), *How to Do Everything: iPhone 5* (McGraw-Hill Professional, 2012), *How to Do Everything: Digital Photography* (McGraw-Hill Professional, 2011), *How to Do Everything: Kindle Fire* (McGraw-Hill Professional, 2012), *Your iPad 2 at Work: Third Edition* (Que), *iPad and iPhone Tips and Tricks: Second Edition* (Que), and *The Ultimate Guide to YouTube for Business* (Entrepreneur Press).

To read more than 175 feature-length how-to articles about the iPhone and iPad, visit www.iOSArticles.com, and click on the Articles tab. Jason's work also appears in a wide range of other national magazines, major daily newspapers, and popular websites.

Please follow Jason R. Rich on Twitter (@JasonRich7), or if you're an iOS mobile device user, be sure to check out his blog, *Jason Rich's Featured App of the Week*, to learn about new and innovative iPhone and iPad apps (www.FeaturedAppOfTheWeek.com).

About the Technical Editor

Joshua Fleetwood has been taking things apart since he learned to crawl. As he acquired better and better motor skills, he even learned to put them back together occasionally. While actually a superhero, he daylights as a mild-mannered computer technician and photographer in Boston.

How to Do
Everything™

iCloud®
Second Edition

Jason R. Rich

New York Chicago San Francisco
Athens London Madrid Mexico City
Milan New Delhi Singapore Sydney Toronto

Cataloging-in-Publication Data is on file with the Library of Congress

McGraw-Hill Education books are available at special quantity discounts to use as premiums and sales promotions, or for use in corporate training programs. To contact a representative, please visit the Contact Us pages at www.mhprofessional.com.

How to Do Everything™: iCloud®, Second Edition

1234567890 QFR QFR 10987654

ISBN   978-0-07-182504-7
MHID   0-07-182504-5

Sponsoring Editor Roger Stewart	**Technical Editor** Joshua Fleetwood	**Composition** Cenveo Publisher Services
Editorial Supervisor Jody McKenzie	**Copy Editor** Lunaea Weatherstone	**Illustration** Cenveo Publisher Services
Project Manager Nidhi Chopra, Cenveo® Publisher Services	**Proofreader** Paul Tyler	**Art Director, Cover** Jeff Weeks
Acquisitions Coordinator Amanda Russell	**Indexer** Valerie Perry	**Cover Designer** Jeff Weeks
	Production Supervisor James Kussow	

This book is dedicated to the late Steve Jobs,
as well as to my niece Natalie, and my former foster son, Nick.

Contents at a Glance

Contents

x Contents

xii   Contents

Acknowledgments

Thanks to my former editor Megg Morin for inviting me to work on the first edition of this book, and to Roger Stewart at McGraw-Hill Education for inviting me to work on this all-new second edition. It's great to be working with Roger again! Thanks also to Amanda Russell, and everyone else at McGraw-Hill who contributed their talents and publishing know-how as this book was being created.

My gratitude also goes out to Joshua Fleetwood for lending his expertise to this project. He truly is an Apple "genius" in every sense of the word.

I'd also like to thank everyone at Apple who helped to create iCloud, as well as the iPhone, iPad, iMac, MacBook, Apple TV, and the other computers and devices I spend so much of my days using.

Thanks also to my friends and family for their endless support and encouragement. A special thank you and shout-out goes out to Nick O'Brien. Nick: Please know that wherever our paths lead in the future, you will always be an important part of my life and be considered a part of my family.

Introduction

This all-new second edition of *How to Do Everything: iCloud* provides a comprehensive overview of iCloud's features, plus offers step-by-step directions on how to use each of these features, including Shared Photo Streams, the iWork for iCloud apps, and iCloud Keychain, which were among the newest features added to Apple's online service in conjunction with the release of the OS X Mavericks operating system (Mac) and iOS 7 operating system (iPhone, iPad, and iPod touch).

Keep in mind, all of the content in this book focuses on how to use iCloud in conjunction with a Mac that's running OS X Mavericks or iOS mobile devices that are running the latest version of iOS 7. If you have an Apple TV device, it too will need to be running the latest version of its own operating system in order to fully utilize all of iCloud's features and functions, which you'll soon be reading about.

The concept of "cloud-based computing" is nothing new or revolutionary. However, as Apple has been developing and improving iCloud, it took the concept of online-based file sharing and cloud-based computing and dramatically improved upon it for its Mac, iOS mobile device, and Apple TV users.

Once iCloud is set up (which you'll learn how to do in this book), you'll discover that it's never been easier to transfer and sync app-specific data, documents, files, photos, music, and other content between your computers and iOS mobile devices (including your iPhone and iPad). In fact, much of the synchronization happens automatically and behind the scenes.

As you're using your iPad to create or edit a document using the Pages word processor, for example, as soon as you're done working with the file, it automatically becomes accessible on your other computers and iOS mobile devices via iCloud. Or if you're out and about, and you update an event with the Calendar app on your iPhone, that modified appointment information will automatically synchronize with your schedule that's maintained on your primary computer, as well as on your other iOS mobile devices. Thanks to iCloud, your files and data will always be up to date.

iCloud is designed primarily for Apple users. It works with all Mac-based computers running the OS X Mavericks operating system. It's also designed to work in conjunction with Apple TV, and all versions of the iPhone and iPad, as well as the more recent models of the iPod touch. As long as each computer or device has Internet connectivity and is linked to the same iCloud account, all of the various iCloud-related features and functions take traditional cloud-based computing and online file sharing to a new level of sophistication and convenience (especially when it comes to transferring and syncing information among your computers and iOS mobile devices).

In addition to the functionality iCloud offers, you can begin using it within minutes, and it's free. Once you set up a free iCloud account, it comes with 5GB of online storage space, an email account, plus as much additional online storage space as is necessary to store your iTunes Store, iBookstore, and App Store content purchases (music, TV show episodes, movies, audiobooks, apps, ebooks, and so on). As you'll soon discover, additional (and unlimited) online storage is also provided for your digital photos.

As soon as your personal iCloud account is set up, everything you've ever purchased from the iTunes Store, iBookstore, or App Store becomes instantly available on all of your computers and iOS mobile devices that are linked to the same iCloud account, without your ever having to repurchase any content.

What's in This Book?

This book covers all you need to know to get the most out of Apple's iCloud service. The book contains 15 chapters, and is divided into five parts.

Part I: Learn About Online File Sharing and Apple's iCloud

- Chapter 1, "Learn About Cloud-Based Online File-Sharing Services," explains the basics of what cloud-based computing offers, and provides an overview of the unique features of Apple's iCloud service.
- Chapter 2, "How Mac Users Can Utilize iCloud," explains the core features of iCloud that can be used by Mac (and in some cases Windows-based PC) users.
- Chapter 3, "How iPhone, iPad, iPad mini, and iPod touch Users Can Utilize iCloud," explains the core features of iCloud that can be used by iOS mobile device users.
- Chapter 4, "How to Use the New OS X Mavericks and iOS 7 iCloud Features," introduces you to everything that's been newly added to the iCloud service, including Shared Photo Streams, iWork for iCloud online apps, iCloud Keychain, and much more.

Part II: Manage Your Music, Multimedia Content, and Photos in the Cloud

- Chapter 5, "Manage Your Digital Music Library and iTunes Purchases," focuses on how to access all of your iTunes Store music purchases from any computer or device that's linked to the same iCloud account.
- Chapter 6, "Use the Premium iTunes Match Service," shows you how to use this fee-based service to access your entire digital music collection (not just iTunes Store music purchases) from all of your computers and iOS devices.

- Chapter 7, "Store and Manage Your Digital Photos with My Photo Stream," explains how to use iCloud's My Photo Stream feature with your own collection of digital photos.
- Chapter 8, "Share Your Digital Images with Others Using Shared Photo Streams," explains everything you need to know to manage and share select groups of your digital images with specific people you choose.

Part III: Share Documents, Music, Data, and More via iCloud

- Chapter 9, "Manage and Sync Your Safari Bookmarks, Reading List, and Passwords," teaches you how to utilize the iCloud-related features available to you as you use the Safari web browser to surf the Internet.
- Chapter 10, "Working with iWork for iCloud," explains how to use the online-based Pages, Numbers, and Keynote apps that are available via the iCloud.com website, in conjunction with the Pages, Numbers, and Keynote apps running on your Mac and iOS mobile devices. You'll also learn how to use Microsoft Office files and documents with the iWork for iCloud apps.

Part IV: Discover More Uses for iCloud When Used with Your Mac and iOS Mobile Devices

- Chapter 11, "Manage Apps, App-Related Data, and Ebooks with iCloud," explains how to sync and share apps and app-specific data among iOS mobile devices and your computers via iCloud.
- Chapter 12, "Back Up Your iPhone and iPad," introduces you to the iCloud Backup feature, which is used to create and maintain a remote backup of your iOS mobile devices.
- Chapter 13, "iCloud and Apple TV: The Perfect Entertainment Combination," shows you how to use your iOS mobile device and/or Mac in conjunction with Apple TV to stream content to your HD television or home theater system.

Part V: Additional iCloud Features and Functions

- Chapter 14, "Locate a Lost Mac, iPhone, iPad, or iPod touch with iCloud's Find My... Feature," explains how to keep tabs on the whereabouts of your compatible Apple equipment, and potentially recover your computers and iOS mobile devices if they get lost or stolen.
- Chapter 15, "Manage Your iCloud Email Account," explains how to utilize the free iCloud-related email account that's provided when you set up your iCloud account.
- Appendix A, "Troubleshoot iCloud-Related Problems," helps you diagnose and solve problems you might encounter when setting up or using iCloud.

Conventions Used in This Book

To help you better understand some of the more complex or technical aspects of using iCloud, as well as focus your attention on particularly useful iCloud-related features and functions, you'll discover Note, Tip, and Caution paragraphs throughout this book that highlight specific tidbits of useful information.

Plus, throughout this book, you'll discover "How To..." and "Did You Know?" sidebars that provide additional topic-related information and advice that pertain to the issues covered in the chapter you're reading.

PART I

Learn About Online File Sharing and Apple's iCloud

1

Learn About Cloud-Based Online File-Sharing Services

HOW TO...

- Learn about Apple's iCloud cloud-based file-sharing service and how it can be used.
- Discover how iCloud has evolved in conjunction with OS X Mavericks and iOS 7.
- Determine whether you want or need to use a cloud-based file-sharing service, such as iCloud.
- Determine what equipment you'll need to use iCloud and how much it costs.

The concept and technology related to cloud-based file-sharing services are nothing new. However, it wasn't until Apple designed and launched its iCloud service that most everyday computer users began discovering how this type of online service can be used. Since it was first launched, iCloud has evolved a lot—and it continues to improve.

As an Apple Mac, iPhone, iPad, iPod touch, and/or Apple TV user, you can begin using iCloud immediately, and you'll probably discover that it makes your everyday computing easier and more reliable.

If you're a Windows-based PC user, you can also take advantage of some of iCloud's functionality and features, especially when it relates to syncing app-specific data (such as your contacts and calendar), iTunes-related purchases, and working with the new iWork for iCloud apps—all of which you'll learn more about later.

How to Do Everything: iCloud, Second Edition is all about how you can best utilize the various features and functions of iCloud, especially if you use more than one computer or mobile device that's compatible with the service. As you're about to discover, as long as each of your compatible computers and mobile devices has Internet access, each can utilize iCloud to handle an ever-growing array of tasks. Plus, once the various features of iCloud are set up and activated, which typically only needs to be done once per device, that feature will work continuously, in the background, and automatically.

First, let's focus on which Apple products iCloud can be used with. Next, we'll explore what a cloud-based service, like iCloud, actually is, and focus a bit on how it works. Then, later in this chapter, you'll read an overview of the specific functions iCloud can be used for in conjunction with your computers and mobile devices. In subsequent chapters, you'll discover exactly how to use each of iCloud's features and functions, based on the computers and mobile devices you'll be using it with.

iCloud Works with Many Apple Products

Just about any Apple computer or iOS mobile device that can connect to the Internet can now utilize one or more of iCloud's features. This includes all of the latest iMac, Mac mini, and Mac Pro desktop computers, as well as MacBook Pro and MacBook Air notebook computers, the iPhone, iPad, iPod touch (3rd generation or later models), and Apple TV. In addition, some iCloud functionality can also be accessed and utilized from a Windows-based PC that's connected to the Internet or directly from the iCloud website.

What you'll soon discover is that if you only use one compatible Apple product or Windows-based PC, iCloud can be used for certain tasks, such as backing up your compatible app-specific files or data, including all of your iTunes Store content purchases. However, iCloud really comes in handy when you use two or more compatible computers or iOS mobile devices (and/or Apple TV). Then iCloud can be used to automatically sync multimedia content (music, TV shows, movies, etc.), apps, digital photos, as well as app-specific data and files, with all compatible devices that are linked to the same Apple ID/iCloud account (including Windows-based PCs).

Apple has integrated iCloud functionality into its latest OS X Mavericks operating system for the Mac, iOS 7 used with its mobile devices, and in the operating system that makes Apple TV function. So the capability for your Apple products to access iCloud already exists. Now you just need to turn on the iCloud features and functions you want to utilize on each of your compatible Apple computers and devices, as well as on your Windows-based PCs, if applicable.

Set Up a Free iCloud Account

To begin using iCloud, you'll need to set up a free account. This is typically done using your existing Apple ID and password, and it only needs to be done once, from a computer or mobile device that's connected to the Internet.

 If you've created an Apple ID in the past, but don't remember your username and password, visit https://appleid.apple.com to access and manage your Apple ID account. This includes the ability to look up your username or retrieve a forgotten password.

How to set up your free iCloud account will be discussed later. What you need to understand right now, however, is that you only need one iCloud account, which you will ultimately be able to utilize from all of your various compatible Apple and Windows-based computers and iOS mobile devices, as well as your Apple TV, if applicable.

Use Your Existing Apple ID to Create Your iCloud Account

For reasons you'll discover later, it's best to use your existing Apple ID information to set up your free iCloud account. This allows all past app, iTunes Store content, iBookstore, and Newsstand purchases to be accessed from any computer or mobile device that's linked to the same Apple ID/iCloud account. Apple has kept detailed information about all of your past Apple-related online purchases (such as music, movies, TV shows, ringtones, and ebooks), and through iCloud, allows you to access that already purchased content from any compatible computer or device that's linked to the Apple ID account you used to initially make the purchase.

What Exactly Is iCloud Anyway?

iCloud is an online-based service that's owned and operated by Apple. It operates in cyberspace ("in the cloud") and is run from many powerful Internet servers that are housed within Apple's massive data centers located around the world.

Unlike other cloud-based file-sharing services, however, iCloud does a lot more than simply allow you to store data on the Web and then retrieve it remotely from various computers or devices that are connected to the Internet.

Yes, among its many uses, iCloud can easily be used as an online-based file-sharing service. However, it's also designed to handle many other tasks, depending on which Apple products it's being used with. One of the things that sets iCloud apart from other cloud-based services is that the functionality it offers is built directly into the operating system of the Apple computer or iOS mobile device you're using.

iCloud functionality is also built into many Mac, iPhone, and iPad apps created by Apple and its third-party developers. Thus, once they're initially set up, many iCloud features are designed to work continuously, automatically, and in the background in conjunction with the apps (programs) you're probably already using or soon will be using.

If you're using some type of Mac or an iPhone, iPad, or iPod touch, the computer or device has some type of internal storage in which the operating system as well as your apps, files, documents, digital photos, data, and other content are stored. If you're using a Mac, for example, you also have the ability to connect an external storage device to that computer, such as a hard drive or USB flash drive, onto which you can store data or create backups of your important data.

Instead of physically connecting an external storage device to your computer or taking advantage of its internal storage, when the device is connected to the Internet you have the ability to store all kinds of data in the cloud, which in this case is Apple's online-based iCloud service. Thus, when content is stored in your iCloud account online, this is often in addition to it being stored in the internal storage of your Mac or iOS mobile device.

When you set up your free iCloud account, it comes with 5GB of online storage space. Any additional online storage you need for your digital photos—or for any purchases you have made in the past or will make in the future from the iTunes Store, App Store, Mac App Store, iBookstore, or Newsstand—is automatically provided free of charge. Thus, the 5GB of online storage that's provided can be used to store your personal backup files or app-specific data, for example.

Note   If you need additional online storage space for your personal data, documents, and files, beyond the 5GB that's provided, it can be purchased for an annual fee.

Think of iCloud and other cloud-based file-sharing services as a way to store copies of important files, documents, photos, and data from your computer (or an iOS mobile device) in cyberspace (the cloud). So when your computer or device is connected to the Web, files and data can be uploaded, either automatically or manually, to the cloud-based service. At the same time, your computer or device can securely download files and data from the cloud as needed. This is in addition to storing all of the content in the computer or device's internal storage, such as a Mac's hard/flash drive. Easily sharing and synchronizing files, documents, photos, and data is what cloud-based computing is all about. However, iCloud is capable of doing much more than just that.

Note   Many cloud-based file-sharing services are available to consumers. Dropbox, for example, can be used for sharing general files and documents, as well as photos. Amazon Cloud Drive is more specialized. It allows you to store and access Amazon music purchases while managing your digital music library, as well as other content and files. Microsoft SkyDrive can be used to manage your Microsoft Office files and documents in the cloud, while Adobe's Creative Cloud can be used to share and sync images and artwork that are created using popular Adobe applications, such as Photoshop.

In its most basic form, a cloud-based file-sharing service allows you to create and maintain a remote backup or copy of your data and files. If your computer or device gets damaged, lost, or stolen, a copy of your important information is always safely and securely stored on a web-based server in cyberspace (the cloud).

As you'll discover, cloud-based file-sharing services, particularly Apple iCloud, offer a handful of features and functions that are designed to make much of what you do on your Mac, iPhone, and iPad more efficient and easier. Using iCloud, you can more easily share and sync data between computers and iOS mobile devices that you frequently use.

Did You Know?

Terms Used Often in This Book

In this book, any mention of iOS mobile devices refers to any and all models of the iPhone, iPad, or iPod touch (3rd generation or later). References to iTunes Store purchases refer to music, TV shows, movies, and ringtones, for example, purchased or acquired for free from Apple's iTunes Store, as well as ebooks from iBookstore, digital publications from Apple's Newsstand, Mac apps acquired from the Mac App Store, and iOS mobile device apps acquired from the App Store.

Note   Taking advantage of iCloud requires no programming knowledge whatsoever. Apple has introduced many new ways that everyday computer users can easily utilize cloud-based computing without having to pay a fortune or become more computer savvy than they already are.

What iCloud Can Do

iCloud is designed to work seamlessly with the tasks you handle every day on your Mac, iPhone, iPad, iPod touch, and/or Apple TV. Let's take a look at some of the ways iCloud may be immediately useful to you.

iCloud Works with iTunes

Every time you make a purchase from the iTunes Store, App Store (for your iOS mobile device), Mac App Store, iBookstore, or Apple Newsstand, which are all online businesses operated by Apple, a copy of the digital purchase is automatically stored in your iCloud account. That content can later be downloaded to any computer or compatible device that's linked to the same iCloud account.

Figure 1-1 shows the iCloud icons displayed next to content that's already been purchased by the user and that can be downloaded (for no additional fee) to the computer (or in this case, the mobile device) the user is working on. This includes free content you acquire from one of Apple's online business ventures. This free content gets treated like purchased content.

So if you purchase a song, album, ringtone, TV show episode, or movie from the iTunes Store using your iPhone, for example, a copy of what you purchased automatically gets stored in your iCloud account at the same time it gets downloaded to the device it was purchased on. It can then either automatically or manually (depending on how you have adjusted the related settings) be downloaded to your Mac, iPad, iPod touch, or streamed to Apple TV. You will not have to repurchase the content multiple times. If you later delete the purchase from the device it was purchased on, you can redownload your purchases at any time.

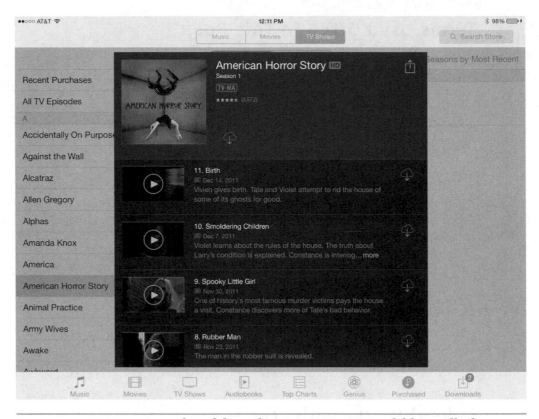

FIGURE 1-1 Content purchased from the iTunes Store is available on all of your devices that are linked to the same Apple ID/iCloud account.

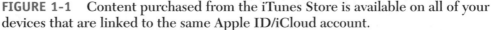

Note See Chapter 5 for more information on how to use this iCloud functionality and to learn more about how you can benefit from it.

Just as iCloud keeps track of all of your iTunes Store purchases, it does the same for all of your Mac App Store and App Store (for iOS) purchases. As a result, if you purchase an iPhone/iPad hybrid app on your iPhone, for example, you can download that same app onto your iPad for no additional fee. Plus, if you ever delete the app from one or more of your devices, you can always reinstall it, for free, via iCloud.

When it comes to managing your personal ebook library (the books you purchase from Apple's iBookstore service), once you purchase an ebook (or download a free ebook), it becomes part of your digital book library, a copy of which is automatically maintained in your iCloud account. Thus, you can use the free iBooks app on any of your Macs or iOS mobile devices that are linked to the same iCloud account to download or redownload any of your past ebook purchases.

iCloud keeps track of your bookmarks as you're reading an ebook. Any time you exit out of iBooks while reading, the page where you left off gets synced with iCloud. You can then continue reading that same ebook on another computer or device and pick up exactly where you left off.

Manage Your Entire Music Library with Premium iTunes Match Service

The free iCloud service can be used to manage all of your digital music purchases that you acquire from the iTunes Store, and then allows you to sync that music with all of your compatible devices that are linked to the same iCloud account. For an annual fee, you can upgrade to the premium iTunes Match service.

iTunes Match allows you to manage and sync your entire digital music library, including music you "rip" from your own audio CDs, music you compose using GarageBand, and music you purchase or download from other online sources.

  In Chapter 6, you'll learn all about the benefits of iTunes Match and discover how to use this fee-based iCloud service.

Store, View, and Share Your Photos Online

The Mac comes with the iPhoto app built in, but it can be upgraded to Apple's Aperture software if you need additional photo organization and editing capabilities. In addition to storing your images on your computer, up to 1,000 of your most recently shot images can be stored online in your iCloud My Photo Stream. Those images can then be accessed from any Mac, Windows-based PC, iOS mobile device, or Apple TV that's linked to the same account.

However, if you want to be able to share groups of digital images with other people, you can take advantage of iCloud's Shared Photo Stream feature. This allows you to create an unlimited number of online galleries (each of which can contain an unlimited number of images), and then invite specific people via email to view your digital photo galleries online—without giving them full access to the rest of your iCloud account.

Figure 1-2 shows a Shared Photo Stream that was created on a Mac, but that's being viewed on an iPad mini. Shared Photo Streams are a great way to share groups of photos online with specific people whom you choose and ultimately invite to view your images.

iCloud Can Make Surfing the Web Easier Too

Apple's web browser, called Safari, comes bundled with OS X Mavericks and iOS 7. It also nicely and automatically integrates with iCloud. Using this functionality when you're surfing the Web, you can create a comprehensive list of bookmarks, manage your favorites bar, or add web pages to your Reading List. All of this saved content

FIGURE 1-2   A Shared Photo Stream is an online gallery that you can invite people to view without giving them access to the rest of your iCloud account.

will then automatically sync with iCloud and become almost instantly available on any other computer or iOS mobile device that's also running Safari (or a compatible web browser).

Tip   Your open tabbed web browser windows within Safari can also be synced, so you can begin viewing a web page on one computer, and then switch to another computer or device that's linked to your iCloud account in order to pick up exactly where you left off.

Thus, a fully updated listing of your favorite bookmarked websites, for example, is always available on any computer or device that's linked to the same iCloud account. In addition, one of the new features added to iCloud is called iCloud Keychain. Now, any time you enter a username or password in order to log in to a website, iCloud will remember that log-in information (if you turn on this feature), and automatically log you in to that website every time you visit it. You no longer need to remember countless usernames and passwords in order to visit and revisit your most frequented websites.

Use iCloud to Back Up and Sync App-Specific Data

OS X Mavericks, as well as iOS 7, comes bundled with a handful of apps, including Contacts, Calendar, Reminders, and Notes. All of these apps fully integrate with iCloud. When you turn on iCloud functionality to work with Contacts on each of your compatible computers and iOS mobile devices, for example, the service will automatically sync your personal contacts database and keep it up to date, in almost real time.

As a result, if you create a new contact entry on your iPhone using the Contacts app, that new entry will get uploaded to iCloud and then automatically be synced with the version of Contacts that's running on your Macs and/or iPad. This app-specific data syncing also works with Calendar, Reminders, and Notes, as long as each device is linked to the Internet and you've turned on the iCloud functionality on each computer or device.

Another way iCloud can be used in conjunction with the Contacts, Calendar, Reminders, and Notes apps is to use any computer's web browser to visit www.iCloud .com. From this website, you can log in using your Apple ID and password, and then have full access to online-based versions of these apps (shown in Figure 1-3), which will all be populated with your own data. Thus, even if you forget your iPhone at home, you can still access your complete Contacts database, your personal schedule (stored within Calendar), your to-do lists (created using Reminders), and your digital notes (stored within Notes) directly from the Internet.

FIGURE 1-3   The iCloud website features fully functional, online-based versions of apps which you can access from any compatible web browser.

iCloud Can Be Used in Conjunction with the iWork Apps

Similar iCloud integration, which includes file, document, and data syncing, is also built into Apple's optional iWork apps, including Pages (for word processing), Numbers (for spreadsheet management), and Keynote (for digital slide presentations). Versions of these three iWork apps are available for the Mac, as well as for the iPhone and iPad. As of October 2013, Apple offers all versions of the iWork apps for free, and they are all fully compatible with one another. For example, whether you use Pages on the Mac, on your iPhone, on your iPad, or access the online version (which will be explained shortly), your documents will all be automatically synchronized and accessible. Plus, the latest version of these iWork apps allow for document or file collaboration with other people via iCloud.

When you turn on iCloud functionality in any or all of these apps, your work will automatically be backed up to iCloud and synced with your other computers or mobile devices that you have the iWork apps installed on.

One of the newest features of iCloud is called iWork for iCloud. It includes fully functional, online versions of Pages, Numbers, and Keynote, which you can access and use from any compatible Mac or Windows-based web browser, such as Safari (Mac), Microsoft Internet Explorer (Windows), or Chrome (PC/Mac). These apps can be accessed by visiting www.iCloud.com, and by logging in using your Apple ID and password.

Note How to use the iWork for iCloud apps (Pages, Numbers, and Keynote) is covered in Chapter 10.

Use iCloud to Track the Exact Location of Your Mac, iPhone, or iPad

If your iPhone, iPad, iPod touch, or even your MacBook Air gets lost or stolen, as long as it's turned on and can connect to the Internet, the Find My iPhone/iPad/Mac feature that's built into iCloud will display a detailed map that shows the exact location of your equipment. Once the computer or device is located, the Find My iPhone/iPad/Mac feature (or optional app) offers a handful of options to password-protect the device, erase its content, or lock it down so a thief can't easily resell or use it. Shown in Figure 1-4 is the iPhone version of the free Find My iPhone app, which shows some of the options you can use to recover or lock down your computer or device once it has been located.

The nice thing about the Find My iPhone/iPad/Mac feature is that it only needs to be turned on once per device.

FIGURE 1-4 The Find My iPhone app is shown here running on the iPhone. You can also visit www.cloud.com/#find to access similar device location functionality.

Note See Chapter 14 for more information about how to use this useful iCloud feature.

Caution As you will discover, access to iCloud, as well as your iTunes Store, App Store, Mac App Store, iBookstore, and Apple Newsstand purchases, and your FaceTime and iMessage usernames, are all associated with your Apple ID (which you must link with a major credit card or debit card in order to make online or in-app purchases). Your Apple ID is also used in conjunction with the Find My iPhone/iPad/Mac feature. Thus, it is essential that you keep the password associated with your Apple ID confidential. Otherwise, someone could access your private files stored on iCloud, make online purchases, and even track your exact whereabouts in real time.

Maintain Full Backups of Your iOS Mobile Devices Using iCloud

Maintaining a full backup of your iPhone or iPad is essential for a variety of reasons, which we'll discuss in Chapter 12. To create and maintain a backup, you can connect your iOS mobile device to your primary computer via the supplied USB cable, and then use the iTunes Sync backup feature. In this case, your iOS mobile device's backup files will be stored on your primary computer's hard drive. However, you can also automatically create and maintain a backup of your mobile device wirelessly using the iCloud Backup feature.

The benefit to using iCloud Backup is that if you ever need to restore your mobile device, this can be done from anywhere there's a Wi-Fi Internet connection. Your primary computer is not needed, since the backup files are securely stored in the cloud.

Once the iCloud Backup feature is activated, a backup will be created automatically once per day, as long as your iOS mobile device is connected to the Internet via Wi-Fi, plugged into an external power source, and in sleep mode. You can manually create an updated backup at any time from within Settings (as shown in Figure 1-5). How to do this is covered in Chapter 12.

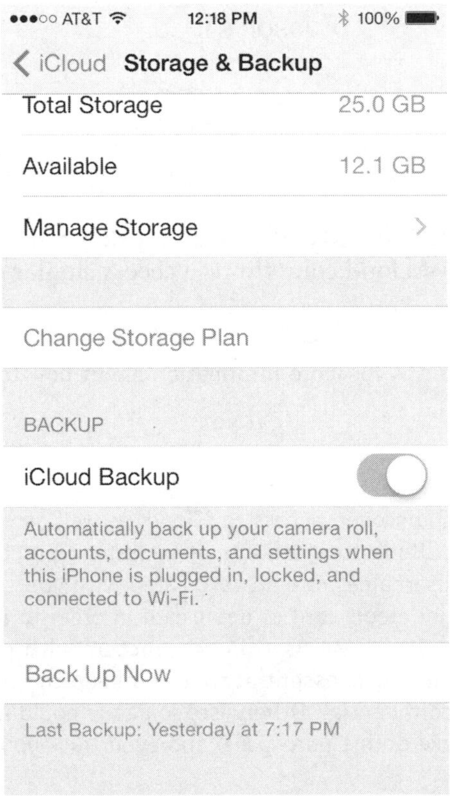

FIGURE 1-5 Tap the Back Up Now option to manually create a backup of your iOS mobile device from within Settings.

iCloud Comes with Its Own Email Account

As soon as you establish your free iCloud account, you'll be given a free email account. This email account can be used with the Mail app that's built into OS X Mavericks or iOS 7, or you can manage this email account directly from the iCloud.com website.

When it comes to using your iCloud email account (username@icloud.com), iCloud automatically syncs your incoming and outgoing messages, as well as your various message folders across all of the computers and devices that are linked to the same iCloud account. Keep in mind, however, that this functionality only works with your iCloud email account, not with the other email accounts you may utilize in conjunction with the Mail app.

Note   You'll learn how to use your iCloud email account in Chapter 15.

iCloud Works Nicely with Apple TV Too

Apple TV (www.apple.com/appletv) is one of Apple's least hyped devices, yet it's one of the more useful, especially for people who purchase iTunes Store content or opt to utilize iCloud's My Photo Stream and Shared Photo Stream features.

Apple TV, which costs just $99, connects directly to your HD television set and the Internet. It allows you to acquire, sync, and watch (or listen to) iTunes Store content on your HD television, as well as access your iCloud My Photo Stream and Shared Photo Streams and view your digital images on your HD television.

Note   See Chapter 13 for more information on how to use Apple TV in conjunction with iCloud, as well as your Macs and iOS mobile devices.

Pick and Choose Which iCloud Features You Want to Use

Apple has taken the cloud-based file-sharing concept, vastly improved upon it, added features, and created a service that works seamlessly with its Mac desktop and notebook computers, as well as iPhones, iPad tablets, iPod touch, and Apple TV devices. What sets iCloud apart from other cloud-based services is that iCloud fully integrates with OS X and iOS 7, and you can pick and choose which features and functions you want to utilize, as well as on which Apple devices you want to use those features.

For example, if you have no interest in syncing your digital photos with your various computers and mobile devices, and don't need a way to share your digital photos with others via online galleries, you can turn off the iCloud My Photo Stream and Shared Photo Stream options and never have to deal with them.

In reality, most people will not want or need to use all of the functionality that iCloud offers. You can choose which features will be most useful to you and then customize those features. You can turn off the features you're not interest in using. Options for personalizing and turning on and off individual iCloud features are discussed throughout this book.

Tip   It's important to understand that while iCloud can work seamlessly with all of your Macs, Windows-based PCs, iOS mobile devices, and Apple TV, each iCloud feature must be turned on and customized on each of your computers and devices separately. For example, if you want your Contacts database on your Mac to sync with your iPhone and iPad, you must turn on this feature on all three devices individually.

Note   Keep in mind that iCloud was designed primarily for everyday computer users, not for business applications. If you're operating a midsize to large business, and you want to tap into what cloud-based computing offers, another cloud-based file-sharing service will probably be more appropriate. However, you may still find certain iCloud features, such as iWork for iCloud, very useful.

Yes, iCloud is one of many cloud-based file-sharing services available, and while the specific focus of this book is on Apple's iCloud service, you'll also learn about some of the other useful cloud-based file-sharing services available to consumers.

Plus, if you're a Windows-based PC user, you'll soon discover that more and more iCloud features are available to you as well, even though your computer is running the Microsoft Windows operating system. In some cases, you'll need to install free Apple software on your Windows PC in order to add iCloud functionality and integration.

Tip   To download the free iCloud Control Panel software onto your Windows-based PC, visit http://www.apple.com/icloud/setup/pc.html. You'll learn how to utilize this software later in the book.

Remember, once iCloud is set up to work with your computers and iOS mobile devices, most of its functionality works automatically in the background. Your computer or device will upload and download relevant data or files to and from iCloud as needed.

Did You Know?   **You Must Have Internet Access to Use iCloud**

To use iCloud, or any cloud-based file-sharing service, your computer or device must have access to the Internet. If you're using iCloud with an iOS mobile device, such as an iPhone or iPad, some of iCloud's functions will work using a 3G or 4G (LTE) cellular Internet connection. However, to use all of iCloud's functionality for file sharing, data backup, and synchronizing data, a Wi-Fi Internet connection is necessary.

Discover What Using a Cloud-Based File-Sharing Service Costs

In addition to offering many different features and uses that have now been fully integrated into your Mac or iOS device's operating system, as well as popular software and apps you're probably already using, Apple has made getting started with iCloud extremely inexpensive. In fact, it's free!

As you learned earlier, when you set up a free iCloud account, you're given immediate access to 5GB of online storage space, plus an unlimited amount of extra online storage space for all of your iTunes Store, iBookstore, App Store, Mac App Store, and Apple Newsstand purchases, plus your digital photos.

Not only does this provide you with an automatic backup of the content you purchase or download from Apple, it also makes that content available to all of your Mac computers and iOS devices, as well as your Apple TV device, and in some cases your Windows-based PC, for no additional charge. Sharing music and apps among computers and mobile devices is only one of the features built into iCloud.

For most people, the features and functionality offered using a free iCloud account will be more than adequate. However, if your online storage needs go beyond 5GB, you can purchase additional storage space for an annual fee. An additional 10GB of online storage costs $20 per year (giving you 15GB of online storage space total). You can purchase 20GB of extra storage space for $40 per year, or 50GB of extra storage space for $100 per year.

Note Purchasing additional online storage space on iCloud can be done directly from your Mac, iPhone, or iPad. The fee associated with the extra online storage space will be billed to the credit or debit card that's linked to your Apple ID account.

To upgrade your online storage capacity from your iPhone or iPad, for example, launch the Settings app from the Home screen, and then from the main Settings menu, tap the iCloud option. When the Storage & Backup screen appears within Settings, tap the Buy More Storage option. Then, from the Buy More Storage window, tap the amount of storage you want (as shown in Figure 1-6). Your in-app purchase will be charged directly to the credit or debit card that's associated with your Apple ID, and the additional storage space will instantly become available to you.

If you want to make your entire digital music collection available to your computers and devices (including content that was not purchased through the iTunes Store), you can upgrade to the iTunes Match service for $24.99 per year.

Note If you plan to use many of the features offered by iCloud and maintain complete backups of two or more iOS mobile devices via your iCloud account, chances are you'll need to add to the 5GB of free online storage that's provided. However, if you're using iCloud with just your Mac and one iOS mobile device, for example, chances are the 5GB of online storage that's provided will be adequate.

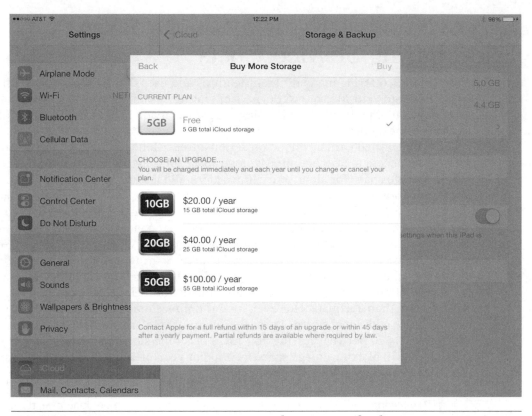

FIGURE 1-6   At any time, you can increase the amount of online storage space available to you on iCloud for an annual fee.

What You'll Need to Start Using iCloud with a Mac

What will be required to begin using iCloud will depend in part on how you'll be using it. If you're a Mac user, you'll first need to upgrade to OS X Mavericks in order to be able to utilize all of iCloud's newest features. You can upgrade your OS X from Lion or Mountain Lion to Mavericks directly from the Mac App Store. The upgrade is free.

In addition, you'll need to upgrade some of your Mac's software (apps) to the latest versions. You can do this by clicking the Apple logo icon that's displayed in the upper-left corner of your Mac's screen, and then clicking the Software Update option.

 You can also update Mac software (apps) by launching the Mac App Store and then clicking the Updates button that's displayed near the top-center of the screen.

Beyond upgrading your Mac's operating system and making sure your Mac is running the most recent version of the iTunes software, if you'll be using iCloud to create a My Photo Stream or Shared Photo Stream, you'll need to upgrade to the latest version of iPhoto. Meanwhile, if you want to use iCloud to keep your iWork files and documents synchronized, and be able to easily share those files and documents with your other Macs and iOS mobile devices, upgrading to the latest versions of Pages, Numbers, and Keynote will be necessary, on both your Macs and your iOS mobile devices.

Note Many third-party software developers are also now making their applications iCloud-compatible. Thus, it may be necessary to upgrade to the latest versions of those software packages (apps) as well.

The good news is that updates to all of Apple's operating systems and apps, including those apps that are part of iLife and iWork, are free. These software updates are necessary to use much of the new functionality built into iCloud. (Before updating your OS X or any software, be sure to create a backup of the computer. On a Mac, this can easily be done using Time Machine.)

Note When you upgrade to OS X Mavericks on your existing Mac, or purchase and begin using a new Mac and set up the computer for the first time, you will be prompted to either set up a free iCloud account or link your existing iCloud account to your Mac, using your Apple ID. At any time, however, you can create a new iCloud account or link your existing iCloud account to your Mac. To do this, launch System Preferences and click the iCloud icon.

What You'll Need to Start Using iCloud with an iPhone or iPad

Your Apple iPhone, iPad, or iPod touch operates using Apple's cutting-edge iOS operating system, which is among the most powerful and robust operating systems available for any mobile devices. In October 2013, iOS 7 was released, providing iPhone, iPad, and iPod touch users with the most significant upgrade to the iOS operating system yet. Literally hundreds of new features, including better integration with iCloud, along with a nice selection of preinstalled apps, are part of iOS 7. In addition, the look and user interface of iOS 7 has been completely revamped and updated.

When you begin using iOS 7 for the first time, you'll be prompted to set up a free iCloud account, or you can easily link to your existing iCloud account with your iOS mobile device using your Apple ID. However, to use some of iCloud's features, you will need to adjust settings on your iPhone, iPad, or iPod touch, and make sure the apps that are compatible with iCloud (such as Pages, Numbers, and Keynote) also get updated to the most current versions.

Once you have the latest version of iOS 7, and install other iCloud-compatible apps onto your iOS mobile device, you'll need to adjust certain settings manually. In many cases, you'll use the Settings app that can be launched from your mobile device's Home screen. You may also need to adjust iCloud-related settings when using specific apps. How and when to adjust the various iCloud-related settings on your iOS mobile devices and in the apps running on your devices will be explained in applicable chapters of this book.

Let's Get Started

Just reading about the various features offered by iCloud may have already set off a light bulb in your mind, as you contemplate the various ways this service will soon be helpful to you. Although you'll find plenty of other cloud-based file-sharing services out there, none have been integrated into the core operating system of your computer or device, and none (other than iCloud) have managed to keep the service easy to use and extremely customizable based on how you personally use your computer or iOS mobile device.

When set up and used correctly, iCloud can provide a secure and reliable remote backup option for your compatible app-specific data and files, plus ensure that the data and files you need are readily available to you on whatever iCloud-compatible computer or device you're using. iCloud will also ensure that you can always listen to and watch your iTunes Store purchased content on any compatible device, as long as a web connection is present.

Welcome to the world of cloud-based computing, where your important files, documents, photos, data, and content get remotely stored on an online-based server via the Internet, and become continuously accessible from multiple computers and mobile devices linked to the same Apple ID/iCloud account.

Since so many Mac users have also become iPhone and iPad users, and a growing number of these people have discovered what Apple TV offers to their home entertainment system, the need to keep data, files, documents, photos, and multimedia content synced is more important than ever, and iCloud makes this possible.

Caution If you opt to access your iCloud account using someone else's computer (from an Internet café or a hotel's business center, for example), and you access www.iCloud.com in order to use the online versions of Contacts, Calendar, Reminder, Notes, Mail, Pages, Numbers, and Keynote, make sure you log off from the iCloud.com website when you're done in order to prevent unauthorized people from accessing your iCloud account and your personal data.

2

How Mac Users Can Utilize iCloud

HOW TO...

- Set up your Macs to work with iCloud using OS X Mavericks.
- Activate the Back to My Mac feature of iCloud.
- Use the Find My Mac feature of iCloud.
- Share data, files, and documents between Macs (such as an iMac and MacBook).

In the process of developing the latest OS X Mavericks operating system for the Mac, Apple continued to incorporate iCloud functionality into its operating system. For people who enjoy music, for example, iCloud makes it extremely easy to share all of your iTunes Store music purchases among all of the computers and mobile devices that are linked to the same iCloud account, without your having to repurchase the same songs multiple times.

Did You Know?

You Need to Create an iCloud Account and Log into It with Your Mac

Before you can begin using an iCloud account with your Mac, you'll need to set up the free account (just once). Then sign into that iCloud account from the Mac you're using. Once the Mac is linked to your iCloud account, it's possible to turn on and activate the individual iCloud features and functions you want to use.

To link your existing iCloud account with your Mac, from the Dock, launch System Preferences. Next, click the iCloud icon. When prompted, enter your Apple ID (or the email address used to create the iCloud account) and the corresponding password.

Much of iCloud's functionality is designed to make wireless communication between your Macs and iOS mobile devices more efficient, since iCloud allows you to exchange data, documents, and files via the Web, rather than using the iTunes Sync process. If you're a Mac user but have not yet invested in an iPhone, iPad, or iPod touch, you can still use iCloud for a variety of tasks, some of which are described in this chapter.

Manage Your Music via iCloud

In Chapter 5, you'll discover that all your past iTunes Store music purchases are immediately accessible from iCloud, using any of your computers and iOS mobile devices that are linked to the same iCloud account. Using the iTunes software to access the iTunes Store on your Mac, it's easy to see a listing of all your past purchases (as shown in Figure 2-1).

It's possible to set up your Macs—including your iMac or Mac Pro desktop computer and/or your MacBook Pro or MacBook Air notebook computer—so that any time you purchase any new music from the iTunes Store, on any computer or iOS mobile device, it will immediately be downloaded and stored on all of your separate Macs or iOS devices. By default, iCloud can be used to easily and automatically synchronize and share your iTunes Store purchases.

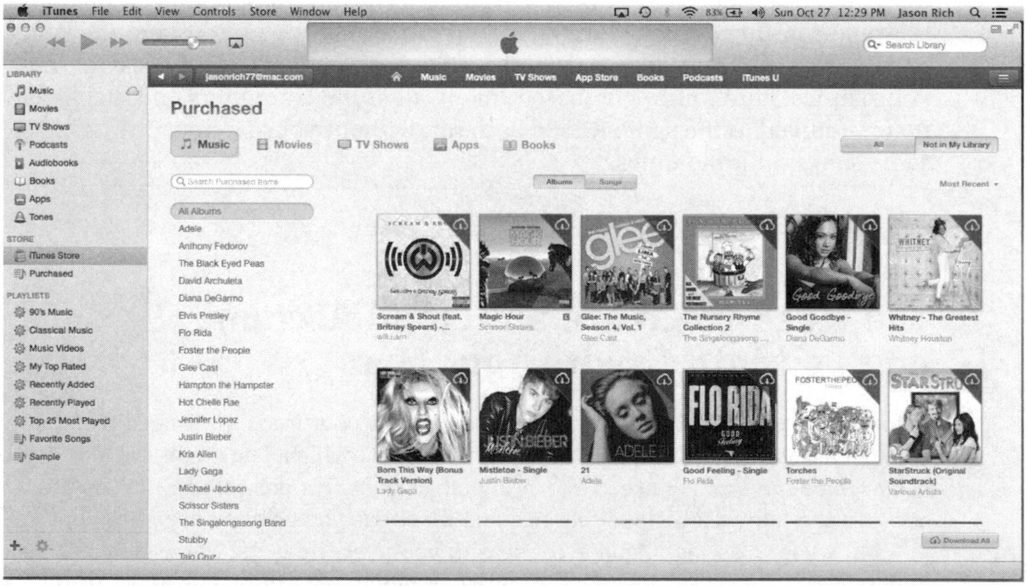

FIGURE 2-1 View a listing of all iTunes Store purchases, even if they were purchased from another computer or iOS mobile device.

How to... Set Up iCloud to Automatically Sync Music Purchases with Your Macs

To quickly set up iCloud so that it syncs your music library automatically as you acquire new music from the iTunes Store, follow these steps:

1. After you have set up a free iCloud account and have set it up to work with your Mac, launch the iTunes software on your Mac.
2. From the iTunes pull-down menu that's displayed near the top-left corner of the screen, select the Preferences option.
3. Click the Store option that's displayed near the top-center of the General Preferences window.

Store option

4. Near the top of the Store Preferences window, add a checkmark to the checkbox that's associated with the Always Check For Available Downloads option.

(Continued)

5. Under the heading Automatic Downloads in the Store Preferences window, add a checkmark to the checkbox that says Music. If you also want the iTunes software to download and sync all of your newly acquired apps (Mac software) and ebook purchases (from iBookstore), add checkmarks to the checkboxes labeled Music, Apps, and Books as well. (The Books option will only appear if you use iBookstore.)

Automatic Downloads options

6. Look toward the bottom of the Store Preferences window and add checkmarks to the checkboxes associated with any of the additional user-adjustable options to customize what content is downloaded and displayed when using the iTunes software.
7. Click OK to save your changes.
8. Repeat this process on each of your Macs that are linked to the same iCloud account.

If you invest $24.99 per year to subscribe to the iTunes Match service, all of your music, including songs and albums not purchased from the iTunes Store, can be stored in your iCloud account and made available on all of your computers and iOS devices. This includes music you "rip" from your own music CDs, acquire from other online music services (such as Amazon.com Music), or that you compose using Apple's GarageBand software, for example.

Note   Chapter 6 shows you how to use the iTunes Match service.

Manually Access Past iTunes Store Purchases via iCloud

In addition to music that's been purchased from the iTunes Store, you can use iCloud to access any other content that you've previously purchased, such as TV show episodes, movies, or music videos. This includes purchases made on other computers or devices using the same Apple ID used to create your iCloud account.

If you choose to skip turning on the automatic syncing and downloading of new content purchased from the iTunes Store feature, you can still manually access your past iTunes Store purchases. To do this from a Mac, launch the latest version of the iTunes software (version 11 or later) and click the iTunes Store option that's displayed on the left side of the screen under the Store heading (shown in Figure 2-2). Then, under the Quick Links heading on the right side of the iTunes screen, shown here, click the Purchased option.

iTunes Store option   Purchased option

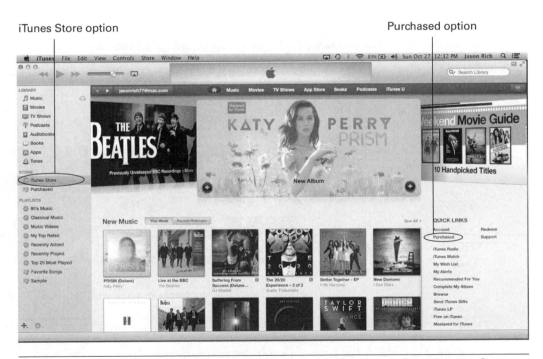

FIGURE 2-2   The online-based iTunes Store is accessible using the iTunes software on your Mac.

When the Purchased screen is displayed, near the top of the screen select the type of purchased content you want to find and download, such as Music, Movies, TV Shows, Apps, or Books (as shown in Figure 2-3). If you click TV Shows, for example, on the left side of the Purchased screen, the names of each TV series that you've purchased episodes of in the past will be displayed.

Click a TV series name to reveal individual episodes (or entire seasons' worth of episodes) that you've already purchased (as shown in Figure 2-4). On the right side of the screen, click the TV series icon to reveal individual episode listings that you can download.

If the episode is not already stored on the Mac you're currently using, to the right of each episode listing will be a Download button. Click it to download that specific episode. Once downloaded, the episode will be added to your iTunes library on the Mac you're using, so you can watch that show anytime. Keep in mind that the TV show file will be saved on your Mac's hard drive and will be accessible from the computer you're using until you manually delete the file.

After the TV show, movie, or music that was originally acquired from the iTunes Store is transferred to your Mac, you can watch or listen to it using the iTunes software. An Internet connection is no longer required.

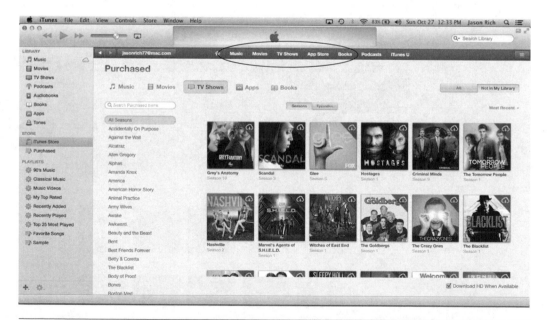

FIGURE 2-3 Click the type of purchased content you want to access. Shown here are purchased TV show episodes.

FIGURE 2-4   Click a TV series name to see a listing of episodes or entire seasons of that show that are stored in your iCloud account.

Sync and Share Digital Photos Using iCloud

As a Mac user, you can also benefit from iCloud by using its My Photo Stream feature, which allows you to sync up to 1,000 of your most recently shot or imported digital photos, via the Internet (and iCloud), among your various Mac and PC computers, Apple TV, and iOS mobile devices.

Or, if you want to share groups of photos you currently have stored in the iPhoto or Aperture software running on your Mac (or the Photos or iPhoto app on your iOS mobile device), you can use iCloud's Shared Photo Stream feature.

While iCloud's My Photo Stream and Shared Photo Stream features have similar names, each feature functions a bit differently. The My Photo Stream feature is used exclusively to sync your own photos between your own Apple computers and devices, as well as to help you automatically establish a backup of those images.

The Shared Photo Stream feature is designed to offer you an alternative to email or using an independent online photo sharing service (such as Flickr) for sharing groups of images in online galleries stored in iCloud, which become accessible to the people you invite to view them.

Sync App-Specific Data with iCloud

By default, if you're an iPhone, iPad, or iPod touch user who also uses a Mac, you can benefit from being able to synchronize your data from the Contacts, Calendar, Reminders, and Notes apps that come bundled with the iOS 7 and OS X Mavericks (for the Mac) operating systems. Plus, you can automatically sync and share data, documents, and files associated with Apple's Pages, Numbers, and Keynote applications, which are also available for the Mac, as well as for the iPhone, iPad, and iPod touch.

In the past, syncing app-specific data was only possible using the iTunes Sync process. With iCloud, however, you can sync app-specific data wirelessly via the Internet, so your computers and iOS devices never need to be physically connected using a USB cable in order to synchronize data or exchange information.

Note A growing number of third-party Mac OS X and iOS apps support syncing data between your computers and iOS mobile devices via iCloud.

Surf the Web More Efficiently

In addition to sharing and syncing app-specific data that's associated with Contacts, Calendar, Reminders, and Notes, as well as the optional Pages, Numbers, and Keynote apps, iCloud can automatically sync email information that's associated with your free iCloud email account, as well as sync bookmarks and other information that's associated with the Safari web browser.

For example, in Chapter 9, you'll learn all about the new iCloud Keychain feature, which can be used in conjunction with Safari. Once activated on each of your Macs and iOS mobile devices, as you visit new websites and are required to create a username and password to access them, Safari will automatically remember that login information and sync it with your other compatible computers and mobile devices. Then, any time you revisit a website from any computer or mobile device that's linked to the same iCloud account, you will automatically be logged into websites and never need to remember your usernames or passwords.

Beyond storing and syncing usernames and passwords, iCloud continues to integrate with Safari in order to sync bookmarks, entries to your Bookmarks bar, contents saved to Safari's Reading List, as well as open (tabbed) web browser windows. Thus, you can

Did You Know?

Windows PC Users Can Also Use iCloud

First and foremost, Apple's iCloud service was designed for Apple Macs (including iMacs and MacBooks), as well as Apple's iOS mobile devices and the Apple TV device. If you're a Windows PC user, you can download the free iCloud Control Panel software in order to take advantage of iCloud's ability to synchronize data between your computer and your iPhone, iPad, or iPod touch.

Plus, you can access your iTunes music purchases from iCloud from your Windows-based PC, as well as access your My Photo Stream and Shared Photo Stream, for example. However, if you're a Windows PC user who is not also an Apple iOS mobile device user, plenty of other cloud-based file-sharing services might be more suitable to your needs. Throughout this book, you'll learn how Windows PC users can use various iCloud features.

To download the free iCloud Control Panel software for a Windows-based PC, visit www.apple.com/icloud/setup/pc.html.

start surfing the Web on one Mac or iOS mobile device using Safari, and then switch to another computer or mobile device and pick up exactly where you left off.

Access App-Specific Data from Any Web Browser

From any computer or mobile device that's connected to the Internet, it's possible to securely access your Contacts, Calendar, Reminders, Notes, Pages, Numbers, and Keynote-related data, documents, and files, as well as manage your iCloud email account, simply by pointing any web browser to www.iCloud.com. Once you reach this iCloud website, log in using your iCloud username and password (which is typically your Apple ID and the password associated with it).

Online-based applications that are almost identical to the Contacts, Calendar, Reminders, Notes, Pages, Numbers, and Keynote apps (which are part of OS X Mavericks and iOS 7) are available for free. These online versions of the apps grant you full access to your data and files (for these apps) that are stored in your iCloud account, even if the computer or mobile device you're currently using to surf the Web is not ordinarily linked to your iCloud account.

Use the Find My Mac Feature via iCloud

If your iPhone or iPad gets lost or stolen, and you've preactivated iCloud's Find My iPhone or Find My iPad feature, you can visit the iCloud website (www.iCloud.com/#find) from any computer or device that's connected to the Internet and quickly pinpoint the exact location of your missing iOS mobile device. Once it's located, you are given a variety of options to recover your device, lock it down, and/or erase it to keep your personal and private data away from authorized parties.

For Mac users, Apple offers the equally useful Find My Mac feature. It works in conjunction with Find My iPhone and Find My iPad. As long as your iMac, Mac Pro, MacBook Pro, or MacBook Air is connected to the Internet via Wi-Fi, you can pinpoint its exact location on a map via the iCloud website, and then perform a handful of tasks remotely to retrieve your lost or stolen computer. At the same time, you can remotely lock down or protect the data stored on that computer to keep it away from authorized users.

Obviously, the Find My Mac feature will be more useful for locating a MacBook, which is extremely mobile, as opposed to an iMac or Mac Pro that probably sits on a desk in your home or office. However, this feature works with any Mac computer that's running the latest version of OS X Mavericks.

 Tip   If you use an iPhone or iPad, download the free Find My iPhone app from the App Store, which can also be used to pinpoint the location of your Mac, as long as your iOS device and Mac have access to the Internet.

How to... Activate and Use the Find My Mac Feature

For the Find My Mac feature to work, you must first activate it on each of your Macs. Then, to pinpoint the location of your computers, the computer must be connected to the Internet via a wireless network.

To turn on the Find My Mac feature, which you need to do only once, launch System Preferences from your Mac's Dock or from the Applications folder. Then, from the System Preferences window, click the iCloud icon.

When the iCloud window (in System Preferences) is displayed, if prompted to do so, log in to your iCloud account using your Apple ID and password. Then, in the iCloud window, click to add a checkmark next to the Find My Mac option.

Click the red dot displayed in the upper-left corner of the iCloud window to exit System Preferences. Or, from the System Preferences pull-down menu displayed near the top-left corner of the Mac's screen, select the Quit System Preferences option to save your changes and exit System Preferences.

Be sure to turn on the Find My Mac feature on each of your Mac computers separately, after each is linked to your iCloud account.

When you access www.iCloud.com/#find from any computer or mobile device that's connected to the Internet, and then log in to your iCloud account using your Apple ID and password, the Find My Mac feature will pinpoint and display the exact geographic location of your Mac on a detailed map.

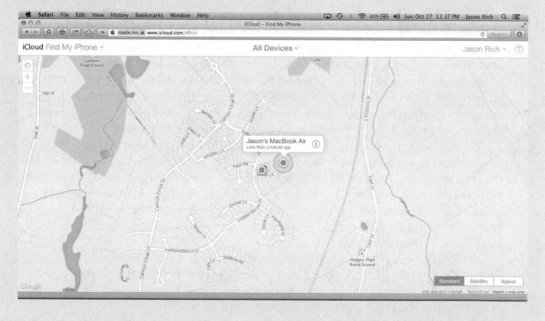

(Continued)

As you're looking at the map, click the Devices button to see the location of each of your Apple devices that have the Find My ... feature activated. To zoom in or out on the map, click the Zoom In (+) or Zoom Out (–) icons displayed near the upper-left corner of the iCloud map screen. To recenter the map based on the location of your "found" computer or device, click the target-shaped icon that's displayed just above the Zoom In icon.

The illustration below shows a Hybrid map view after the Zoom In feature has been used to display more detail. You can also click the Standard or Satellite map view option to change the map's appearance.

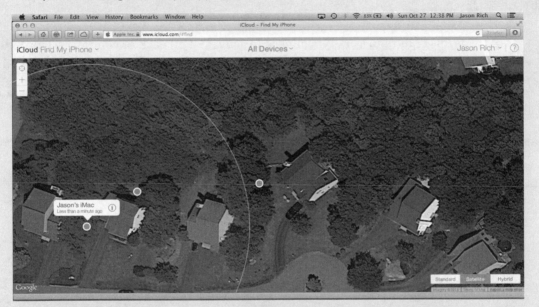

Once the Find My Mac feature locates your Mac, click the green dot on the map that's associated with your device's location. The name of the device will be displayed in a text bubble. In this bubble, click the Info icon ("i") to open a separate window that allows you to remotely take control of the missing computer or device.

From within this window, click the Play Sound option to have the computer or iOS mobile device play a sound so you can more easily find it as you get closer to it. Click the Erase [iPhone/iPad/Mac] option to remotely erase all of the content on that computer or device. This will protect your data. Later, when you recover your computer or device, you can fully restore your data from a recent backup.

If you're locating an iOS mobile device, click the Lost Mode option to immediately and remotely activate the computer or iOS mobile device's Passcode feature. This will prevent anyone from using your lost equipment without first entering the four-digit passcode you create. If you're locating a Mac, click the Lock option, which will prevent anyone from accessing your computer without knowing the correct password.

Share Files Using the Back to My Mac Feature

The Back to My Mac feature allows you to transfer documents and files between Macs over the Internet or control a Mac from a remote location using another Mac. This useful feature is now offered through iCloud.

> **Note**   When you use the Back to My Mac feature to share files, documents, or data, you must do so manually. It will not automatically sync files between two or more machines.

For this feature to work, you'll need to activate it on each of your Macs. Once it's activated, whenever you access the Finder on your Mac, you'll see a Shared heading displayed on the left side of the Finder window (shown in Figure 2-5). Below that Shared heading is a listing for the Macs that are accessible wirelessly using the Back to My Mac feature.

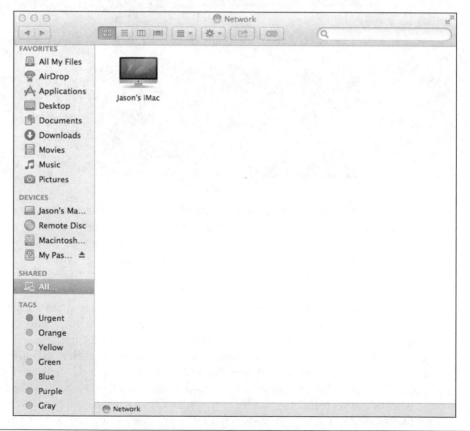

FIGURE 2-5   Once the Back to My Mac feature is activated, you can access a Mac remotely by clicking its listing under the Shared heading in the Finder window. Shown here is an iMac being accessed by a MacBook Air.

You can then manually drag and drop or copy files between the Mac you're using and any other wirelessly connected Mac that's listed under the Shared heading in the Finder window. Basically, the folder displayed in the Finder for other Macs with which you're sharing acts like an external hard drive or thumb drive. As you copy files to the folder, they're accessible on the other machine (and vice versa).

To activate the Back to My Mac feature on each of your Macs, follow these steps:

1. Launch System Preferences from the Mac's Dock or Applications folder.
2. From the main System Preferences window, click the iCloud icon.
3. When the iCloud window (in System Preferences) becomes available, log in to your iCloud account if you're prompted to do so.
4. Click to place a virtual checkmark next to the Back to My Mac option displayed in the iCloud window in System Preferences (shown in Figure 2-6).

 It might be necessary to make adjustments on your wireless Internet router to use the Back to My Mac feature with the maximum possible file transfer speeds.

5. Exit System Preferences to save your changes.
6. Repeat this step on each of your Macs.

 For the Back to My Mac feature to function properly, all Macs must be using the same version of the OS X operating system, and they need to be linked to the same iCloud account. This feature is different from the AirDrop feature that's also built into OS X Mavericks and iOS 7. AirDrop allows two Apple computers or mobile devices to share information wirelessly, as long as they're in close proximity and have the AirDrop feature turned on.

FIGURE 2-6   Add a checkmark to the Back to My Mac option in the iCloud window of System Preferences to turn on this feature.

Sync Your Ebooks Library via iCloud

In conjunction with the release of OS X Mavericks, Apple also released a Mac version of its popular iBooks app, which was previously available exclusively to iPhone, iPad, and iPod touch users. The iBooks app serves two primary functions. First, iBooks serves as a conduit for accessing Apple's iBookstore (one of the largest online ebookstores in the world). Second, iBooks works as a full-featured ebook reader, allowing people to manage and then read the ebook titles they acquire from iBookstore, as well as access and read PDF files acquired from other sources.

The Mac edition of iBooks works very much like the iOS edition. As a result, it also fully integrates with iCloud, allowing for bookmarks, notes, annotations, and other information pertaining to each of your ebooks to be automatically synced with iCloud.

Using this functionality, you can begin reading an ebook on one computer or device, and then pick up exactly where you left off by launching iBooks on another computer or device that's linked to the same iCloud account. Once you purchase (or acquire) an ebook title from iBookstore, it can be downloaded to all of the computers and mobile devices that are linked to the same iCloud account.

To download the free iBooks app for your Mac, launch the App Store app. In the Search field that's displayed near the upper-right corner of the App Store screen, enter the search word "iBooks." When a listing for the iBooks app is displayed, click the Free icon to download and install the iBooks software on your Mac.

If you're already an iPhone or iPad user who has discovered how enjoyable it is to read ebooks using iBooks, and you've established a personal ebook library, you can sync that ebook library with the iBooks software on your Mac without having to repurchase any of those ebook titles.

Note Only ebooks that are formatted to be read using iBooks will load into the iBooks software and sync with iCloud. If you have ebooks formatted for a Kindle (from Amazon) or a Nook (from Barnes & Noble), for example, you'll need to download and install an alternate ebook reader on your Mac, such as the free Kindle app, which can be used for reading Kindle-formatted ebooks on your Mac and syncing ebook titles with your Kindle ebook reader.

Use iCloud's Documents in the Cloud Feature to Sync iWork Data, Documents, and Files

In Chapter 10, you'll learn all about how you can use iCloud's Documents in the Cloud feature to share documents and files created using Apple's iWork software on your Mac with other computers, as well as with the iWork apps running on your iOS mobile devices. All versions of the iWork apps can link automatically to your iCloud account.

When you use this functionality, your iWork-related documents, data, and files automatically get synchronized and backed up in the cloud. There's no need to copy or drag and drop files manually, as you must do with the Back to My Mac feature.

iWork for Mac includes three software packages: Pages, Numbers, and Keynote. Pages is a word processor that is compatible with Microsoft Word. Numbers is a spreadsheet management program that's compatible with Microsoft Excel, and Keynote is a digital slide presentation tool that's compatible with Microsoft PowerPoint.

From your Mac, you can import a Microsoft Word file into Pages, for example, and then automatically share it with other computers and iOS mobile devices via the iCloud integration that's built into the software.

Note Thanks to the online-based versions of Pages, Numbers, and Keynote, which anyone can access for free by visiting www.iCloud.com and signing in using their Apple ID and password, Microsoft Office documents and files can be imported into any of the iWork apps, automatically converted into a Pages, Numbers, or Keynote file, and then shared (via iCloud) with all computers and iOS mobile devices linked to the same iCloud account. Those files can also be manually shared with others using email.

Additional iCloud Functionality for Your Mac

Third-party software developers are continuing to make their applications compatible with iCloud, so you'll be able to transfer and sync files, documents, and data associated with other apps with ease.

Over time, Apple and a variety of third-party software developers will introduce new features and functionality that can be used on your Mac in conjunction with iCloud to handle a wider range of tasks.

Note Keep in mind, while you can use iCloud to back up the entire contents of your iOS mobile device (using the iCloud Backup feature), this functionality does not currently work on a Mac. While iCloud can back up, sync, and store app-specific data from Contacts, Calendar, Reminders, Notes, Mail, Safari, Pages, Numbers, and Keynote, this does not constitute a full backup of your computer. You should still maintain a reliable backup solution for your Mac, whether it involves using OS X Mavericks' Time Machine feature or a third-party online-based data backup service.

3

How iPhone, iPad, iPad mini, and iPod touch Users Can Utilize iCloud

HOW TO...

- Discover what iCloud can do in conjunction with your iOS mobile devices.
- Learn about new iCloud features introduced in conjunction with iOS 7.
- Turn on iCloud functionality on your iOS devices.

These days, most people don't have just one Apple product. They own and regularly use several. This might include a Mac desktop and notebook computer, as well as an iPhone smartphone, iPad (or iPad mini) tablet, or an iPod touch. Now, thanks to iCloud, all of the Apple computers and devices you regularly own and use can sync information, automatically and in the background.

Note Even if you just use one iOS mobile device and nothing else, as you'll learn from this chapter, iCloud offers a handful of extremely useful functions that can greatly expand what's possible using that device.

When you combine iCloud's functionality with the power and portability of your iPhone, iPad, iPad mini, or iPod touch (all of which are among Apple's mobile devices that run the latest iOS 7 operating system), you gain the ability to back up, sync, share, and access your own data, music, files, documents, photos, and other content almost instantly, any time, and from anywhere an Internet connection is available.

Only One iCloud Account Is Needed: Multiple Accounts Are Optional

Even if you have multiple Macs, as well as an iPhone, iPad, or iPod touch, along with an Apple TV device, you only need one iCloud account. This single account will allow you to sync and share information among all of your computers or iOS mobile devices that are linked to the same iCloud account.

When you set up your free iCloud account, Apple encourages you to use the same Apple ID username and password as you've used in the past to take advantage of Apple's other online-based services, such as making purchases from the App Store or iTunes Store, or using FaceTime, Game Center, or iMessage, for example. By using your existing Apple ID username and password for your iCloud account, everything you do related to Apple utilizes the same account information.

However, some people opt to create one iCloud/Apple ID account for all content purchases (allowing family members to share all purchased content between their computers and devices), and a separate iCloud/Apple ID for everything else (allowing each family member to maintain, back up, and sync their own app-specific databases for Contacts, Calendar, Reminders, Notes, etc., plus have their own identity when using services like FaceTime, iMessage, or Game Center).

If you opt to use two separate iCloud accounts/Apple IDs, it will be necessary to sign in and out of each account as it's needed. You will also need to adjust options in the Settings app a bit differently. Begin by launching Settings and tapping the iTunes & App Stores option. Near the top of the iTunes & App Stores menu, tap the Apple ID field. Tap the Sign Out option, if necessary, and then sign in using the iCloud account/ Apple ID you want to use with all Apple-related content purchases.

Next, return to the main Settings menu and tap the iCloud option. Tap the Account field that's displayed near the top of the screen. Here, enter the iCloud username and password (or Apple ID and password) you want to use for all iCloud-related functions, such as data syncing and data backups related to Contacts, Calendar, Mail, Reminders, Safari, Notes, Passbook, iCloud Keychain, Photos, Documents & Data (Pages, Numbers, and Keynote), and the Find My... feature.

Note Keep in mind, it is not currently possible to later merge two separate Apple ID accounts into one account. However, it is possible to change the email address that's associated with some Apple ID accounts, as long as they don't end with @mac.com or @me.com.

Tip If you have previously purchased iTunes Store, App Store, iBookstore, or Newsstand content using several different Apple IDs, you can merge that content to be accessible from a single Apple ID/iCloud account. To do this, first transfer and download all of the related content to a single Mac or PC that's running the latest version of the iTunes software. Be sure to authorize the computer to be able to access the content from each Apple ID account. (The Authorize command is found under the Store pull-down menu when running the iTunes software on your PC or Mac.) When all of the content is stored on the single computer within iTunes, you can then sync it to one iCloud account, and by default all of your other computers and iOS mobile devices that are linked to that same iCloud account. In the future, if you ever need to restore this data, you will be prompted for the Apple ID password associated with each account you used to acquire content. To keep things simple, consider using the same password for all of your Apple ID accounts.

What an iOS Mobile Device User Can Do with iCloud

iCloud, when used in conjunction with your iOS mobile devices, can handle a variety of tasks, including:

- iCloud gives you instant access to all your iTunes music purchases (via the iTunes Store and Music app that comes preinstalled with iOS 7). Music you own can be downloaded to your iPhone, iPad, or iPod touch, even if that music was not originally purchased on that iOS device or isn't currently stored on it. You'll discover how to access your iTunes Store–purchased music and how to manage your digital music library via iCloud in Chapter 5.
- iCloud can grant you access to your entire digital music library, including non-iTunes Store purchases, if you upgrade to the optional iTunes Match service for $24.99 per year. You'll learn about the iTunes Match service in Chapter 6.
- iCloud lets you access and update your iCloud-based My Photo Stream. As you snap photos using the cameras built into your iOS mobile device (or import photos into your iPhone, iPad, or iPod touch from other sources), your most recent images can automatically be added to My Photo Stream and then shared, almost immediately, with your other iOS mobile devices and computers. You'll learn more about how to create and manage your iCloud My Photo Stream in Chapter 7.
- Quickly and easily share selected groups of digital photos with other people using iCloud's Shared Photo Stream feature. With Shared Photo Stream, it's possible to create and manage an unlimited number of separate online galleries, and then decide exactly who will be able to view each of them.
- Using iCloud's Documents in the Cloud functionality, you can create or edit documents and files using the iWork for iOS apps (or other iCloud-compatible apps), and then wirelessly and automatically sync them with your other computers or iOS devices that are linked to the same iCloud account.

- With iCloud, you can synchronize app-specific data related to Contacts, Calendars, Reminders, Notes, Mail (for your iCloud-related email account only), and other iCloud-compatible apps that you purchase from the App Store. This sync process is done wirelessly.

- The iBooks app serves as both a way to shop for ebooks through Apple's online-based iBookstore, as well as a feature-packed ebook reader that allows you to read full-length books (as well as PDF files) on your iPhone or iPad's screen. Thanks to iCloud, your personal ebook library (ebooks you've acquired from iBookstore) automatically get stored in your iCloud account and will sync with your other computers and iOS mobile devices that utilize the iBooks app. At the same time, your bookmarks and ebook annotations, for example, also get synced automatically. Thus, you can begin reading an ebook on your iPad and pick up exactly where you left off on your Mac or iPhone.

- When it comes to surfing the Web, iCloud is now more fully integrated with the Safari web browser than ever before. In addition to syncing your bookmarks and favorites bar, iCloud will sync your open (tabbed) browser windows, as well as content saved to Safari's Reading List. Using iCloud with Safari on your Macs and iOS mobile devices is covered in Chapter 9.

Note The iCloud Keychain feature also works seamlessly with Safari on an iPhone, iPad, or iPod touch.

- iCloud Backup lets you wirelessly create and maintain a backup of your iOS device. This replaces the iTunes Sync process for making backups. In Chapter 12, you'll discover the advantages of using iCloud Backup, as opposed to iTunes Sync, to maintain a backup of your iOS devices. When you use iCloud Backup, your backup files are stored online (in the cloud), rather than on your primary computer's hard drive. As a result, if it becomes necessary, you can perform a restore from anywhere with a Wi-Fi Internet connection.

Note Keep in mind, you can restore from an iCloud backup to your existing iOS mobile device or to a replacement device of the same type. For example, if your iPhone gets stolen, or you upgrade from an iPhone 4S (or iPhone 5) to an iPhone 5S, you can use iCloud Backup to restore your data from your old iPhone to your new (replacement) iPhone. If you have both an iPhone and an iPad, you will need to maintain two separate backups using the iCloud Backup feature, both of which will take up some of your 5GB of free online storage space that Apple provides for your personal data as part of your iCloud account.

- If your iOS mobile device gets lost or stolen, iCloud's Find My iPhone [iPad] feature can help you locate it using either the free Find My iPhone app, or by accessing the iCloud website (www.iCloud.com/#find) and logging in using your iCloud username and password. New features added to Find My iPhone [iPad] allow you to remotely erase or lock down your device. The focus of Chapter 14 is on how to track the whereabouts of your Macs and iOS mobile devices using iCloud's enhanced Find My... feature.

As you'll discover throughout this book, after iCloud functionality is established, you can pick and choose which iCloud-related features and functions you want to use, and then customize that functionality so it best meets your needs.

Set Up Your iOS Devices to Work with iCloud

If you're a Mac or Windows PC user who also owns and uses an iOS mobile device, your best bet is first to establish an iCloud account on your primary computer. You'll need to establish an iCloud account only once, and only one account is needed to connect all of your computers and iOS mobile devices together via iCloud.

Did You Know?

You Can Create Your iCloud Account from Your iOS Device (or Computer)

You can also establish an iCloud account directly from your iOS mobile device. However, only one iCloud account needs to be created. That account then needs to be activated on each computer and iOS mobile device that you want to be wirelessly linked together. Only then can the computers and devices wirelessly share and synchronize data, files, documents, photos, and other content via the Internet.

How to...

Make Sure Your iOS and Apps Are Up to Date

After you've established an iCloud account, make sure each of your iOS mobile devices has been upgraded to the most recent version of iOS 7. If you've already upgraded to iOS 7, check to see if a more recent update to the operating system has been released.

To check for iOS updates, launch Settings, tap the General option, and then tap the Software Update option. If the following message appears on your screen, you're all set: "iOS 7.#. Your software is up to date." However, if a more current version of the iOS operating system is available, you'll be given the opportunity to download and install it for free, providing a Wi-Fi Internet connection is available. Before upgrading to a new version of the iOS, be sure to back up your device first.

Keep in mind, any time a major update to the iOS is released by Apple, many of the apps on your mobile device will also need updating. iOS 7 now automatically updates your apps as needed, provided an Internet connection is available. To determine if there are any outstanding updates that need to be installed, while your iPhone or iPad is connected to the Internet, launch the App Store app and tap the Updates option.

Turn On iCloud Functionality on Your iOS Devices

Now that you've created an iCloud account and you have iOS 7 (or later) running on your iPhone, iPad, or iPod touch, you need to turn on iCloud functionality on each device separately. On each device, you'll then need to choose which iCloud features and functions you want to activate and, in some cases, turn on iCloud functionality in specific apps.

To turn on iCloud functionality on an iOS device, follow these steps:

1. Launch the Settings app from the Home screen.
2. From the main Settings menu, tap the iCloud option.
3. When the iCloud menu screen appears within Settings, tap the Account option that's displayed near the top of the screen.
4. Near the top of the Account screen, enter your Apple ID and password that was used to create the iCloud account (shown in Figure 3-1 on an iPhone). It's essential that you use the same iCloud/Apple ID account on all devices you want to link together via iCloud.

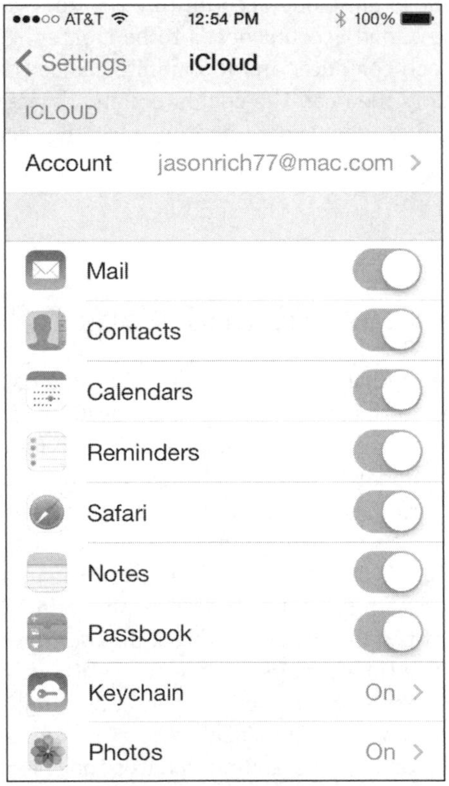

FIGURE 3-1   Turn on iCloud functionality by entering your iCloud account information in the Settings app, shown here on an iPhone 5.

5. Tap the Done icon after you've finished entering the account information. iCloud functionality is now activated on that device.

6. Return to the iCloud screen within Settings. Below the Account option are options for Mail, Contacts, Calendars, Reminders, Safari, Notes, Passbook, Keychain, Photos, Documents & Data, and Find My iPhone [iPad]. To the right of each of these options is a virtual on/off switch. One at a time, tap the virtual switch that corresponds to the iCloud features you want to turn on or off.

Note
If you turn on the virtual switch that's associated with Contacts, for example, that device will immediately begin syncing your Contacts app-related data with iCloud. Then iCloud will sync your Contacts data with all other Macs, Windows-based PCs, and other iOS mobile devices that are linked to the same iCloud account and that have the Contacts feature turned on. Unless the Contacts feature is turned on in the iCloud menu found within the Settings app (or on the Mac in System Preferences), the Contacts app will not sync data with your iCloud account, or with your other computers or mobile devices linked to your account.

7. One at a time, choose which iCloud features and functions you want to turn on and begin using on the iOS devices you're currently working with. Each of these features is explored in other chapters in this book.

8. Repeat this process on each of your iOS devices.

Did You Know?

Once App-Specific Syncing Is Turned On, Your Data Will Automatically Be Synchronized

As soon as you turn on an iCloud feature, such as Contacts, your iOS device will immediately begin syncing your Contacts app-related data with iCloud. Then any time you make changes to your Contacts database, and your iOS device has access to the Internet, those changes will be synced with iCloud.

Once your Contacts data is stored on iCloud, it will be synced automatically with any other iOS devices or computers that are linked to that iCloud account. So any changes now made to your Contacts database on your computer or on another iOS device will be downloaded from iCloud and synced with the information on the device you're currently using. This all happens automatically, almost instantly, and in the background once the feature is activated.

Keep in mind, if you delete an entry from your Contacts database on your iPhone, for example, that deletion will also take effect in the Contacts app that's running on each of your Macs and other iOS mobile devices that are linked to the same iCloud account. The deletion will also impact your Contacts database, which is accessible from the iCloud website (www.iCloud.com). There is no undo function.

Turn On iCloud Functionality for Specific iOS Apps

If you turn on the Documents & Data feature, you will also need to turn on iCloud functionality related to the specific apps you want to use with this feature, such as Pages, Numbers, or Keynote (each of which is sold separately from the App Store).

To do this, return to the main Settings menu on your iOS mobile device and scroll down to the listing of apps. Here, you'll discover listings for the apps you can use with iCloud to sync data between your iOS mobile device and iCloud.

For example, tap the Pages option (shown in Figure 3-2).

Tap the virtual switch associated with the Use iCloud feature, displayed near the top of the Pages menu screen, and turn it on. Repeat this process for each app that's capable of syncing files or data with iCloud, including Numbers and Keynote.

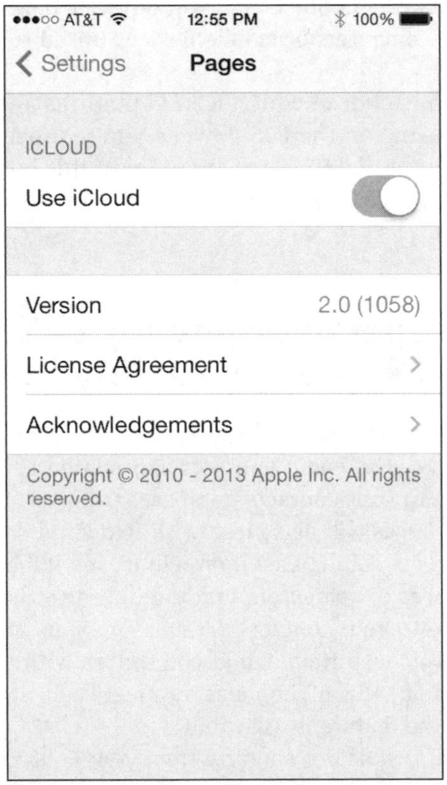

FIGURE 3-2 The Pages menu within Settings allows you to turn on (or off) iCloud functionality for that specific app, on the iOS mobile device you're currently using.

Your iTunes Content Is Always Accessible via iCloud

After you establish your iCloud account, you can access any previously purchased iTunes Store content, even if it was purchased on another computer or device. This includes music, TV show episodes, movies, ringtones, and audiobooks, as well as ebooks purchased from iBookstore, and apps acquired from the App Store.

It's possible to redownload any of this content to the iOS mobile device you're currently using, anytime. For music, a cellular Internet connection will work. However, to transfer TV show episodes, movies, or content with a large file size, a Wi-Fi connection will be required.

Once you launch the Settings app, tap the iCloud option, enter your iCloud account information once, and turn on the virtual switches associated with each of the listed iCloud features, your iOS device is ready to begin utilizing the features and functions of iCloud.

Keep in mind that all iCloud features require that your iOS device has access to the Internet via a cellular or Wi-Fi connection. However, to use My Photo Stream, Shared Photo Stream, or the iCloud Backup feature, for example, you must use a Wi-Fi connection.

If you plan to use your iOS device in conjunction with Apple's AirPlay feature (to stream content between your iOS device and your Apple TV) or Apple's Home Sharing feature (to transfer data between your iOS device and primary computer), the two devices will need to be connected to the same wireless home network. How to do this is explained in greater detail in Chapter 13.

Did You Know?

App-Specific Data You Delete Gets Synced Almost Instantly

If you delete any content (such as a song) that was purchased from the iTunes Store, you can redownload it any time from iCloud. However, if you delete any of your own data that is being synchronized via iCloud—such as an entry from your Contacts database, an event from your Calendar database, a bookmark that was previously saved in Safari, a Pages document, a Numbers spreadsheet, or a Keynote presentation file—that data, document, or file will almost immediately be deleted permanently from the device you're using, and within seconds, from the other computers and iOS mobile devices that are linked to your iCloud account. There is no "undo" command after you've deleted app-specific data and your app data has been resynced with iCloud. To retrieve that deleted file, you'll need to refer back to a recent backup (if one exists). Otherwise, that data or file could be lost forever. Before deleting data or files that are being synchronized with iCloud, make sure you won't need that information in the future on the device you're using, or on your other computers or iOS devices.

Share Content With and Without iCloud

iCloud is designed to make it easy for you to share your own data, documents, files, photos, music, and content with your other computers and iOS mobile devices. It is not, however, useful for sharing most types of content with other people or with computers or devices that are not linked to your personal iCloud account.

That being said, to share photos or iWork-related documents and files with other people (including Pages, Numbers, and Keynote documents and files), you can use Apple's iWork for iCloud functionality in conjunction with the Pages, Numbers, or Keynote apps running on your Mac, iPhone, iPad, or iPod touch. To share photos, you can use the Shared Photo Stream feature in conjunction with the Photos or optional iPhoto app.

From any computer or device that has Internet access, you can also access fully functional online versions of the Contacts, Calendar, Reminders, and Notes apps, manage your iCloud email address, and work with online versions of Pages, Numbers, and Keynote. To do this, use any web browser to visit www.iCloud.com and log in using your iCloud account username and password. When you do this, all of your app-specific data, documents, and files will be accessible to you from the online versions of the various apps, which work just like their Mac or iOS mobile device counterparts.

 If you want to share your personal documents, files, and data with others, take advantage of the Share menu options that are offered in many iOS 7 apps. Depending on the app, these options allow you to share data, files, content, or photos, for example, with other people via email, text/instant message, AirDrop, or in some cases using online social networking or file-sharing services, such as Facebook, Twitter or Flickr (for sharing photos).

If you need to share data, documents, and files with other people, and want to utilize a cloud-based file-sharing service to accomplish this, consider using a third-party service, such as Dropbox. A service like Dropbox is somewhat similar to iCloud in that it offers some overlapping functionality. However, Dropbox also offers functionality for securely sharing specific files or documents with other people.

4

How to Use the New OS X Mavericks and iOS 7 iCloud Features

HOW TO...

- Discover the new ways Apple has integrated iCloud functionality into its OS X Mavericks operating system for the Mac.
- As an iPhone, iPad, or iPod touch user, learn about the newest iCloud features added to iOS 7 and a growing number of apps.
- Learn how to sync app-specific data with your computers and mobile devices, and in some cases, share content with other people.

In October 2013, Apple released OS X Mavericks, a newly enhanced version of its operating system that runs on all new Macs, including the iMac desktop computers, high-end Mac Pro desktop computers, and all MacBook notebook computers. As you will discover, some of the new features incorporated into the operating system itself, as well as the apps that come preinstalled on all Macs, now more fully integrate with iCloud. This is a free upgrade and is necessary to utilize all of iCloud's latest features and functions.

Meanwhile, in conjunction with the iOS 7 operating system that was also released in October 2013, Apple introduced a handful of new ways iPhones, iPads, and iPod touch devices are able to utilize iCloud. There was even an OS update for Apple TV that allows the device to benefit from expanded integration with iCloud. Of course, the latest iCloud features and functions work with all of Apple's latest iOS mobile devices, including the iPhone 5S, iPhone 5C, and iPad Air and iPad mini with Retina display. These same features also work with most (but not all) older iPhone and iPad models.

If you're a Mac and iOS mobile device user, what you'll quickly discover is that many of the newest iCloud features allow you to more freely exchange content, files, and data between your computers and mobile devices that are linked to the same iCloud account and that have Internet access. In many cases, iCloud-related file and data syncing happens automatically and in the background once a particular feature is turned on and set up on each of your computers or devices.

In addition, iCloud functionality now works with a larger selection of core (preinstalled) apps running on your Macs and iOS mobile devices, as well as a growing number of optional third-party apps. So if you're using a third-party app such as PDFpen, for example, your PDF files can be wirelessly transferred and synced between your computers and mobile devices, as long as you have the PDFpen app running on each computer or iOS mobile device and you have iCloud functionality turned on. Figure 4-1 shows PDFpen running on an iPad. From the Settings menu within this app, you can turn on or off iCloud file syncing functionality.

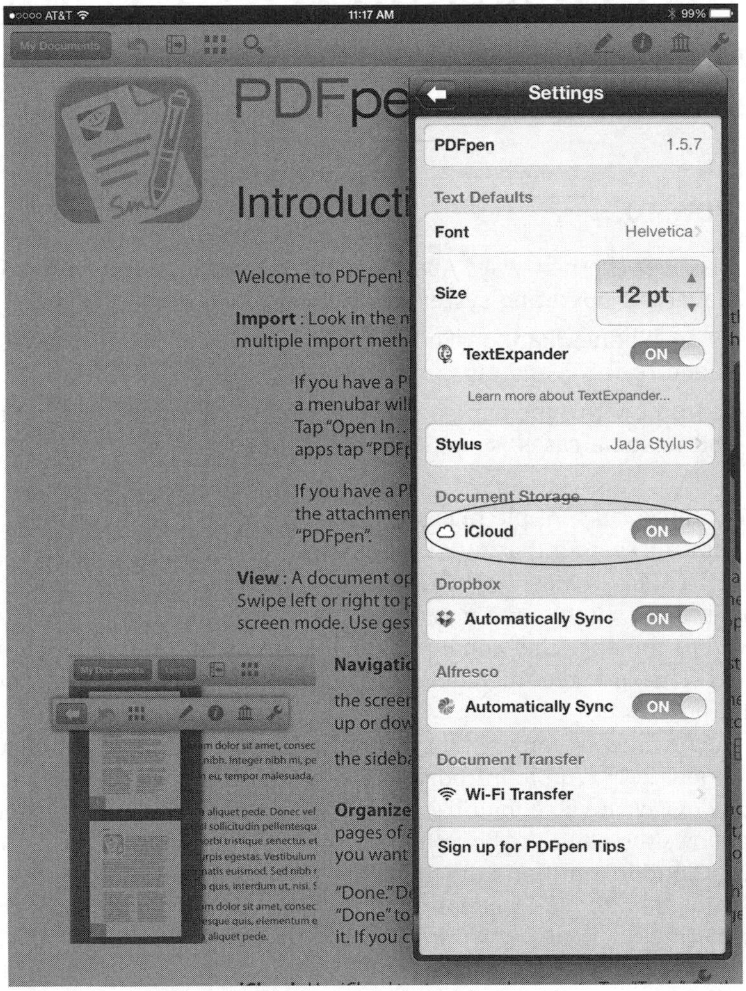

FIGURE 4-1 PDFpen is one of a growing number of third-party apps that allow files to be synced with iCloud and shared across multiple iOS mobile devices and computers.

Did You Know?

Find My iPhone Has Been Improved

In the past, the Find My iPhone feature could be used to help you pinpoint the exact location of a lost or stolen iPhone, iPad, iPod touch, or Mac. Now, in addition to helping you locate your computers or devices and then giving you the ability to remotely lock them down to prevent unauthorized access, additional functionality has been put into place to help deter thieves from stealing iPhones by making is much more difficult for iPhones that are reported stolen to be unlocked and reactivated by a thief.

Once you turn on Find My iPhone or Find My iPad on your iOS mobile device, that feature cannot be turned off without someone knowing your Apple ID and password.

Tip   When using a third-party app with iCloud, the iCloud feature typically needs to be turned on and set up from within the app itself, not from within System Preferences (Mac) or Settings (iPad).

Third-party apps, such as FileMaker (a database app, www.filemaker.com), Evernote (a note-taking and information organization app, www.evernote.com), iAWriter (a word processor, www.iawriter.com), Todo (a to-do list manager, www .appigo.com/todo), DayOne (a scheduling app, http://dayoneapp.com), and Memo Sticky Notes (a sticky note app, http://memo.bloop.info), each have a Mac and an iOS mobile device version available and allow you to sync app-specific data wirelessly and automatically via iCloud.

Note   In some cases, a Windows version of the software is also available, allowing software-specific data or files to sync with iCloud and be shared with a Mac and/or iOS mobile device.

The Mac versions of these apps are available from the Mac App Store, while the iPhone/iPad versions of each are available from the App Store. To quickly locate, purchase, and download any of these apps, enter the app name in the Search field of either the Mac App Store or iOS App Store.

To sync third-party app-specific data, the latest version of each app must be running on your Macs or iOS mobile devices. For example, a PDF file you annotate using PDFpen on your iPad will not automatically sync with your Mac unless the Mac version of PDFpen is running on your Mac and both the Mac and iPad have Internet access.

iCloud Works Much the Same Way on Macs and iOS Mobile Devices

As you know, one of iCloud's core functions is to make it easier, and in many cases effortless, for all of your Mac computers and mobile devices to share information wirelessly via the Internet and your iCloud account. This ability to share and sync data is more prevalent than ever and can be utilized in even more ways.

As a result, your data, files, documents, photos, ebooks, multimedia content (including music, movies, and TV show episodes purchased from the iTunes Store), and other important information are always available to you, regardless of where you are or what computer or device you're using.

Note In the past, this data and file syncing and sharing applied to all computers and mobile devices linked to the same iCloud account. Now, however, it's possible to use any Internet-enabled computer or mobile device to access much of your iCloud account from www.icloud.com, in order to view or work with files and data related to the Contacts, Calendar, Reminders, Notes, Mail, Pages, Numbers, and Keynote apps.

Note While photos can be synced and shared using iCloud, this is done using the iPhoto app that comes bundled with the Mac, the optional Aperture software for the Mac, and/or with the Photos or optional iPhoto app for the iPhone and iPad. Access to these images if you use My Photo Stream is done directly through the previously mentioned photography apps, while Shared Photo Streams is done through unique website URLs (addresses), not from the iCloud.com website. Apple TV devices have their functionality for displaying images stored within an iCloud account.

At the same time, your digital photos can be synced between computers using iCloud's My Photo Stream feature, and it's easier than ever to share photos with others using iCloud's Shared Photo Stream functionality.

When your computers are linked to the same iCloud account, app-specific data can automatically be synchronized and shared between computers and mobile devices—not just from preinstalled apps associated with OS X Mavericks and iOS 7 but with a growing number of third-party apps as well.

Some of the newest iCloud-related features also make it much easier to quickly switch between computers and mobile devices that are linked to the same iCloud account, allowing you to pick up exactly where you left off. This applies to Safari, iBooks, iPhoto, Pages, Numbers, and Keynote, and other popular apps.

For example, when surfing the Web using any version of Safari (on a Mac or iOS mobile device), all of your saved bookmarks, website URLs saved to your favorites bar, content stored on your Reading List, and even the actual web browser windows you have open when using the tabbed browsing feature immediately and automatically sync with iCloud.

So if you begin surfing the Web on a Mac, you can continue on the iPad (shown in Figure 4-2) or iPhone, for example, and all of the web pages you had open and were viewing on your Mac will automatically be accessible on the other device.

iCloud Features Need to Be Activated on Each Computer or Device

When it comes to working with iCloud, there are two important things to remember. First, once your iCloud account is set up, it needs to be linked with each of your computers and compatible iOS mobile devices (as well as your Apple TV, if applicable).

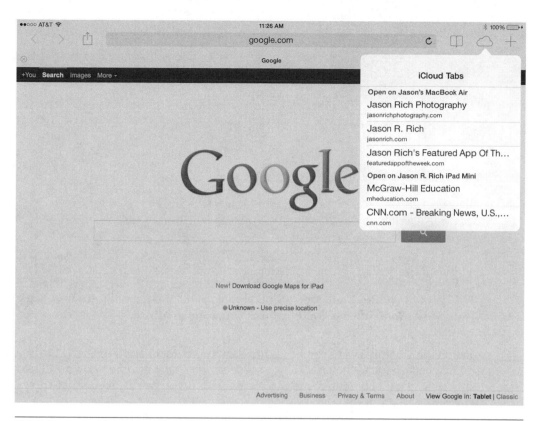

FIGURE 4-2 When surfing the Web using Safari and the tabbed browsing feature on a iPad, for example, you can view open browser windows on your Mac or iPad mini and iPhone.

> **Note** In order for your iCloud account to share data with all of your Macs, PCs, Apple TV, and iOS mobile devices, you only need one iCloud account, but that single account needs to be linked separately to each computer or device.

Second, you can then opt to turn on, customize, or turn off each individual iCloud feature, based on your computing needs and whether or not you want to utilize it.

Link Your Mac to Your iCloud Account

You can link your iCloud account to a Mac when you initially set up a new Mac after purchase, as you upgrade to OS X Mavericks from an older version of OS X, or any time by launching System Preferences and then clicking the iCloud option. Linking a Mac to your iCloud account only needs to be done once. From the left side of the iCloud window in System Preferences, enter your Apple ID and password. Then, from the right side of the System Preferences window, manually turn on or off individual iCloud features, including Mail, Contacts, Calendar, Reminders, Notes, Safari,

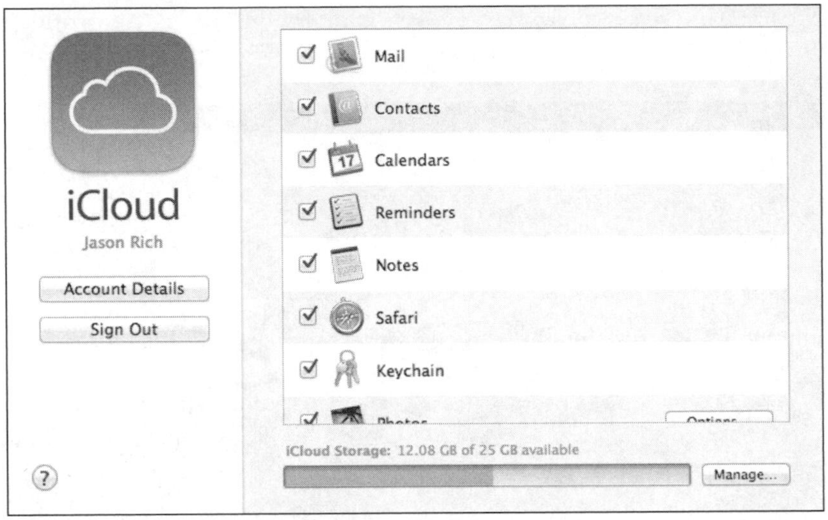

FIGURE 4-3 Once your Mac is linked to your iCloud account, it's necessary to turn on the individual iCloud features you want to utilize.

Keychain, Photos, Documents & Data, Back to My Mac, and Find My Mac. When you add a checkmark to the checkbox associated with each option (shown in Figure 4-3), this activates it. Then, in some cases, a submenu will be displayed that allows you to customize that option.

Note Remember, if you have multiple iMacs, Mac Pros, MacBook Pros, or MacBook Air computers that you want to link to the same iCloud account, you need to link each computer separately, and then turn on each iCloud feature separately (on each computer).

Link Your iPhone and iPad to Your iCloud Account

Just as you need to link each Mac to your iCloud account, you also need to link each of your iOS mobile devices to that same iCloud account. Again, this can be done when you set up a new iOS mobile device, when you upgrade to iOS 7, or at any time by launching Settings, tapping the iCloud option, and then entering your Apple ID and password when prompted.

Link Your Windows-Based PC or Apple TV to Your iCloud Account

To link your Windows-based PC to your iCloud account, it's necessary to download and install the free iCloud Control Panel software from Apple's website (www.apple .com/icloud/setup/pc.html). When you launch the iCloud Control Panel, enter your

Apple ID and password when prompted on the left side of the window, and then turn on/off individual iCloud features from the right side of the Control Panel window.

Tip To learn more about using iCloud with your Apple TV, be sure to read Chapter 13.

iCloud Keychain Remembers Your Website Usernames and Passwords

The new iCloud Keychain feature is fully compatible with all versions of Safari running on Macs or iOS mobile devices. As soon as you turn on this feature on each of your Macs and iOS mobile devices, any time you visit a new website and create a username and password to access that site, Safari automatically remembers that login information. Then, when you return to that site in the future, Safari logs you in without you having to remember your sign-in details.

Once this feature is turned on, iCloud Keychain automatically syncs all of your username and password data with your iCloud account. It then shares and syncs it with all of the computers and iOS mobile devices linked to the same account. As a result, if you create a new website account when surfing the Web on your iPad, for example, when you next access that same site from your iMac, MacBook, or iPhone, Safari will access your account information from iCloud and log you in automatically. (There are some websites, such as online banking sites, where this feature does not work. This is an effort to maximize security.)

iBooks Now Works with iCloud

iBooks was originally available only on iOS mobile devices and was used to acquire ebooks from Apple's iBookstore and then read them on the screen of an iPhone, iPad, or iPod touch. The iBooks for iOS app was (and continues to be) compatible with iCloud.

For example, when you purchase or acquire a new ebook from iBookstore, in addition to immediately downloading that ebook to the device it was purchased on, the acquisition gets saved in your ebook library on iCloud. All of your other iOS mobile devices can access your ebook library and automatically download new acquisitions, regardless of on which device it was purchased.

As you're reading an ebook, you can mark pages with virtual bookmarks, highlight text, or add notes, and then allow iCloud to sync that information with all of your other iOS mobile devices. So you can start reading an ebook on your iPad and automatically pick up exactly where you left off on your iPhone.

In conjunction with OS X Mavericks, iBooks is now available for the Mac. Thus, all of the same functionality for acquiring, syncing, and sharing your ebook library now extends to your Macs as well. To set this up, access the iTunes or iBooks apps, choose Preferences, click the Store option, and then add a checkmark that's associated with the Books option.

Shared Photo Stream Is Improved

Apple's My Photo Stream and Shared Photo Stream features are separate but related, as you'll discover in Chapters 7 and 8. In an effort to make sharing digital photos as easy as possible, this functionality has been improved upon.

For a Mac or iOS mobile device user who is using the iPhoto or Aperture apps on the Mac or Photos or iPhoto app on an iOS mobile device, it's now possible to create Shared Photo Streams. These are basically online galleries (stored online in your iCloud account) that become accessible to others. This allows you to share groups of photos with people you choose.

In addition to sharing photos via a Shared Photo Stream, it's now possible to share videos (up to five minutes in length) that become viewable in up to 720p HD resolution. Plus, as you share your photos and videos with others, those people can post comments, "Like" photos, and upload their own images or video clips to your Shared Photo Stream.

Everything that other people post or share becomes accessible to you and everyone else who is able to view that Shared Photo Stream. As an iCloud user, you can create an unlimited number of Shared Photo Streams to share groups of images with individuals you choose.

Note   Creating, editing, managing, viewing, and using Shared Photo Streams is done using the iPhoto or optional Aperture app on a Mac, or the Photos or optional iPhoto app on an iOS mobile device. People you share a Shared Photo Stream with can access it using one of these apps, or directly from their Internet web browser using a special website URL that's supplied with the email you send that invites them to view the Shared Photo Stream.

The latest versions of the iPhoto and Aperture apps for the Mac, as well as the Photos and iPhoto app for iOS mobile devices, all offer multiple ways to share one or more photos with others from directly within the app. For example, you can send photos via email, text message/instant message, publish them on Facebook or Twitter, transmit them to someone else via AirDrop, or publish them online (via iCloud) as a Shared Photo Stream. Images can also be uploaded from within these apps directly to Flickr (a free online photo-sharing service).

From an iPhone or iPad that's running iOS 7, select the photo or photos you want to share and then tap the Share button that's displayed in the app. The new and expanded Share menu screen (shown in Figure 4-4) will be displayed, which allows you to select how you want to share the selected images.

To share the images via an iCloud Shared Photo Stream using the Photos app that comes preinstalled with iOS 7, simply tap the iCloud icon, add appropriate comments/captions, choose the specific Shared Photo Stream to add the selected photos to (or create a new one), and then tap the Post option.

On a Mac that's running iPhoto, select the photos you want to share and then click the Share button that's displayed near the lower-right corner of the screen. The Share menu (shown in Figure 4-5) offers a handful of options, including Order Prints, Twitter, Flickr, Facebook, Email, Messages, and Photo Stream. You'll learn more about using iPhoto's Share option in conjunction with iCloud's Shared Photo Stream features in Chapter 8.

FIGURE 4-4   The Share menu screen has been expanded with the iOS 7 version of the Photos app.

Click on the Share icon to access the Share menu

FIGURE 4-5   The Share menu in iPhoto on a Mac allows you to easily share images via an iCloud Shared Photo Stream.

How to... **Activate the My Photo Stream and Shared Photo Stream Features on Each of Your Macs and iOS Mobile Devices**

Once again, be sure to separately set up the My Photo Stream and Shared Photo Stream features on each computer and iOS mobile device you're using.

On the Mac, launch System Preferences and click the iCloud option. Next, add a checkmark to the Photos option, and then click the Options button to turn on the My Photo Stream and Photo Sharing options separately (by adding a checkmark to each feature's respective checkbox).

On an iOS mobile device, launch Settings, tap the iCloud option, and then tap the Photos option. Turn on the My Photo Stream and Photo Sharing options separately by tapping each feature's respective virtual switch.

iCloud Still Stores All of Your Content Purchases

Any time you acquire content from one of Apple's online business ventures, that purchase automatically downloads to the computer or device it was purchased on. However, it also gets stored in your iCloud account. Plus, Apple has kept track of all of your past purchases and acquisitions and has added them to your iCloud account as well.

This includes:

- App purchases for your iOS mobile device from the App Store
- Mac app/software purchases from the Mac App Store
- Music, movies, TV shows, audiobooks, ringtones, and music videos from the iTunes Store
- Ebooks from iBookstore
- Digital editions of newspapers and magazine from Newsstand
- Free podcasts acquired from the iTunes software running on your Mac or the Podcasts iOS app
- iTunes U lessons for online courses and personal enrichment programs you've registered for via the free iTunes U service. (On an iOS mobile device, install the free iTunes U app.)

As always, when you make a new acquisition (which includes free content from one of these online business ventures), you can delete and then reinstall that content at any time from the device it was acquired on. You can also either manually or automatically wirelessly install that content onto all of your compatible computers and devices via iCloud, without having to repurchase the content. To do this, your other Macs and iOS mobile devices need to be linked to the same iCloud account and have Internet access.

So if you buy a song from the iTunes Store on your iPhone, it downloads directly to your iPhone in less than one minute and is stored there. At the same time, you can set up your other computers and mobile devices, as well as your Apple TV, to automatically download that new song. Thus, when you launch iTunes on your Mac or the Music app on your iPad, the song will be ready to play.

Note Movies that you rent from the iTunes Store can only be downloaded and stored on one device at a time. From the iTunes software running on a Mac or PC, you can transfer a rented movie from one computer or device to another as long as you're within the 30-day storage period or 24-hour viewing period for that movie. However, movies that are purchased from the iTunes Store can be copied via iCloud to any and all of your linked computers or devices.

Access iCloud from Any Computer

In addition to being able to access data from Macs and iOS mobile devices running specific apps, such as Contacts, Calendar, Reminders, and Notes, from any computer that's connected to the Internet, it continues to be possible to access your app-specific data by launching that computer's web browser and visiting www.icloud.com. Once you log in to iCloud's website, click the app icon for Mail, Contacts, Calendar, Notes, or Reminders (shown in Figure 4-6) to access fully functional online versions of those apps that are populated with your own personal data.

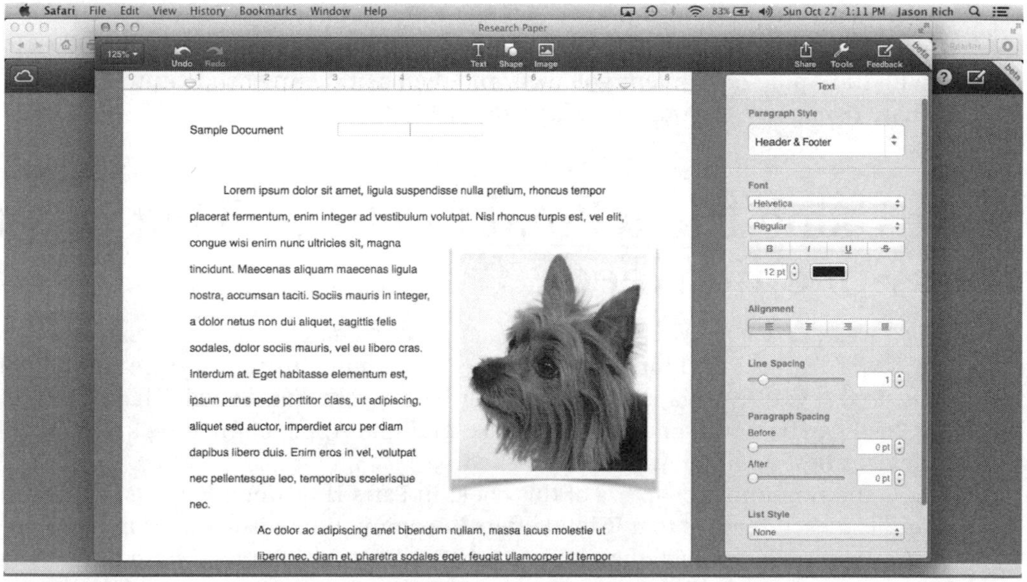

FIGURE 4-6   Access your app-specific data directly from iCloud's website using online versions of the apps. Shown here is the online version of the Pages app.

One of the newer features of the iCloud website is more robust compatibility and integration with the three iWork apps—Pages, Numbers, and Keynote. Now, in addition to just syncing Pages, Numbers, and Keynote documents and files and storing them online in your iCloud account, it's possible to run fully functional online-based versions of these apps from any computer (a Mac or PC), and have full access to your documents and files. Thanks to iCloud and new features added to the iWork apps, it's also now possible to collaborate on documents and files in real time with other people who are using any version of the same iWork app. For example, you can be working on a document using Pages on your Mac, while your coworker is reviewing and editing the same document on their iPad. Windows PC users can access the online edition of Pages and work on the same document at the same time, if they're invited to do so.

iWork for iCloud also provides an easy way for Windows PC computers to share documents and files with Mac computers, as it's possible to import Microsoft Word, Excel, or PowerPoint documents or files into Pages, Numbers, or Keynote respectively, and export Pages, Numbers, or Keynote documents or files to Word, Excel, or PowerPoint format so they can be accessed and used on a PC or Mac running Microsoft Office.

iCloud Works a Bit Differently with Each App

iCloud has evolved into a powerful online file- and data-sharing, syncing, and backup service that can be used for many different purposes, regardless of what your everyday computing needs involve. As always, once each feature of iCloud is turned on and set up, it's usually designed to work automatically and in the background. The tricky part, which is one core focus of this book, is understanding exactly how iCloud can be used with the Apple equipment you own, and then setting up each feature to work in a way that's conducive to your everyday work habits.

Start Using the iCloud Features That Meet Your Specific Needs

In Part I of *How to Do Everything: iCloud, Second Edition*, you have read an overview of iCloud's features and functions and discovered how this free service can potentially be used if you're a Mac, iPhone, iPad, or iPod touch user. You also have learned how iCloud can be very beneficial if you use multiple Apple computers and iOS mobile devices or if you use Apple TV.

The remaining chapters of this book, in Parts II through V, focus on how to set up and use each feature that iCloud offers in conjunction with your Macs, Windows-based PCs, Apple TV, and iOS mobile devices. We'll start in Chapter 5 with how to manage your digital music library and sync it with all of your computers and devices.

If you don't listen to digital music, you can always skip using this iCloud functionality and focus on iCloud functions that are more useful to you, such as managing and syncing a Contacts database or your schedule.

The thing to remember is that iCloud is designed to make transferring and syncing data, files, documents, photos, and content among your Macs, PCs, iOS mobile devices, and Apple TV a faster and easier process, plus the service offers certain functionality just for iOS mobile devices, such as the iCloud Backup feature.

At the same time, while much of iCloud's functionality is designed to allow an Apple computer or iOS mobile device user to sync and share data, files, documents, photos, and content with their own computers and iOS mobile devices that are linked to the same iCloud account, new functionality allows for certain types of information and data to be shared with others, without granting someone full access to everything stored in your iCloud account.

PART II

Manage Your Music, Multimedia Content, and Photos in the Cloud

5

Manage Your Digital Music Library and iTunes Purchases

HOW TO...

- Set up an Apple ID to work with iTunes.
- Install and use the iTunes software on your Mac or PC to manage and acquire music.
- Link iTunes to iCloud to share your iTunes Store music purchases with your other computers and iOS devices.

Apple has designed iCloud to handle many different tasks, mostly behind the scenes, to ensure that a wide range of files, data, and information is constantly available to you from your computers, Apple TV (for compatible content, such as music, TV shows, and movies), and/or all of your iOS mobile devices (including the iPhone, iPad, and iPod touch). Nowhere is this data syncing functionality more prevalent than with Apple's iTunes software for the Mac and PC, and the Music app for iOS mobile devices. Thanks to iCloud, your iTunes music purchases are accessible when and where you want to listen to them.

Note The new iTunes Radio service streams audio programming to your computer or iOS mobile device for free. However, it's possible to use iCloud to sync details about your favorite stations, as well as stations you custom create.

The iTunes software, which actually serves a handful of purposes, is free and should be downloaded to your Mac or PC. This extremely versatile software was designed to help you manage your entire music library, sync data between your primary computer and iOS mobile devices, and serve as a portal for accessing the iTunes Store to acquire and manage a wide range of content, including music, TV show episodes, movies, music videos, ringtones, audiobooks, and ebooks.

After you purchase content from the online-based iTunes Store, App Store, iBookstore, or Newsstand, it's immediately downloaded to the computer or device from which it was purchased, but it's also saved to your iCloud account. Thus, it becomes immediately accessible on all of your computers and iOS mobile devices that are linked to that account and that have access to the Internet. So, for example, if you purchase a song from the iTunes Store, and you have a computer, iPhone, and iPad, you do not need to repurchase the same song three times to enjoy listening to it on all three devices.

 All of the online storage space in your iCloud account that's needed to store your iTunes Store and related purchases (from the App Store, iBookstore, and Newsstand) is provided for free. The 5GB of online storage space that's also provided by Apple is used for your backup files and other personal content (excluding photos) that you store on the service.

Note To use iCloud with your Mac, you must first install OS X Mountain Lion or the latest edition of the Mac operating system, called OS X Mavericks. You'll also need to download and install the latest version of iTunes (v11 or later) and have an active Apple ID account. On a PC running Windows, in addition to the latest version of the iTunes software, you'll need to download and install the free iCloud Control Panel software (available from the Apple website at www.apple.com/icloud/setup/pc.html).

Did You Know?

You Can Make Your Content Purchases from Apple's iTunes Store

You can shop for content from Apple through the online-based iTunes Store, which is accessible via the iTunes software. From the iTunes software running on a Mac or PC, it's possible to purchase or acquire apps for your iPhone, iPad, or iPod touch, as well as ebooks, TV shows, movies, music videos, ringtones, audiobooks, and digital publications. You can also subscribe and listen to podcasts.

When you shop for similar content from your iOS mobile device, use the iTunes Store app to purchase music, movies, TV shows, music videos, or ringtones. Use the App Store app to acquire and install apps. The iBooks app is used to access Apple's iBookstore service, and you can use Newsstand to find and acquire digital editions of newspapers and magazines. To download and enjoy podcasts, use the optional (free) Podcasts app on your iOS mobile device.

Movies can also be rented by accessing the iTunes Store using the iTunes software from a Mac or PC, or by using the iTunes Store app on an iOS mobile device.

iBooks Is Now Available for the Mac

In addition to purchasing and reading ebooks from Apple's iBookstore using the iBooks app on the iPhone, iPad, or iPod touch, a version of iBooks is now available for free for the Mac. It can be downloaded and installed from the Mac App Store, and it works very much like the iOS edition of iBooks. (iBooks for the Mac will automatically be installed when you upgrade to OS X Mavericks.) All of your iBookstore ebook purchases can now be read on your Macs and iOS mobile devices.

Note   If you're a Mac user, don't confuse the iOS App Store with the Mac App Store. The iOS App Store is where you get apps for your iPhone, iPad, and iPod touch. The Mac App Store is where you can acquire Mac software via the Web. The Mac App Store is accessible by clicking the Mac App Store icon that's displayed on your Mac's Dock.

Using the iTunes software on your computer (or the iTunes Store app on your iOS device), you can browse through Apple's vast and ever-growing music selection, which currently includes more than 20 million songs. As you're music shopping, it's possible to preview music for free, and then, with a click of the mouse (on a computer) or the tap of a finger (on an iOS device), purchase individual songs or entire albums in digital format. Once music is purchased and downloaded, it can be enjoyed almost instantly using the iTunes software on a Mac or PC, or the Music app on an iOS mobile device.

Shop for Music from the iTunes Store

The iTunes Store allows you to browse for music by genre, artist, song title, and a wide range of other options, so you can quickly find and purchase what you're looking for. Or you can utilize the iTunes Genius feature, which allows the iTunes Store to recommend music based on your past music purchases and listening habits.

Note   The iTunes Store is online-based, so to use it, your computer, Apple TV, or iOS mobile device requires access to the Web. After the music has been downloaded to your computer or device, a web connection is no longer needed to enjoy listening to it at any time, because it is saved in the internal storage space of your computer, Apple TV, or iOS device. (On a computer, content can also be stored on an external hard drive or flash drive, for example.) Keep in mind, when you listen to music via iTunes Radio, that audio programming is streamed from the Internet to your computer or mobile device. It is not stored on your computer or mobile device, so a continuous Internet connection is required.

Whether you're looking for the latest chart-topping hit from your favorite artist, a classic "oldies" song, or music from an unsigned or up-and-coming band or artist, chances are you'll find it for sale in the iTunes Store.

From your Mac or PC, after you launch the iTunes software and then select the iTunes Store option, click the Music option to begin shopping for music (shown in Figure 5-1). For suggestions about what to purchase and download, check out the Albums and EPs, Singles, Genius Recommendations, and What's Hot music sections. If you know what you're looking for, enter the song title, album title, artist, or any other keyword related to that music into the iTunes Search field.

Each individual song or complete album offered by iTunes has its own listing in the iTunes Store. When you click a song or album listing, this leads directly to an album or song description page (shown in Figure 5-2), which then displays all the information you need to know about the song and/or album on a single screen.

When viewing an iTunes Store listing for an album, the album cover artwork, artist, music genre, number of tracks on the album, and the album's average star-based rating are displayed. You'll also discover a price icon, along with Songs, Ratings and Reviews, and Related tabs.

Click the price icon to purchase the complete album and download it to the device you're currently using. You'll need to enter your Apple ID to confirm the purchase. Instead of immediately purchasing the entire album, however, you have the option to view a listing of individual songs from the album and listen to a free preview of them, one song/track at a time.

FIGURE 5-1 Shop for music and other content from the online-based iTunes Store, using the iTunes software on your Mac or PC.

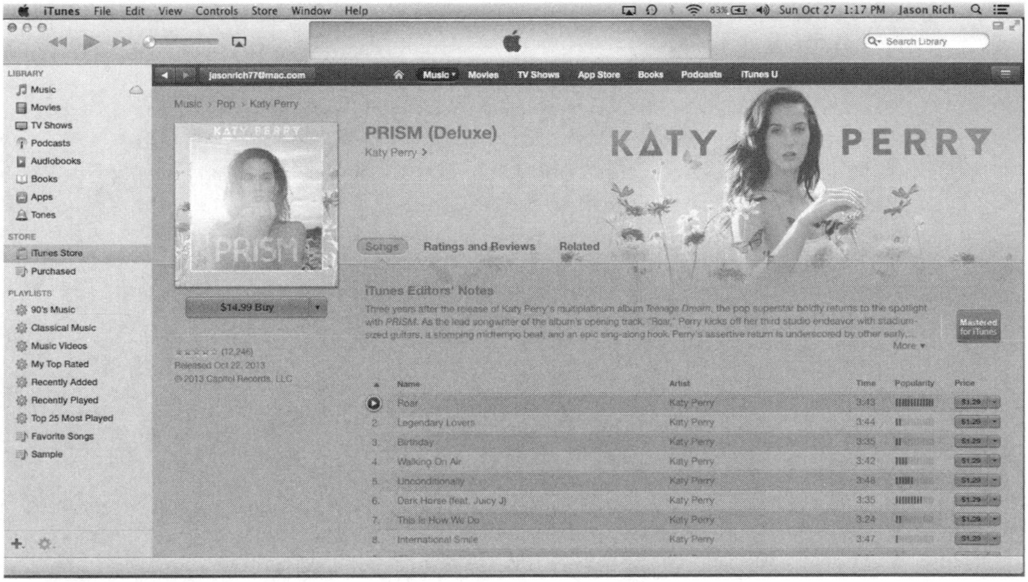

FIGURE 5-2   Every album or song offered by the iTunes Store has its own detailed description associated with it.

Tip   As with any Apple-related online purchase, when you purchase a new song or album by tapping the price icon, the credit or debit card that's linked to your Apple ID account will immediately be charged. You can also pay for iTunes Store purchases using a prepaid iTunes Store gift card. A gift card needs to be redeemed before you can use it to make online purchases. To redeem an iTunes Gift Card, while exploring the iTunes Store using the iTunes Store app on your iOS mobile device, scroll down to the bottom of the screen after tapping the Music, Movies, TV Shows, or Audiobooks option, and then tap the Redeem button. When accessing the iTunes Store using the iTunes software on a Mac or PC, click the Redeem option that's listed under the Quick Links menu on the right side of the screen.

In conjunction with each song track, you'll see either a price icon or an Album Only icon. If you click the price icon for an individual song listing, it's possible to purchase and download just that song, as opposed to the entire album. If you see an Album Only icon, this means that the song can only be acquired by purchasing the entire album (as shown in Figure 5-3).

If you already own one or more individual songs from an album, the songs you own will be shown with either an Open icon or an iCloud icon. An Open icon means you already own the song and it's already stored on the device you're using. In other words, you can play it right away. When you see an iCloud icon in conjunction with a song listing, this means you own the song, but it's not currently stored on the device you're using. Click the iCloud icon to download the song (for free, since you already own it).

Click the Ratings and Reviews tab to "like" a song or album on Facebook, write a review that will be published in the iTunes Store, view the star-based ratings the song

Album Only option

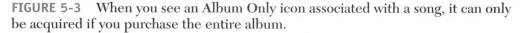

FIGURE 5-3 When you see an Album Only icon associated with a song, it can only be acquired if you purchase the entire album.

or album has received, and read reviews posted by other iTunes customers (shown in Figure 5-4). You can also enter your own star-based rating (between one and five stars).

Click the Related tab to see listings for other songs and albums that are somehow related to the artist or music genre of the song or album you're currently viewing.

FIGURE 5-4 Click the Ratings and Reviews tab to learn what other iTunes Store customers think about a song or album. You can also create your own review or star-based rating, or "Like" the content on Facebook.

How to... Discover Chart-Topping Music

To discover the most popular music currently available from the iTunes Store, access iTunes Top Charts. From your web browser, visit www.apple.com/itunes/charts/ songs to view a listing of the 100 current most popular songs on iTunes (based on purchased iTunes downloads). From the iTunes software on your computer, you can view several different Top Charts (for songs, albums, or music videos). These charts are displayed along the right margin of the main iTunes Store screen when you click the Music option.

From your iOS mobile device, launch the iTunes Store app, and then select the Top Charts option from the bottom of the screen. Near the top of the screen, tap the Music, Movies, TV, or Audiobooks option to see the Top Charts for each type of content. For example, if you tap the Music tab on your iPad, you'll see Top Charts for Songs, Albums, and Music Videos for all genres. To narrow down the Top Charts list and see popular music from a specific genre, tap the All Genres option, and then pick a Music category, such as Pop, Rock, Alternative, or Classical.

As you shop for complete albums from the iTunes Store, the album listings include much of the same information as individual song listings. When you click an album title or album cover artwork, the description screen includes a complete list of all songs from that album, which you can then preview one at a time or purchase individually.

As you're looking at a song listing or the song listings for an entire album, click or tap the song title to stream a sample of that track and be able to listen to it before making a purchase.

Learn More About Music Before Purchasing It

The iTunes Store's star-based rating system is a great way to clue you in as to a song or album's popularity (as shown in Figure 5-5). In fact, this rating system is used for all content that's available from the iTunes Store. Content, such as a song, can be rated from one to five stars, with five stars being the highest possible rating. So if a song has received thousands of ratings, and has an average five-star rating, chances are it's a pretty good song and wildly popular.

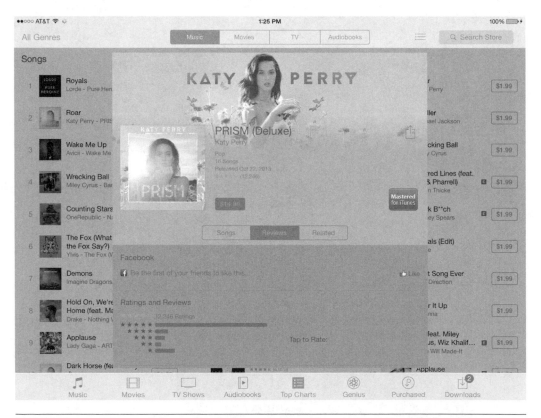

FIGURE 5-5   It's possible to check the ratings and reviews that specific content has received before making your purchase decision.

By clicking an album cover or song title within a listing, you can view a detailed description page or window for that song or album. Then, by clicking the Reviews tab, it's possible to read full reviews written by fellow iTunes Store customers and see more details about how many one-, two-, three-, four-, and five-star ratings that content has received.

Before you make a purchase decision, you can also listen to a preview of a song for free by tapping the song's title from within the description screen. (Similar previews are also available for TV shows, movies, audiobooks, ringtones, and ebooks.) After hearing the preview for a song, if you like what you hear, click the song's price icon to purchase and download that song from the iTunes Store. That purchase will be downloaded directly to the computer or iOS mobile device on which it was purchased; then it will become accessible to all of your computers and iOS mobile devices via iCloud.

The purchase price will be automatically charged to the credit or debit card that's linked to your Apple ID account, or it will be deducted from the iTunes Gift Card balance that's associated with your Apple ID account, if applicable.

To help you stay up to date on the latest music releases from popular artists, as well as new and up-and-coming artists, each week the iTunes Store offers a selection of free music you can download and enjoy. Once you download a free song, you own it (as if you purchased it), and it also becomes available to you via iCloud as part of your digital music library.

Tip   Any time content is offered for free from the iTunes Store, App Store, iBookstore, or Newsstand, the content will display a Free icon instead of a price icon. To acquire that content, tap the Free icon and enter your Apple ID when prompted. That free content will then be treated the same as purchased content. A copy will be downloaded to the computer or device it was acquired on, and a copy of the free content will be stored online in your iCloud account, and become accessible from your other computers or iOS mobile devices.

To find free music using the iTunes software on your computer, click the Music option (displayed near the top of the screen), and then look under the Music Quick Links heading for the Free on iTunes option (shown in Figure 5-6). The Free on iTunes screen will be displayed. Under separate headings, you'll see Music, Movie Featurettes, Featured TV Shows, and Apps, for example, that are being offered as free downloads.

To access free music on your iPad, launch the iTunes app and then tap the Music command icon. Scroll down to the bottom of the screen, and under the Quick Links heading, tap the Free on iTunes option (shown in Figure 5-7). On the iPhone, free offerings are interspersed with regularly priced content listings.

Browse the iTunes Store for Music by Genre

On a PC or Mac, to browse the iTunes Store for music based on genre, click the All Categories pull-down menu that's displayed under the Music heading on the right side

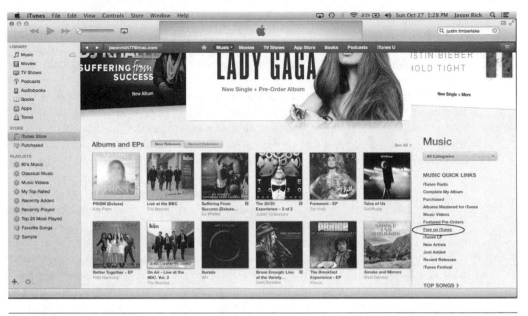

FIGURE 5-6 Discover free music and other content that's offered weekly from the iTunes Store.

FIGURE 5-7 Access free content from the iTunes Store app on the iPad from the Free on iTunes option displayed under the Quick Links heading.

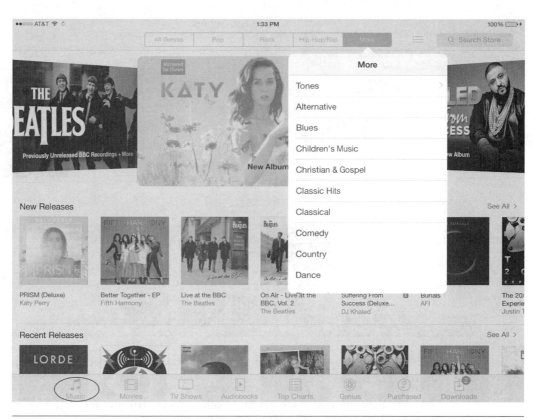

FIGURE 5-8   The music available from the iTunes Store is divided into 25 different music categories or genres.

of the screen after clicking the Music option at the top of the iTunes Store screen. From the pull-down menu, select one of the 25 music genres listed (shown in Figure 5-8).

Tip   On the iPhone, to browse available music based on genre, launch the iTunes Store app, tap the Music option, and then tap the Genres option that's displayed near the top-left corner of the screen. Choose a genre by tapping its listing, and then tap the Featured or Charts tab that's displayed near the top of the screen to view listings for related songs and albums that are available from the iTunes Store.

On the iPad, launch the iTunes Store app, tap the Music option, and then tap one of the music genre tabs displayed along the top of the screen. You'll see tabs that say All Genres, Pop, Rock, Hip-Hop/Rap, and More. Click one of these, or click the More tab to view the rest of the music genre categories (shown in Figure 5-9).

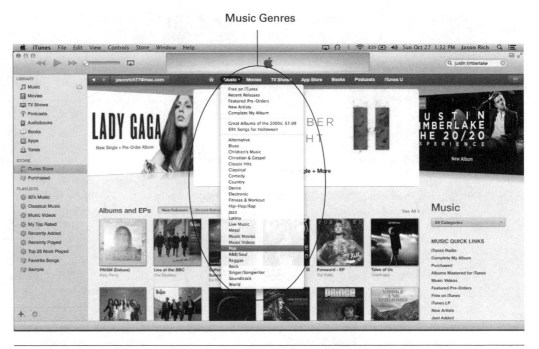

FIGURE 5-9 You can select a music genre from the iTunes Store app running on the iPad (or iPhone).

Like any music store, the iTunes Store offers music from many different genres that are sorted by category. The available categories include:

- All Categories
- Alternative
- Blues
- Children's Music
- Christian & Gospel
- Classic Hits
- Classical
- Comedy
- Country
- Dance
- Electronic
- Fitness & Workout
- Hip-Hop/Rap
- Jazz
- Latino
- Live Music
- Metal
- Music Movies
- Music Videos
- New Artists
- Pop
- R&B/Soul
- Reggae
- Rock
- Singer/Songwriter
- Soundtrack
- World

Save Money Using iTunes' Complete My Album Feature

Once you purchase one or more songs from an album, if you decide that you want to purchase the entire album, the iTunes Store offers the Complete My Album feature. This feature allows you to purchase the remaining songs on an album at a prorated (discounted) price. In other words, you don't have to repurchase music you already own. The discounted price will depend on how many songs from that album you've already purchased from the iTunes Store.

To use this feature from the iTunes software running on your computer, launch iTunes, and click the iTunes Store option (on the left side of the screen). Next, click the Music option (near the top-center of the screen). On the right side of the screen, under the Music Quick Links, click the Complete My Album option. iTunes will analyze your past iTunes purchases and display which albums you can purchase at a discount; it will also display the regular price and discounted price (which is displayed in blue).

To use this feature on an iPhone, access any album description screen from within the iTunes Store. If you already own one or more tracks/songs from that album, instead of the album's full price being displayed in the price icon, the prorated Complete My Album price will automatically be displayed, and to the left of the price icon will be an option (in blue) that says Complete My Album, along with the regular album price.

On the iPad, to access the Complete My Album feature, from the Home screen, launch the iTunes Store app. Tap the Music command icon that's displayed near the bottom-left corner of the screen. Using your finger, scroll down toward the bottom of the screen. Just above the Quick Links menu option, you'll see a heading that says Complete My Album, along with listings for the albums that you own at least one song from but not the entire album. Tap one of these album thumbnails. The album's description screen will display (in blue) the prorated Complete My Album price for that album, along with the regular price. The price displayed in the blue price icon will be the prorated price (shown in Figure 5-10).

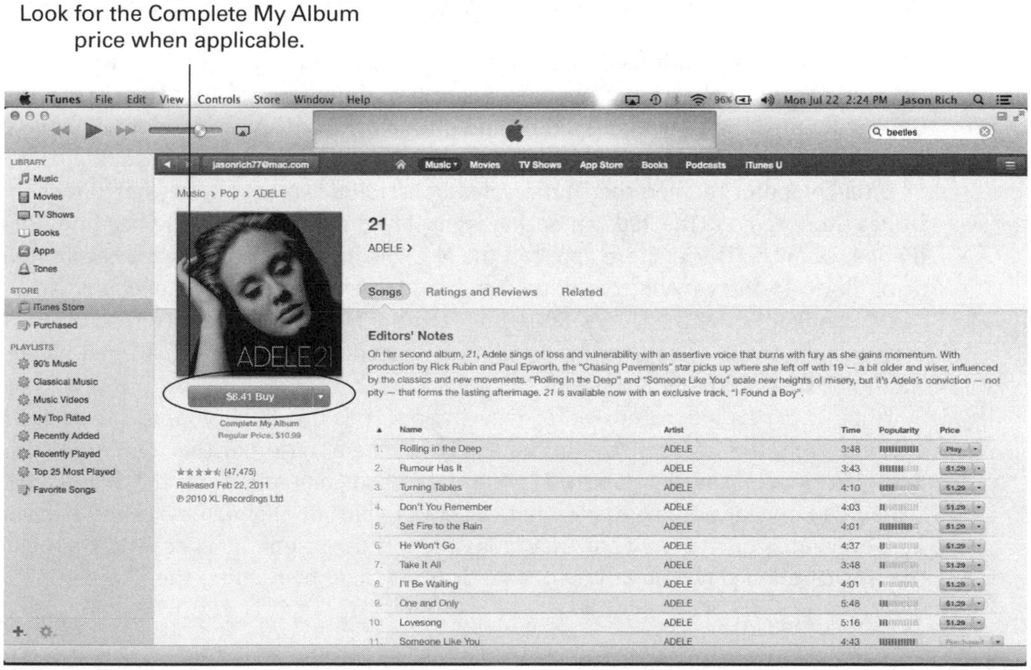

FIGURE 5-10   When appropriate, the iTunes software or iTunes Store app will display the Complete My Album price, in addition to the regular price on an album.

When it comes to purchasing TV show episodes from the iTunes Store, a similar Complete My Season option is available. Thus, you can go back and purchase the rest of the episodes of a television series, from the same season, for a reduced price.

Apple ID Required

When it comes to using your Mac, Apple TV, or iOS mobile device with any of Apple's online-based services or iCloud, a single Apple ID is required. This Apple ID not only identifies who you are and provides you with a free email account, it's also linked to a major credit card or debit card, which allows you to make online purchases from the iTunes Store, App Store, iBookstore, or Newsstand without having to reenter your contact and credit card information with each purchase.

Note If you don't link a credit or debit card to your Apple ID account, you can purchase prepaid iTunes Gift Cards and then redeem them when making online purchases. iTunes Gift Cards are available from Apple Stores, convenience stores, supermarkets, pharmacies, gas stations, or wherever gift cards are sold. They're also available online from Apple's website (www.apple.com/itunes/gifts). iTunes Gift Cards are available in several different denominations, such as $15, $25, and $50.

How to... ## Redeem an iTunes Gift Card and Make Purchases

To redeem an iTunes Gift Card and make purchases from the iTunes Store without using a credit or debit card, select the Redeem option when visiting the iTunes Store. Once you enter the code displayed on the gift card, your iTunes account will have a credit balance, which you can then use to purchase music or other content.

On a computer running the iTunes software, scroll down to the very bottom of the iTunes Store screen. The Redeem option is displayed under the Manage heading. On an iPhone, from the iTunes Store app, tap the Music icon, and then tap the Featured tab. Scroll down to the very bottom of the Featured screen and tap the Redeem button.

On the iPad, from the iTunes Store app, tap the Music command icon, scroll to the very bottom of the screen, and then tap the Redeem button that's displayed under the Quick Links heading.

When using an iPhone or iPad to redeem an iTunes Gift Card, you now have two options. From the Redeem screen, tap the Use Camera option or the You Can Also Enter Your Code Manually option. If you tap the Use Camera option, the Scan Card screen will appear and the rear-facing camera of your iOS mobile device will become active. Scratch off the gray bar that hides the gift card's unique code, and then place the gift card facedown on a flat surface. Scan the card by holding the iPhone or iPad

(Continued)

steady over it, as if you're taking a photo of the gift card's barcode. Once the gift card is recognized, that value of that card will be added to your Apple ID account almost immediately.

Instead of using the camera to scan the gift card and activate it, you have the option to scratch off the gray bar on the card that hides the card's unique code, and then entering that code manually using the iPhone or iPad's virtual keyboard when accessing the Redeem screen.

Keep in mind that iTunes Gift Cards are different from Apple Gift Cards. While an iTunes Gift Card can be used to purchase content online from the iTunes Store, App Store, iBookstore, or Newsstand, an Apple Gift Card is redeemable at Apple Stores (or Apple.com) for purchasing products, such as computers, iOS devices, or accessories.

If you already own a Mac, Apple TV, or iOS mobile device, when you first set up that device, you are prompted to create an Apple ID. You're given this opportunity again any time you attempt to make an online purchase from the iTunes Store, App Store, iBookstore, or Newsstand, or when you first establish an iCloud account.

To establish a free Apple ID, visit https://appleid.apple.com and complete the online form. The process takes just a few minutes. You'll be required to supply your full name, address, and birthday, as well as create a security question and a unique password for the account. Your actual Apple ID can be your primary email address (or your newly assigned iCloud email address), but it will have a separate Apple ID–specific password that you create. Once the Apple ID is established, you're given the option of linking a credit or debit card to the account.

Install and Set Up iTunes to Acquire and Manage Your Music Library

The iTunes software that runs on your Mac or PC can be used to manage your entire digital music library, including the following:

- Music purchased from the iTunes Store
- Music acquired from other online sources, such as the Amazon.com music service
- Digital music files you create ("rip") from your audio CDs
- Music files transferred to your computer (via email, for example)

Get iTunes Running on Your Mac or PC

To be able to use iCloud to access your digital music library (or at least the music you purchase or acquire from the iTunes Store), first install the latest version of the iTunes software on your primary computer, whether it's a Mac or PC. You can download this free software from www.apple.com/itunes.

Install and Use iTunes on a Mac

You'll then need to set up your free iCloud account, if you haven't already done so. Next, turn on iCloud functionality on your computer. On a Mac, access System Preferences and click the iCloud option. When prompted, enter your Apple ID and password that corresponds to your iCloud account. (If you're not automatically prompted to enter your Apple ID, click the Account Details option on the left side of the iCloud window.)

Next, launch the iTunes software (if it's not already running), and from the iTunes pull-down menu that's displayed at the top of the screen, select the Preferences option. The options displayed in the Preferences window that appears on your computer screen (shown in Figure 5-11) allow you to customize operations relating specifically to the iTunes software and the iTunes Store, including how both integrate with iCloud.

Click the Store option (displayed near the top-center of the Preferences window). Under the Automatic Downloads heading, you'll see a message that states, "iTunes can automatically download new purchases made on other devices using [insert your iCloud-related email address]. To change to a different account, sign in to the iTunes Store." Just below this message are three checkboxes, based on the type of content you have stored on your computer: Music, Apps, and Books. Click each option to add a checkmark.

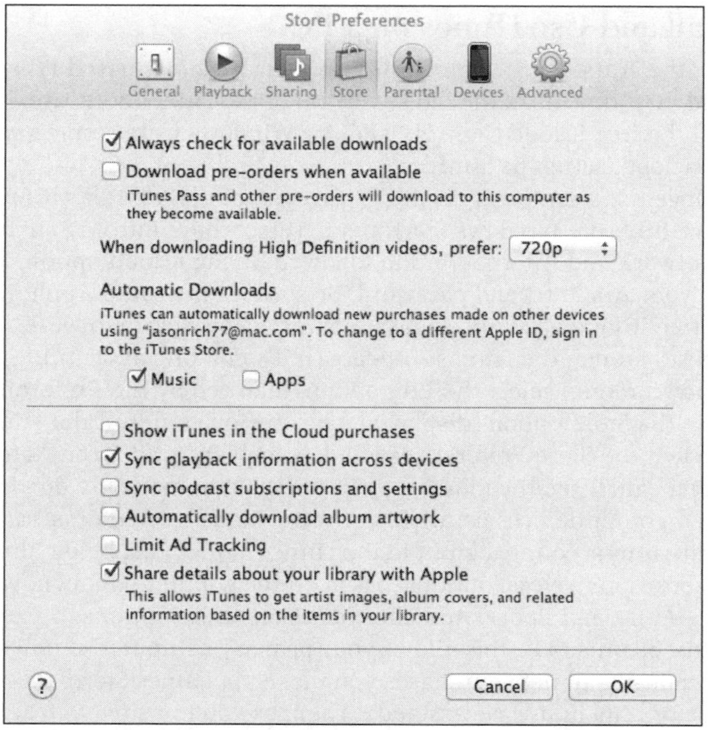

FIGURE 5-11   The Preferences window in the iTunes software.

Doing this allows your primary computer to download and store all new purchases you make via iTunes Store, the App Store, or iBookstore (including Newsstand) automatically. So, as you're using your iPhone or iPod touch, for example, when you download a new song or album, the next time you launch the iTunes software on your primary computer, that music will be downloaded from iCloud and automatically added to your iTunes music library on the computer as well.

Note If you do not add a checkmark to any or all of these checkboxes, the content that's purchased elsewhere will still be accessible from your primary computer via iCloud, but you'll need to select and download it manually.

Likewise, and by default, any time you make a purchase from the iTunes Store, App Store, or iBookstore using your primary computer, that content gets stored on your computer, but it is also saved to your iCloud account, so it becomes accessible from your other computers and iOS devices (and in some cases your Apple TV).

Install and Use iTunes on a PC

To get the iTunes software running on your Windows-based PC so it's able to access iCloud, first download the latest version of the iTunes software. Next, download and install the free iCloud Control Panel for Windows from Apple's website (www.apple .com/icloud/setup/pc.html).

Once the software is installed, turn on your computer's iCloud functionality. To do this, from the Windows Start menu, select the Control Panel option. Then select the Network and Internet option followed by the iCloud option. When prompted, enter your Apple ID and password. Be sure it's the same Apple ID you used to create your free iCloud account. Your computer is now set up to work with iCloud.

Next, launch the iTunes software (if it's not already running). From the iTunes pull-down menu, select the Edit option, followed by the Preferences option, and then choose the Store option (displayed near the top-center of the window).

When the Store Preferences window appears, under the Automatic Downloads heading, you'll see the message, "iTunes can automatically download new purchases made on other devices using [insert your iCloud-related email address]. To change to a different account, sign in to the iTunes Store." Just below this message will be checkboxes for several options, based on the content you own, which may include: Music, Apps, and Books. Add checkmarks to these options.

Just as on a Mac, this allows your primary computer to download and store automatically all new purchases you make via iTunes Store, the App Store, or iBookstore (including Newsstand). Then, as you're using your iPhone or iPod touch, when you download a new song or album, the next time you launch the iTunes software on your primary computer, that music will be downloaded from iCloud and automatically added to your iTunes music library on that computer.

How to... **Automatically Download Music to Another Device**

You can also set up your iPhone or iPad to download automatically from iCloud the music you purchase from the iTunes Store using another computer or device. To do this, launch the Settings app. From the main Settings menu, scroll down to the iTunes & App Store option, and tap it. From the iTunes & App Store menu within Settings, turn on the virtual switches associated with the automatic downloads of Music, Apps, Books, or Updates.

Settings	iTunes & App Store
iCloud	
Mail, Contacts, Calendars	Apple ID: jasonrich77@mac.com
Notes	
Reminders	SHOW ALL
Messages	Music
FaceTime	Videos
Maps	Show all store purchases and iTunes Match uploads in your music and video libraries, even if they have not been downloaded to this iPad.
Safari	iTunes Match
	Store all your music in the cloud with iTunes Match. Learn more…
iTunes & App Store	AUTOMATIC DOWNLOADS
Music	Music
Videos	Apps
Photos & Camera	Books
iBooks	Updates
Game Center	Automatically download new purchases (including free) made on other devices.
	Use Cellular Data
Twitter	Use cellular network for automatic downloads, iTunes Match, and iTunes Radio.

How Digital Music Becomes Accessible from iCloud

When you purchase music from the iTunes Store, it is automatically accessible when you run the iTunes software on your Mac or PC. When the iTunes software is running on your computer, click the Music option that's displayed under the Library heading on the left side of the screen to view your personal digital music library.

Did You Know?

Unless You Upgrade to iTunes Match, Only iTunes Music Purchases Get Synced via iCloud

Music acquired from other sources can be transferred to your iOS devices using the iTunes Sync process from the iTunes software running on your computer. It will not be automatically transferred to iCloud and made available on your iPhone, iPad, or iPod touch, for example, unless you've upgraded to the iTunes Match service.

Music that's acquired from other sources (not the iTunes Store) and saved on your computer's hard drive (or on another form of digital media) needs to be manually imported into your iTunes music library. When the iTunes software is running on your primary computer, access the File pull-down menu and select the Add to Library option. You'll then need to locate the digital music file to import into the iTunes software by selecting the appropriate drive or directory where it is stored.

If you have one or more audio CDs that you want to transform into digital music files that can be stored and played using the iTunes software on your computer (and potentially transferred to your other devices), insert each audio CD into your computer's optical drive while the iTunes software is running on your computer. A pop-up window will appear on your screen that allows you to import each song from that audio CD to your iTunes music library.

The process of transferring music from audio CDs to your computer is called "ripping" the CDs. It takes several minutes to complete the process of converting and then transferring every song from an audio CD to your computer. This process needs to be done only once per song, however.

Note

Although your entire digital music library becomes accessible from the iTunes software running on your computer, by default only the digital music you purchase from the iTunes Store automatically gets saved to your iCloud account and becomes accessible to all the computers and iOS mobile devices that are linked to your iCloud account (including your Apple TV device). If you want access to your entire digital music library via iCloud, including music not purchased through iTunes, you'll need to subscribe to the iTunes Match premium service, which is described in Chapter 6.

Manually Access and Download Past iTunes Purchases from Your PC or Mac

If you've been an iTunes Store customer for a while and have purchased content using a variety of different devices, Apple has kept track of these past purchases and will make them available to all your devices that are linked to the same iCloud account. This includes music, music videos, ringtones, TV show episodes, entire TV show seasons, ebooks, audiobooks, and purchased (but not rented) movies.

To manually access a past iTunes purchase that might not yet have been transferred to your primary computer, from the iTunes software on your computer, click the Purchased option that's listed under the Quick Links heading.

The main area of the iTunes screen will then display a detailed list of everything you've ever purchased from the iTunes Store. Click the Music, Movies, TV Shows, Apps, or Books option (shown in Figure 5-12) to see the content you have purchased in the past. As you're then browsing through the various content listings, items that have an iCloud icon associated with them indicate that the content is not currently stored on the computer you're using. Click the iCloud icon to download (or redownload) the content.

Note If you purchase content on your iPhone, for example, and then subsequently delete it from that iPhone, you can always redownload that content, for no additional cost, from your iCloud account.

When you tap the Music tab, along the left side of the main iTunes screen will be a blank Search field. Below that, you'll see an option labeled All Songs. Using the Search field, enter a song title, artist's name, or any keyword or search phrase that will help you find the music you're looking for. Or tap the All Songs option to view a listing of all individual songs you've previously purchased from iTunes that are now stored in your iCloud account.

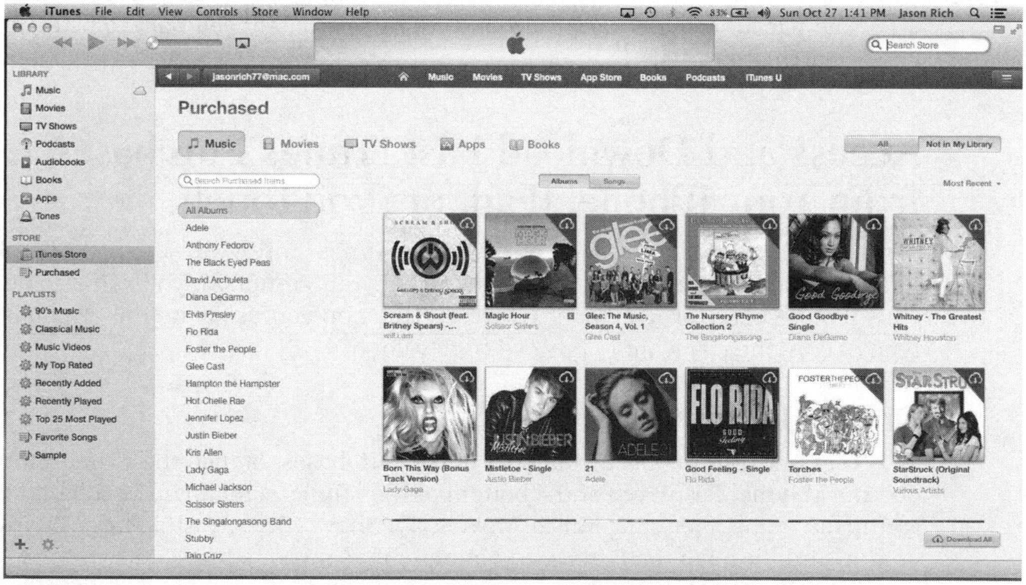

FIGURE 5-12   View all past content purchases you've made from the iTunes Store from your PC or Mac. Shown here are past music purchases.

Below the All Songs option, a listing of recording artists whose music you own will be displayed. Click either the All Songs option or one artist's name to reveal a listing of songs you can download. Each listing will include the song's title, the album title, the artist, and either a Download or iCloud icon. Tap the Download or iCloud icon to download the song to your computer and automatically add it to your music library.

 Instead of downloading one song at a time, click the Download All button to acquire all of the listed music at once.

Next to the Sort By option that's displayed near the upper-right corner of the window, sort the listed iTunes Store purchased content by most recent (based on purchase date) or alphabetically by name. Once you've transferred the previously purchased iTunes music from iCloud that you want stored on your computer, click the TV Shows, Movies, Apps, or Books tab to repeat this process. (Remember, free content you get from the iTunes Store, App Store, iBookstore, or Newsstand is ultimately treated the same as purchased content once it's been initially acquired.)

When you click the TV Shows tab, for example, you can view previously purchased TV show episodes as a comprehensive listing or sort them by series name, season, most recently purchased, or by episode title.

 When you transfer iTunes Store purchased content to your primary computer, these files take up storage space on your computer's hard drive. You can potentially free up a lot of hard drive storage space by allowing your iTunes purchases to be stored on iCloud, and then download only the iTunes content you want to listen to or watch at any time.

Access and Download Past iTunes Purchases from Your iPhone, iPad, or iPod touch

Just as you can easily access all of your past iTunes Store, App Store, and iBookstore (and Newsstand) purchases from iCloud using your computer, you can also do it from your iPhone, iPad, or iPod touch. However, the app you use to do this depends on the type of content you want to retrieve from iCloud.

On the iPhone (or iPod touch)

To access and/or download your past music purchases, launch the iTunes Store app on your iPhone. Displayed at the bottom of the iTunes screen will be a handful of command icons, including Music, Movies, TV Shows, Search, and More. Tap the More option, and then tap the Purchased option to reveal past iTunes Store purchases.

When the Purchased submenu (shown in Figure 5-13) appears on the iPhone, you'll be able to choose from several options, such as Music, Movies, or TV Shows, depending on the type of content that's available. Tap the Music option.

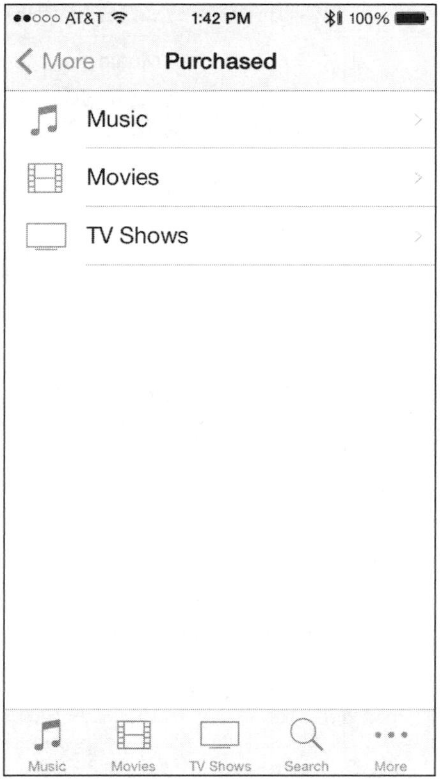

FIGURE 5-13   From the iPhone, choose the type of already purchased content you want to access.

Now the Purchased screen will display two command tabs, labeled All and Not on This iPhone (shown in Figure 5-14). Tap the Not on This iPhone option to display a listing of songs you've purchased that are available to you via iCloud but are not currently stored on your iPhone.

Note   On a PC or Mac, the iTunes software is used to acquire, manage, and play your digital music. On an iOS device, such as an iPhone or iPad, the iTunes Store app is used to acquire music and audiobooks, but the Music app is used to play this content. The Videos app is used to play TV show episodes, music videos, and movies.

You can also find music listed on this screen by tapping the All Songs option to view a listing of songs. It's then possible to sort the music by Most Recent, Name, or Artist Name. Tap the appropriate tab that's displayed near the top of the screen.

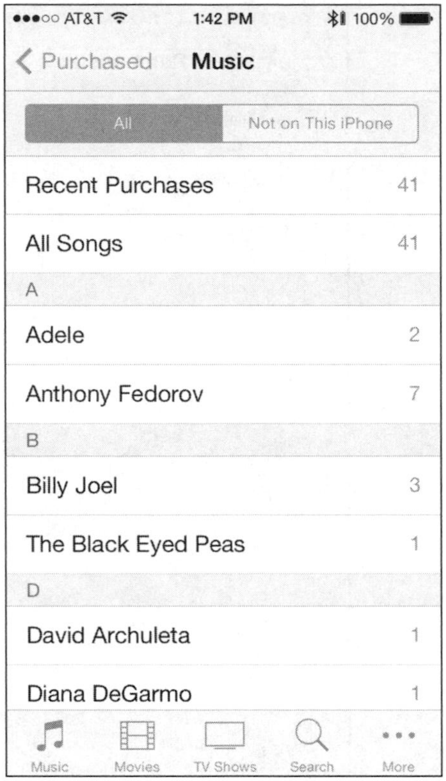

FIGURE 5-14 Tap the Not on This iPhone option to view content you own but that's not currently stored on the iPhone you're using. The All option shows listings for all content you own in that category, such as Music.

When you find the song you want to transfer (download) to your iPhone, tap the iCloud icon that corresponds to that music listing. The song will be downloaded and saved on your iPhone. To listen to it, launch the Music app.

On the iPad

On the iPad, several command icons are displayed along the bottom of the screen in the iTunes Store app, including Music, Movies, TV Shows, Audiobooks, Top Charts, Genius, and Purchased (shown in Figure 5-15).

Tap the Purchased option to view your past iTunes Store content purchases. From the Purchased screen, tap one of the content tabs (Music, Movies, TV Shows, etc.) that are displayed near the top-center of the screen. Then tap the Not on This iPad tab to view content that's not currently stored on your tablet.

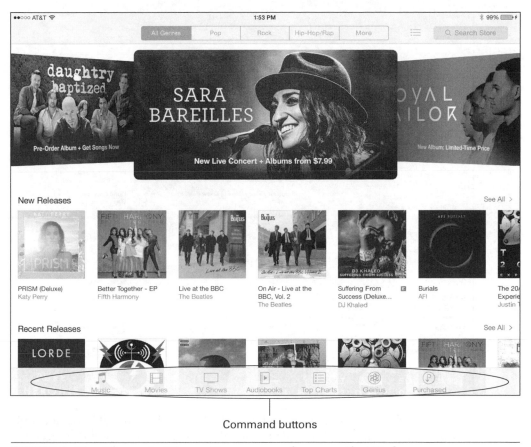

FIGURE 5-15   The main iTunes Store screen shown on the iPad.

If you select Music, for example, along the left margin of the screen, tap the All Songs option to see a listing of songs you've purchased from the iTunes Store. This information will then be displayed on the right side of the screen (shown in Figure 5-16).

Also near the top-right corner of the screen, tap the Songs By pull-down menu to determine how the listed music will be sorted. Options include: Songs by Most Recent, Songs by Name, Albums by Most Recent, and Albums by Name.

While you're viewing the All Songs screen on the iPad, click the iCloud icon that's displayed next to a song title to download it from iCloud to your tablet. Once it's downloaded and stored on your iPad, you can play the song using the Music app. Music that displays a Play icon (instead of an iCloud icon) has already been downloaded to the device you're using and is ready to be played using the Music app.

FIGURE 5-16 View music you own and that's stored in your iCloud account from the iTunes Store app on your iPad. The tabs shown at the top of the screen will reflect the type of content you've purchased in the past.

6

Use the Premium iTunes Match Service

HOW TO...

- Share your entire digital music library with all of your computers, Apple TV, and/or iOS mobile devices.
- Activate an iTunes Match subscription via the iTunes software on your primary computer.
- Discover how to use the iTunes Match feature in conjunction with iCloud.

You already know that one of the most popular features of iCloud is that it lets you share the music and content you acquire from the iTunes Store on all of the computers and mobile devices linked to your iCloud account. This feature is included with the basic iCloud service for free. When using iCloud to manage your digital music library (music that was acquired from the iTunes Store) or other content (such as TV shows, movies, apps, or ebooks) purchased from Apple, your iCloud account is automatically provided with as much online storage space as you need to store that purchased content.

But what about the portion of your digital music library that was not purchased from the iTunes Store? You can purchase and download music from many other online-based music services, including Amazon's MP3 Music store. You can also download music for free (and legally) from some other websites and online services, plus you can create your own MP3s by "ripping" your audio CDs and converting each song on your CDs into digital files that can be used with the iTunes software or the Music app on your iOS mobile device.

By default, the portion of your digital music library that was not acquired from the iTunes Store is not compatible with iCloud. However, you can opt to upgrade your iCloud service, for $24.99 per year, to activate the optional iTunes Match service.

iTunes Match Offers the Highest-Quality Music Files

When iTunes Match determines that music from your personal digital music collection matches songs from the iTunes Store library, the iTunes Match service automatically gives you access to the highest quality recording of that song possible (iTunes Plus quality, which plays back at 256 Kbps), even if the version in your personal music library was saved in a lower quality.

When you purchase music from the iTunes Store, it's provided to you in an AAC format that's fully compatible with the iTunes software for your Mac or PC, as well as the Music app that comes preinstalled on your iOS mobile device. The music is also compatible with Apple TV. To listen to iTunes Store purchased music with another digital audio player, it will first need to be converted into the MP3 file format, which can be done from within the iTunes software on your primary computer.

This premium service allows you to store and access your entire digital music collection on iCloud, regardless of how or where that music was initially acquired, and it includes as much additional online storage space as is needed for this task.

Once activated, iTunes Match examines the digital music collection that's stored on your computer's hard drive. It then compares it to the iTunes Store's library of more than 20 million songs. When matches are found between your personal music collection and songs available from the iTunes Store, those songs automatically become accessible to you on all of your computers and iOS mobile devices via iCloud. This process is repeated on each of your computers and iOS mobile devices that are linked to the same iCloud account. In the end, what you wind up with is all of your music synced among all of your computers and mobile devices.

When matches between your personal music library and the iTunes Store library can't be established, those unmatched songs in your music library (and those that are stored on your Mac, PC, or iOS mobile device) are automatically uploaded to your iCloud account, and within a few minutes, they become fully accessible on all of your computers and mobile devices that are linked to your iCloud account. As always, for this syncing feature to work, all of the computers and mobile devices need Internet access.

Sign Up for iTunes Match

To activate an iTunes Match subscription, first download and install the latest version of the iTunes software on your primary computer. Next, launch the iTunes software on your Mac or PC, and then, from the Store pull-down menu, click the iTunes Match option

FIGURE 6-1   To activate iTunes Match, click the iTunes Match option displayed under the Store pull-down menu within iTunes.

(as shown in Figure 6-1). You will be prompted to activate the iTunes Match feature, pay for the feature, and then enter your Apple ID password to confirm your purchase.

Tip   To ensure you have the latest version of iTunes installed on your computer, launch iTunes, and from the iTunes menu near the top-left corner of the screen, select the Check for Updates option. If a newer version of the iTunes software than the one installed on your computer is available, you'll be prompted to download and install the latest version.

Note   As soon as you purchase an iTunes Match subscription, you will receive a confirmation email from Apple that includes the date of purchase. Keep in mind that your subscription will automatically renew each year unless you turn off the auto-renew option.

Once activated, the iTunes Match service will begin a three-step process of analyzing your personal digital music library, matching it with the song library offered by the iTunes Store, and then uploading any songs from your library that could not

How to... **Turn on Music Match on Each Computer and iOS Mobile Device**

After you complete this process on your primary computer, turn on the iTunes Match service on each of the other computers, iOS mobile devices, and Apple TV devices that are linked to your iCloud account.

On your iPhone and/or iPad, to turn on iTunes Match, launch Settings, tap the iTunes & App Store option, and then turn on the virtual switch associated with iTunes Match. If you want your iOS mobile device to be able to access iCloud using a 3G/4G (LTE) cellular data connection (as opposed to just Wi-Fi), also turn on the virtual switch that's associated with Use Cellular Data. This option is included on the iTunes & App Store menu screen within Settings.

be found in the iTunes Store's vast music collection. Depending on the size of your personal music library, this process will take from several minutes to several hours.

The three-step process occurs only once, when you first activate the iTunes Match service. It begins with iTunes gathering information about your personal music library (as shown in Figure 6-2). The progress meter displayed near the center of the screen

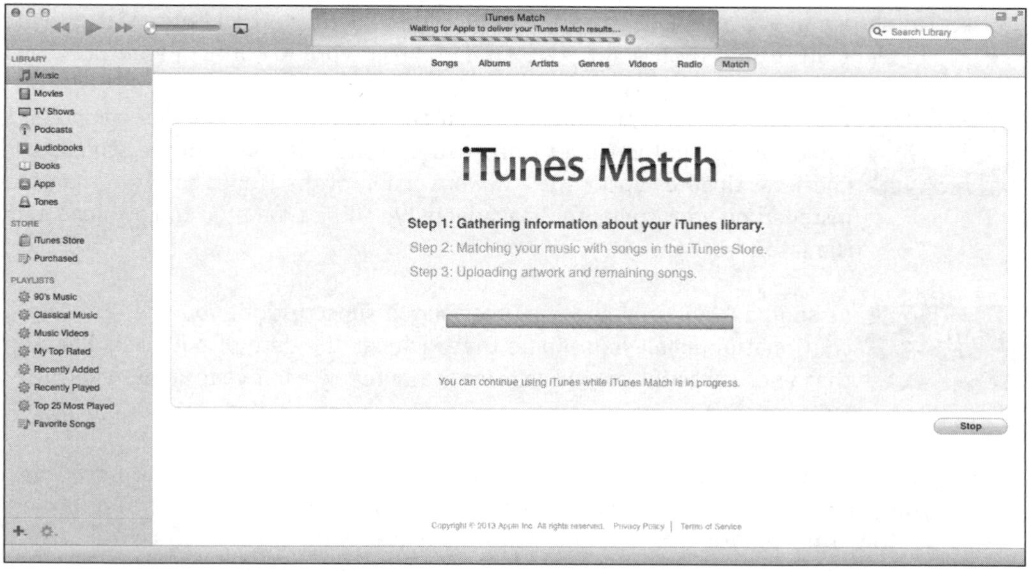

FIGURE 6-2 When iTunes Match is activated, the service gathers information about your personal music library by analyzing the music stored on your computer.

will keep you informed about how long this process will take based on the number of songs in your personal music collection.

As soon as this first step is completed, iTunes Match will immediately begin the second step, which is to match up as many songs in your personal music collection as possible with songs from the master iTunes library. A checkmark appears next to Step 1, and a new progress bar shows how many songs from your collection have already been checked for a match (on the left side of the progress bar) versus how many songs from your personal library still need to be compared to the master iTunes Store library of songs. Once again, how long Step 2 will take to complete will depend on how many songs are in your personal music library.

After the music library comparison is completed, you will discover that all of the songs that matched instantly become accessible to you through your iCloud account (as if they were all purchased from the iTunes Store) and can be enjoyed on any of your computers or mobile devices that are linked to your iCloud account.

Step 3 of the iTunes Match activation process will then commence, and all songs from your personal music library that didn't match up with songs found in the iTunes Store music library are uploaded, one at a time, from your primary computer to your online-based iCloud account.

Again, this process could take a while if many songs didn't match up. For example, if you're a musician and record your own music, or you have downloaded music that didn't include complete information (metadata) about each song within its digital file, those songs will need to be uploaded to your iCloud account.

Near the center of the iTunes screen, yet another progress bar will be displayed. Below this progress bar is a message reminding you to turn on the iTunes Match feature on your iOS mobile devices.

Note iTunes Match devotes as much additional online storage space as is required for all non-matching song uploads to iCloud. This extra online storage is included in the $24.99 annual fee.

As soon as Step 3 of the iTunes Match activation process is complete, your entire music collection, including both iTunes Store purchases and music from your personal digital music collection acquired from other sources, will be available to you via iCloud.

Caution Although you might be tempted to delete the music files on your computer's hard drive to free up space now that your entire digital music collection is stored on iCloud, you're better off transferring these files to an external hard drive and maintaining your own backup. This way, the song files will always be available if your Internet connection fails or, for whatever reason, you can't access iCloud.

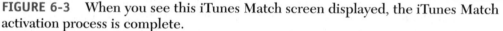

FIGURE 6-3   When you see this iTunes Match screen displayed, the iTunes Match activation process is complete.

When the message "Your iTunes library is now available in iCloud" is displayed near the top-center of the screen (Figure 6-3), the iTunes Match activation process is completed. At this point, you'll want to turn on the iTunes Match feature on your iOS mobile devices. In the meantime, click the Done icon.

How to Cancel Your Auto-Renewing iTunes Match Subscription

Your iTunes Match subscription is auto-renewing, which means that every year you will automatically be charged $24.99 for the service unless you cancel your subscription. To cancel your subscription from your primary computer, follow these steps:

1. Launch the iTunes software on your Mac or PC.
2. On the left side of the screen, under the Store heading, click iTunes Store.
3. Near the upper-left corner of the screen, click your email address or Apple ID account name that's displayed. When prompted, enter your Apple ID password in order to view the Account Information screen.
4. When the Account Information screen appears, scroll down until you see the iTunes in the Cloud heading that's displayed in blue (shown in Figure 6-4).

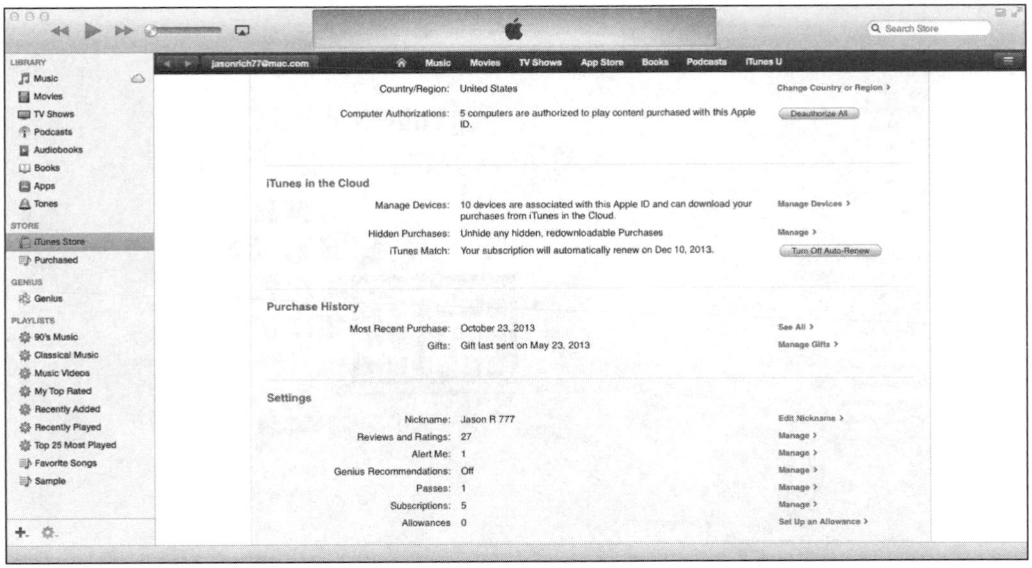

FIGURE 6-4   The Account Information screen in iTunes.

5. To the right of the iTunes Match option, click the Turn Off Auto-Renew option. Remember, to avoid being charged for an additional year, you must do this at least 24 hours before your existing subscription expires. The expiration date for the subscription is displayed within the iTunes in the Cloud section of the Account Information screen.

Tip   As you're looking at the iTunes Account Information screen, under the iTunes in the Cloud heading will also be an option to view all computers and devices linked to your iCloud account. Click the Manage Devices option to access this device listing and to remove one or more of the devices, if you so desire.

Activate iTunes Match on Your Other Macs

To activate the iTunes Match service on your other Macs or PCs running the iTunes software, you have two options. From the Store pull-down menu, select the Turn On iTunes Match option. Then, from the main area of the screen, click the Add This Computer button (shown in Figure 6-5). Or, from the Account Information screen, click the Add This Computer button.

FIGURE 6-5 Click the Add This Computer button to activate the iTunes Match service on your other computers, once you've subscribed to this service from your primary computer.

Activate iTunes Match on Your iPhone or iPod touch

As soon as iTunes Match is activated, you'll also need to turn on this feature on each iOS mobile device you'll be accessing your iCloud account from. The iTunes Match subscription fee allows you to access your music from multiple devices and computers. To activate iTunes Match on your iPhone (or iPod touch) that's running iOS 7, follow these steps:

1. From your iPhone's Home screen, launch Settings.
2. When the main Settings menu appears, scroll down to the Music app option, and tap it.
3. From the Music menu screen within Settings, tap the virtual switch next to iTunes Match (as shown in Figure 6-6) to turn it on.
4. At the bottom of the screen, a pop-up window will appear that displays the message, "iTunes Match will replace the music library on this device." Two options will also appear, labeled Enable and Cancel (as shown in Figure 6-7).
5. Tap the Enable icon, and the music library currently stored on your iPhone will be erased. It will be replaced with access to your entire music library that's now available via iCloud.

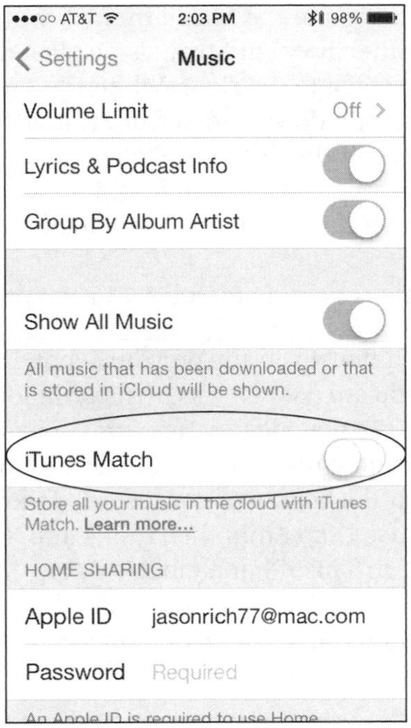

FIGURE 6-6 Turn on the iTunes Match option on your iPhone from within Settings.

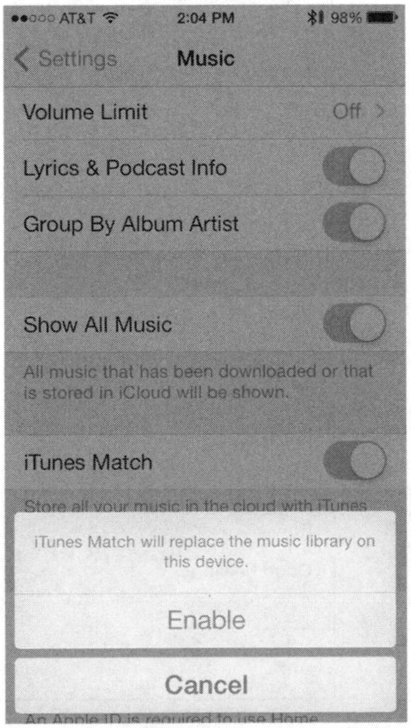

FIGURE 6-7 On the iPhone, confirm your decision to activate iTunes Match.

You will be returned to the Music menu within Settings. Just above the iTunes Match option, the Show All Music is displayed along with a corresponding virtual on/off switch to the right. When the virtual switch is turned off, only music that has been downloaded from iCloud to the iPhone will be displayed in the Music app. If the virtual switch is turned on, all music that has been downloaded, as well as all music stored on iCloud, will be listed in the Music app.

6. Tap the Home button on the iPhone to exit out of Settings and return to the Home screen.

7. From the Home screen, launch the Music app to begin enjoying your music.

When you launch the Music app on your iPhone, all music stored on your iPhone will be displayed when you tap the Playlists, Artists, or Songs option that's displayed along the bottom of the screen. To download songs from your iCloud account (and store them on your iPhone), tap the Store option in the Music app. When the iTunes Store launches, tap the More option (near the bottom of the screen), followed by the Purchased option.

From the Purchased screen in the iTunes app, tap the Music menu option, followed by the Not on This iPhone tab. Next, tap All Songs or one of the Artists listings to find the music you want to download to your iPhone from iCloud. Tap the song listings, and when the iCloud icon appears next to each listing, tap it to download that song (as shown in Figure 6-8).

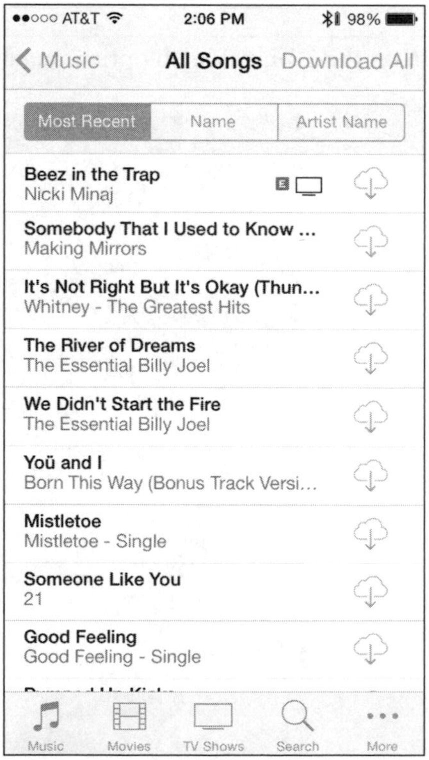

FIGURE 6-8   From the iTunes app on your iPhone, you can download music from your iCloud account and store it on your iOS mobile device.

Activate iTunes Match on Your iPad

As soon as iTunes Match is activated, you'll also need to turn on this feature on each mobile device you'll be accessing your iCloud account from. To activate iTunes Match on your iPad that's running iOS 7, follow these steps:

1. From your iPad's Home screen, launch Settings.
2. Along the left side of the screen, you will see the main Settings menu. Scroll down to the iTunes & App Store option.
3. On the right side of the screen, the iTunes & App Store submenu within Settings will appear (as shown in Figure 6-9). Turn on the virtual switch that's associated with the iTunes Match feature.
4. A pop-up window that says, "iTunes Match will replace the music library on this device" will appear, along with Enable and Cancel options. Tap the Enable option to continue.

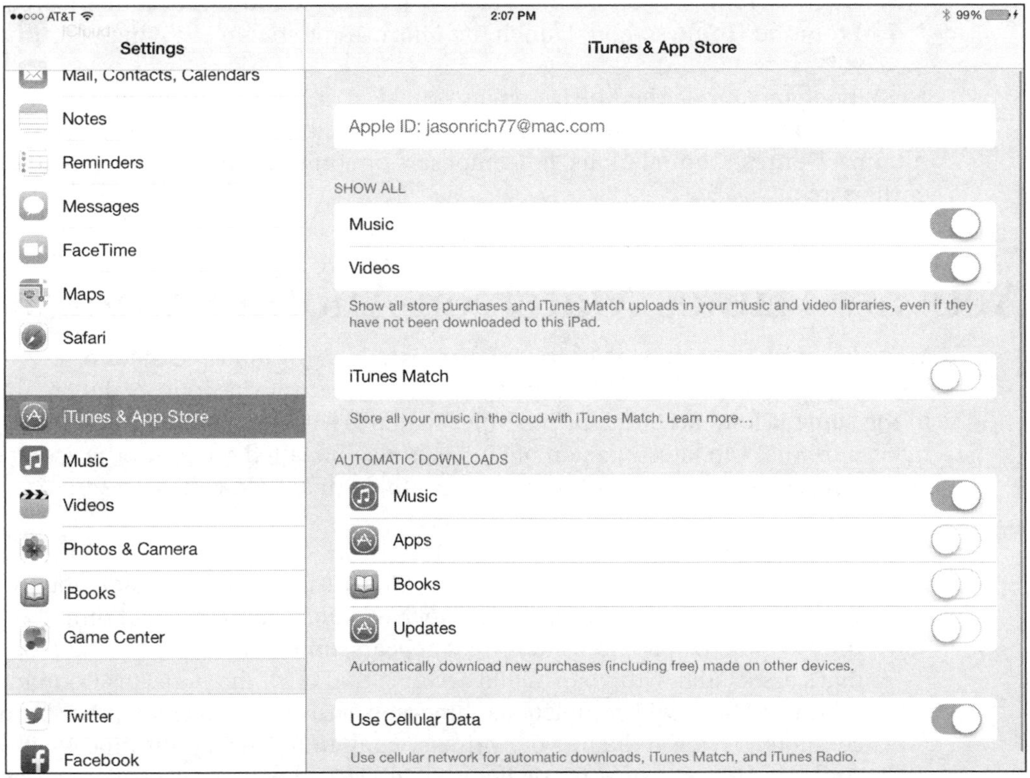

FIGURE 6-9 The main Settings menu shown on the iPad running iOS 7.

How to... **Download Music from iCloud**

To download songs from your iCloud account (and store them on your iPad), while running the Music app, tap the Artists, Songs, Albums, Genres, Compilations, or Composers option that's displayed near the bottom of the screen. Choose which songs you want to download, and then tap the iCloud icon that's associated with each song or album listing.

5. Also on the iTunes & App Store submenu (on the right side of the screen), just above the iTunes Match option, the Show All Music option is displayed. It is also associated with a virtual on/off switch. When turned off, only music that has been downloaded to your iPad will be displayed in the Music app. When turned on, all music that has been downloaded to the iPad or that is stored on iCloud will be shown in the Music app. Turn this virtual switch to the on position by tapping it.
6. Tap the Home button on the iPad to exit Settings and return to the Home screen.
7. From the Home screen, launch the Music app to begin enjoying your music.

When you launch the Music app on your iPad, all music stored on your tablet or accessible from iCloud will be displayed when you tap the Playlists, Artists, Songs, Albums, Genres, Compilations, or Composers option that's displayed along the bottom of the screen.

Activate iTunes Match on Another Computer

You can set up your music library to be accessible from multiple Macs or PCs, including your desktop and laptop computer, for example, as long as they're linked to the same iCloud account. Once iTunes Match is set up on your primary computer, make sure that the latest version of iTunes is also installed on your other computers, and then activate the iTunes Match feature. To do this, follow these steps:

1. Launch iTunes on your secondary Mac or PC.
2. From the Store pull-down menu, select the Turn on iTunes Match option.
3. When the iTunes Match screen is displayed, click the Add This Computer option.
4. In the Apple ID pop-up window that appears, enter the Apple ID and password that's associated with your iCloud account, and click the Add This Computer icon.
   iTunes Match will complete its three-step activation process on the secondary computer, just as it did on your primary computer. During this process, it will compare your personal music library that's stored on your secondary computer with the main iTunes music library. When necessary, it will then upload nonmatching songs to the iCloud service and synchronize your entire personal music library listing. All of the music on your primary and secondary computers will be stored in your iCloud account as one personal music library, which will be accessible from any of your computers and mobile devices.

5. When the message "Your iTunes library is now available on iCloud" is displayed on your secondary computer, click Done.

6. From the main iTunes screen, click the Music option that's displayed near the upper-left corner of the iTunes software screen (below the Library heading). A comprehensive listing of your personal digital music library, including the music stored on iCloud, is displayed. You can access this music by clicking the Songs, Albums, Artists, Genres, or Match tabs, for example, that are displayed near the top-center of the screen.

 When you begin using your secondary computer with the iTunes Match service turned on, a pop-up window will appear once asking if you want to turn on automatic downloads for this computer. By clicking the Turn on Automatic Downloads icon, any time you purchase new content, it will be downloaded to the computer you're currently using, regardless of on which computer or iOS mobile device it was actually purchased on.

When you're looking at a Listing view of your music, look under the Cloud column to see if a song is stored on your computer or is only on iCloud. If an iCloud icon appears next to a song listing, it is available via iCloud but is not yet stored on your computer's hard drive. To download a specific song, click the iCloud icon that corresponds to a song listing.

Keep Your Music Library Up to Date on iCloud

iTunes Match automatically keeps your entire personal music library available via iCloud, regardless of which computer or iOS mobile device you use to acquire new music in the future. For example, if you access iTunes Store or another music service from your iPhone to purchase a few new songs, iTunes Match will sync those new additions to your personal music library stored in iCloud, ensuring that the new additions are accessible from all of your devices and computers.

Note If the auto-update process isn't keeping up with new music added to your personal music library, when running the iTunes software, access the Store pull-down menu and select the Update iTunes Match option on your primary or secondary computer. This might be necessary if your laptop computer hasn't been connected to the Internet for a while, during which time new music was added to your iCloud account or stored on your laptop computer's hard drive after being ripped from a CD, for example.

Using the iTunes software (or iTunes app on your iOS mobile device) in conjunction with iTunes Match and iCloud is only one option when it comes to acquiring music, managing your personal music library, and making your music available to all of your computers and/or mobile devices via a cloud-based service. There are a growing number of other cloud-based services available to you, and each offers a different collection of features at a different price.

If you're a Mac user who wants to make your music library available on other Macs, in addition to your iPhone, iPad, iPod touch, and/or Apple TV, using the iTunes software in conjunction with iCloud and also subscribing to iTunes Match probably makes the most sense in terms of functionality, price, and ease of use. However, be sure to familiarize yourself with other cloud-based options related to managing and enjoying music, including what's available from the Amazon MP3 Music service. You can learn more about these alternative services by surfing the Internet. For example, to learn more about Amazon.com's offerings, visit www.Amazon.com and click on the MP3 Store option or the Cloud Player option that's displayed near the top-center of the screen, as well as under the Shop By Departments heading.

7

Store and Manage Your Digital Photos with My Photo Stream

HOW TO...

- Set up the My Photo Stream feature of iCloud.
- Access and manage My Photo Stream from your iOS mobile devices.
- Use My Photo Stream with iPhoto or Aperture on your Mac.
- View images from your My Photo Stream on a television using Apple TV.

Digital photos are among the various types of data and content that iCloud allows you to share among your Macs, PCs, iOS mobile devices, and your HD television (via Apple TV). You can do this by activating and utilizing iCloud's My Photo Stream feature.

Separate from the digital images stored on your primary computer or mobile devices, your online-based My Photo Stream is a collection of up to 1,000 of the most recently shot or imported images that were taken using any of your mobile devices, imported into your mobile devices, or imported into your primary computer (from your digital camera or its memory card, for example). These images are collected, stored in your iCloud account, and ultimately displayed in reverse chronological order (with your newest images displayed first).

Once My Photo Stream reaches 1,000 images, or after 30 days have passed, the oldest images are automatically removed to make room for new images. These images are then archived on your primary computer's hard drive or on an external hard drive that's connected to your primary computer (you select the destination). The former photo stream images will remain saved there until you manually delete them.

The images that become part of My Photo Stream are stored online in your iCloud account. Thus, they become available on all of your computers and mobile devices that are linked to the same iCloud account.

Did You Know?

iCloud's My Photo Stream and Shared Photo Stream Have Two Different Purposes

The difference between iCloud's My Photo Stream and iCloud's Shared Photo Stream features is that your iCloud account can have one centralized photo stream that is used to sync and share images among all of your own computers and iOS mobile devices. This is referred to as iCloud's My Photo Stream, or simply the photo stream feature.

Shared Photo Streams are online galleries that can be used to share groups of your digital images with other people (who are using computers or mobile devices that are not linked to your iCloud account). You can have as many separate Shared Photo Streams as you like, plus you have the ability to invite whomever you want to view each Shared Photo Stream. How to create and manage Shared Photo Streams is the focus of Chapter 8.

So, if you activate this feature on your iPhone and iMac, for example, almost immediately after you snap a photo on your iPhone, it will automatically be uploaded to My Photo Stream and be accessible from your iMac (via iPhoto or Aperture), as well as on your iPhone and/or iPad (via the Photos or optional iPhoto app), without your having to copy, email, or manually transfer the image, or use iTunes Sync.

For iCloud's My Photo Stream to work, you'll need to be running the latest version of OS X Mavericks, as well as iPhoto or Aperture on your Mac. Older versions of the operating system and Apple's digital photography apps don't have all of the latest iCloud and photo stream functionality or compatibility built in.

Note

For My Photo Stream to work, each of your computers must have access to a high-speed Internet connection (such as broadband or DSL), and/or your iOS mobile devices need Internet access via a Wi-Fi connection. This feature does not work with an iPhone or iPad's cellular Internet connection.

Once an image becomes part of My Photo Stream, you can manually save it to any of your computers or iOS mobile devices that are linked to your iCloud account, so those images can remain on that computer or device indefinitely, until you manually delete them. Plus, you'll then be able to edit any saved images that have been copied from My Photo Stream. Keep in mind, images in My Photo Stream are accessible from your computers or mobile devices, but are not permanently stored on them.

You must manually save individual images from My Photo Stream to whichever computer or device you're using in order to work with them using the iPhoto or Aperture software (on your Mac) or the Photos or iPhoto app (on your iOS mobile device).

How to...   **Add Images to My Photo Stream**

From an iOS mobile device, there are a handful of sources from which you can access digital photos to include in My Photo Stream that's managed using the Photos app (or optional iPhoto app). For example, it's possible to snap a photo using the built-in camera on your iPhone, iPad, or iPod touch. You can also import an image to the mobile device's Photos app, or you can use Apple's optional Camera Connection Kit ($29, http://store.apple.com/us/product/MC531ZM/A) to import images from your digital camera's memory card into your mobile device. Similar adapters (available from the Apple Store or www.Apple.com) are available to connect an SD card reader to your iOS mobile device, or link your digital camera directly to your iOS mobile device using a USB cable connection.

As you're surfing the Web, you can also place and hold your finger on most images, and then tap the Save Image option to store that image or graphic in the Camera Roll album of the Photos app, at which time it can also be added to My Photo Stream.

Once you save a new image to your iOS device, if the My Photo Stream feature is turned on, that image will be uploaded to iCloud and almost immediately added to My Photo Stream.

On a Mac or PC, you can manually drag and drop or copy images stored elsewhere on your computer into the My Photo Stream album within iPhoto or Apple's optional Aperture software ($79.99, www.apple.com/aperture/), after which time those images get uploaded to iCloud and become part of My Photo Stream.

Note   As you'll discover, all new images added to your computer or mobile device can automatically become part of My Photo Stream once this feature is turned on. You can then access My Photo Stream and manually delete images from it, if you choose to do so. How to do this will be explained shortly.

The up to 1,000 images that can automatically be stored using My Photo Stream on iCloud do not use up any of the free 5GB of free online storage space that's provided by Apple. You can feel free to use My Photo Stream with the highest-resolution digital images possible, regardless of their individual file sizes. iCloud displays your images in a resolution that's "optimized" for the computer or device you're using.

First Turn On the My Photo Stream Feature

Just as with all other iCloud-related features, you must manually turn on the My Photo Stream feature on each of your computers and iOS mobile devices separately, and make sure they're each set up to log in to the same iCloud account. Note that even if this feature is turned on within your iPhone or iPad, it will not work unless a Wi-Fi Internet connection is present.

Pros and Cons of Using My Photo Stream

With My Photo Stream, as soon as you shoot a photo on your iOS mobile device or import a photo from your digital camera to your computer, it immediately becomes accessible, viewable, and potentially editable on your primary computer and iOS mobile devices, and viewable on your television screen (via Apple TV). You do not have to transfer or copy your images manually among computers or devices that are linked to the same iCloud account.

By default, this feature also creates a temporary (30-day) online backup on iCloud of your newest images. The drawback of this feature, however, is that My Photo Stream gathers and stores all of your new photos, or none of them, based on whether you turn on or off the My Photo Stream feature.

Thus, when the My Photo Stream feature is turned on, in addition to your favorite photos being added to My Photo Stream, all of the blurry, redundant, overexposed, or underexposed images also get uploaded to iCloud. They can later be manually removed, however.

You can pick and choose which images remain in My Photo Stream, but as you're shooting photos on your iPhone or iPad, for example, anyone who uses your Mac will be able to view all of your images almost immediately as they're added to My Photo Stream (or vice versa).

Turn On My Photo Stream on Your Mac

On a Mac, before setting up the My Photo Stream feature, you'll need to create and activate a free iCloud account. It's then necessary to turn on iCloud's My Photo Stream feature on the Mac itself, and then in whichever photo management/editing software you'll be using on your Mac. This process needs to be done only once (on each Mac).

To turn on the My Photo Stream feature on your Mac, follow these steps:

1. Launch System Preferences on your Mac from the Dock or the Applications folder.
2. From the System Preferences window, click the iCloud icon.
3. When prompted, sign in to iCloud using your Apple ID and password when the iCloud window appears in System Preferences. If you're already signed in to your iCloud account, this step is not necessary.
4. Once you're signed in, add a checkmark to the checkbox displayed next to the Photos option.
5. Click the Options button that's associated with the Photos menu option.
6. From the iCloud Photo Options pop-up window that's displayed (shown in Figure 7-1), add a checkmark to the My Photo Stream checkbox.

The My Photo Stream option on your Mac is now turned on. However, you still need to turn on this functionality in the iPhoto and/or Aperture software.

FIGURE 7-1 Turn on the My Photo Stream feature by adding a checkmark to the appropriate checkbox.

To turn on the My Photo Stream feature in iPhoto, follow these steps:

1. Launch the iPhoto software on your Mac.
2. Click the iPhoto pull-down menu that's displayed near the top-left corner of the screen, and select the Preferences option.
3. Click the iCloud icon that's displayed near the top-center of the Preferences window (shown in Figure 7-2).
4. Add a checkmark to the checkbox that's associated with the My Photo Stream option. Then customize how My Photo Stream will function on the Mac you're using by adding (or removing) checkmarks from the checkboxes associated with the Automatic Import and Automatic Upload options.

Note If you add a checkmark to the checkbox that's associated with the Automatic Import option, the My Photo Stream feature will automatically include images from Events, Photos, Faces, and Places. If you add a checkmark to the checkbox associated with Automatic Upload, all images added to iPhoto will automatically be added to My Photo Stream.

At this point, any new photos that have been added to My Photo Stream from other devices will be imported into the My Photo Stream album (which you can access

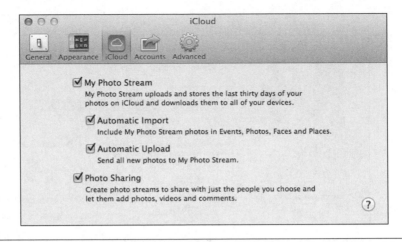

FIGURE 7-2 From within iPhotos Preferences window, click the iCloud icon.

anytime by clicking the Photo Stream option on the left side of the iPhoto window). Depending on how many photos there are, the process could take several minutes.

From this point forward, any new photos you import into iPhoto (from your digital camera's memory card or from other sources) will automatically be uploaded to iCloud, added to your My Photo Stream, and viewable anytime from the My Photo Stream album in iPhoto.

 For instructions on how to set up Aperture on your Mac to work with iCloud's My Photo Stream, visit the Support area of Apple's website at www.apple.com/support/aperture.

Turn On My Photo Stream on Your PC

Once you turn on My Photo Stream functionality to work with your PC, your photo stream images will be stored in a subfolder in your Pictures folder. You can then access, view, edit, print, and share those images using whatever photo management and editing software you typically use on your Windows-based computer.

To turn on My Photo Stream functionality via iCloud on your PC, follow these steps:

1. Download and install the iCloud Control Panel software. You can download this free software from Apple's website at http://support.apple.com/kb/DL1455.
2. Once the iCloud Control Panel software is installed, from the Windows Start menu, choose Windows Control Panel.
3. From Control Panel, click the Network and Internet option.
4. Click the iCloud option, and log in to your iCloud account when prompted by entering your Apple ID (or whichever email address you used to set up the account) and password.

5. When the iCloud Control Panel window appears, add a checkmark next to the Photo Stream option. The iCloud Control Panel looks almost identical to the iCloud window in System Preferences on a Mac.
6. Click the Options icon to the right of the Photo Stream option to customize your settings and activate (or deactivate) Photo Stream's Automatic Import and Automatic Upload features.

Unless you choose an alternative location, by default, your My Photo Stream images will be stored on your PC at the following location: C:\Users\Apple\Pictures\Photo Stream\My Photo Stream.

Note   When your computer or iOS mobile device accesses My Photo Stream from iCloud, it will download any and all new images that have already been added to the My Photo Stream image collection and store them temporarily in a Photo Stream album on your computer or device (in the iPhoto software on a Mac, or the Photos app on your iPhone or iPad, for example). This album will remain synchronized with iCloud and update automatically as new photos are added or deleted.

Turn On My Photo Stream on Your iPhone, iPad, or iPod touch

If you have multiple iOS mobile devices, you'll need to turn on iCloud's My Photo Stream feature on each device separately. To turn on My Photo Stream functionality on any of your iOS mobile devices that are running iOS 7, follow these steps:

1. Create your iCloud account (if you have not already done so).
2. Launch Settings from the Home screen.
3. From the main Settings menu, select the iCloud option by tapping it.
4. When the iCloud menu screen appears within Settings, log in to your iCloud account (if prompted to do so).
5. Tap the Photos option on the iCloud menu within Settings.
6. From the Photos menu screen (shown in Figure 7-3), tap the virtual on/off switch next to the My Photo Stream option to turn it on.

Note   From the Photos menu screen within Settings, you can also turn on or off the virtual switch associated with the Photo Sharing option. This refers to iCloud's Shared Photo Stream feature, which is the focus of Chapter 8. As you can see, although both are iCloud-related features, My Photo Stream and Shared Photo Stream can be controlled separately.

From this point forward, My Photo Stream will automatically upload to iCloud all new photos added to your iPhone, iPad, or iPod touch, and almost simultaneously download and share them to all of your devices that are linked to the same iCloud

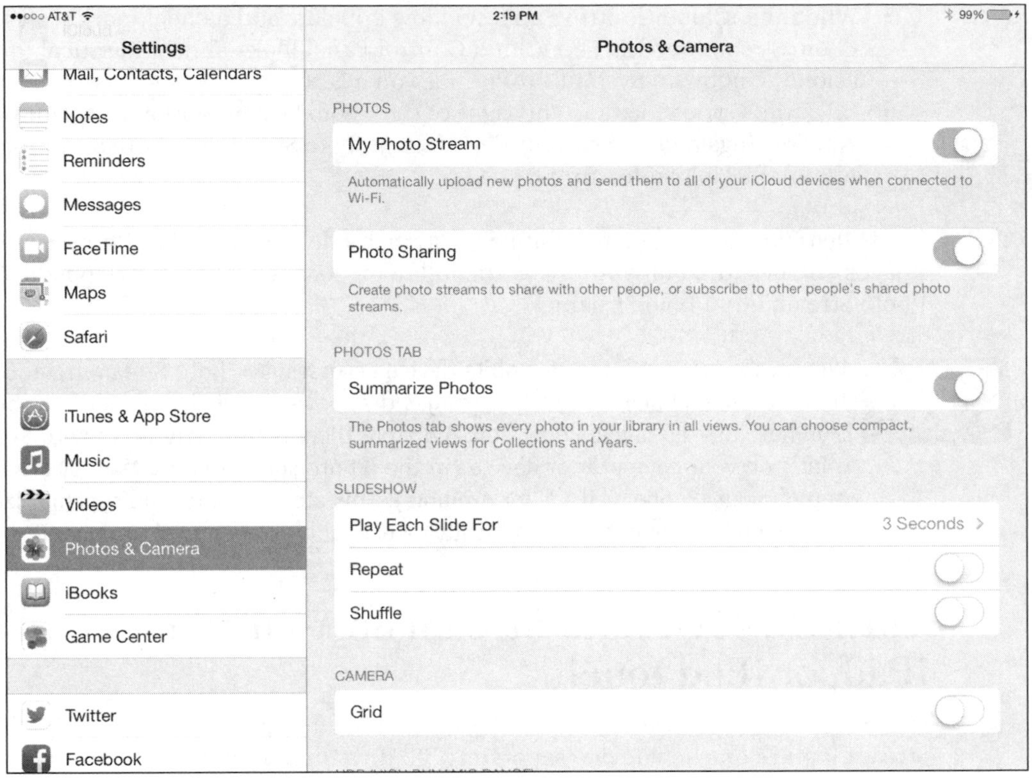

FIGURE 7-3 From the Photos menu screen within Settings, turn on the My Photo Stream option, as shown here on the iPad.

account and that have the My Photo Stream feature turned on. Likewise, any images added to My Photo Stream on your Mac, for example, will become accessible and viewable from your iOS mobile devices.

How to View Your My Photo Stream Images

Images stored in My Photo Stream can be viewed on a Mac, PC, on your HD television or monitor (via Apple TV), or on an iPhone, iPad, or iPod touch. From your computers or iOS mobile devices, it's also possible to edit your My Photo Stream, meaning you can manually add or remove images from it.

It's also possible to edit an image which is part of your My Photo Stream. However, the edited version of the image must first be stored on the computer or device it is being edited on (such as in iPhoto on a Mac, or the Camera Roll album of the Photos app on your iPhone or iPad). Once edited and saved, the updated image will be automatically synchronized with your iCloud account and treated as a newly added image.

View or Delete My Photo Stream Images on a Mac

To view your My Photo Stream images on a Mac, launch the iPhoto or Aperture software, click the iCloud option (on the left side of the iPhoto screen), and then click the My Photo Stream Album option. If no Shared Photo Stream albums are present, after clicking the iCloud option, the My Photo Stream album will open by default (shown in Figure 7-4).

iPhoto displays a thumbnail for each image that's stored in the My Photo Stream album. Click any image thumbnail to display a large version of that image. Keep in mind, to use any of iPhoto or Aperture's features to edit, print, or share an image from My Photo Stream, for example, you'll need to copy the image to your Photo Library first, and then store it in a different album (not the My Photo Stream album).

From within iPhoto, as you're viewing the My Photo Stream album, if you click on any image to view it, or select an image from the thumbnail screen, and then click iPhoto's Edit command icon, a pop-up window will appear (shown in Figure 7-5) instructing you to first import that image from My Photo Stream to your main image library.

Once the image is imported into iPhoto (from My Photo Stream), you have full access to all of the software's viewing, editing, printing, and sharing options. After selecting a My Photo Stream image in iPhoto, if you click the Info command icon, basic metadata information about that image (including the message, "This photo

Photo Stream option

FIGURE 7-4   Select iCloud from the left side of the iPhoto screen and then click the My Photo Stream Album option to view your My Photo Stream images on a Mac (which are shown here).

FIGURE 7-5 Before you can edit an image that is part of your My Photo Stream, you need to import it to the Mac you're currently using.

was downloaded from Photo Stream") will be displayed. However, if you click the Edit, Create, or Add To command icon, you'll be prompted to first import the selected image.

Without first importing the selected images from My Photo Stream, as you're using iPhoto, it is possible to click the Share command icon, and then share those selected images directly from My Photo Stream via Twitter, Flickr, Facebook, or Messages, or use the Order Prints option. Keep in mind, however, that it will be the original (unedited) image you share directly from My Photo Stream.

As you're viewing the My Photo Stream album in iPhoto (or Aperture), you can easily delete images. To do this, select one or more images (or image thumbnails) and then press DELETE on your keyboard. When the pop-up window that says, "These photos will be removed from Photo Stream" appears, click the Delete Photos button (shown in Figure 7-6).

Note Another way to delete an image from My Photo Stream while viewing it using iPhoto on a Mac is to hold down the CONTROL key while clicking on an image thumbnail in order to select it, and then choose the Delete from Photo Stream option.

Keep in mind, once you delete images from the My Photo Stream album on the Mac you're using, the deletion will impact the images stored on iCloud as part of your My Photo Stream. As a result, the images you delete will almost immediately no longer be viewable or accessible from any of your computers, iOS mobile devices, or Apple TVs that are linked to your iCloud account. This deletion process is not reversible.

FIGURE 7-6   It is possible to delete one or more images at a time from My Photo Stream.

Use this deletion feature to remove blurry or unwanted images that were automatically added to My Photo Stream.

View or Delete My Photo Stream Images on Any iOS Device

To view images from your My Photo Stream on your iOS mobile devices, launch the Photos app. Then click the Albums option that's displayed near the bottom of the screen. When viewing thumbnails that represent all of the albums stored in the app, tap the My Photo Stream album (shown in Figure 7-7). As you're looking at image thumbnails, tap one of them to view it in full-size mode.

As you're looking at the My Photo Stream album on your iOS mobile device (with the image thumbnails displayed on the screen), tap the Select option to pick and choose one or more images. After tapping Select, tap on individual image thumbnails to select them. A checkmark icon will appear in the lower-right corner of each selected image's thumbnail.

Once images are selected, they can be saved to the iOS mobile device you're using, deleted altogether from My Photo Stream, or shared. Simply tap one of the command icons displayed along the bottom of the screen.

Your options include tapping the Share icon, which allows you to share selected images via AirDrop, Messages, Mail, iCloud, Facebook, or Flickr, as well as copy an

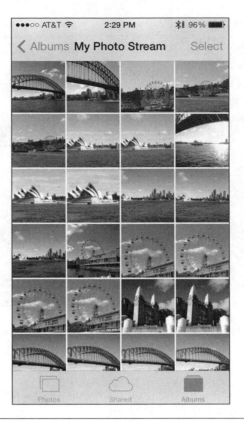

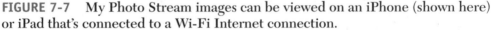

FIGURE 7-7 My Photo Stream images can be viewed on an iPhone (shown here) or iPad that's connected to a Wi-Fi Internet connection.

image, save it to the Photo app's Camera Roll, or use the Print option. Also displayed near the bottom of the screen is the Trash icon (used to delete the selected images) and the Add To option (which allows you to copy the images from the My Photo Stream to another existing album or create a new album).

As you're looking at the My Photo Stream thumbnail screen, tap on a single thumbnail to view that image. In some cases, you can see an even larger version of the image by rotating your iOS mobile device from portrait mode to landscape mode. Tap on the image again to make the available command icons appear.

Tap the Edit icon that's displayed near the top-right corner of the screen (shown in Figure 7-8) to use any of the Photo app's photo editing and enhancement tools (shown in Figure 7-9). Once you edit an image, however, you must save it to the Camera Roll album in the Photos app (so the image gets stored on the iOS mobile device you're using). It will then be treated as a new image and can automatically be uploaded to My Photo Stream, allowing it to be shared with your other computers and iOS mobile devices.

Edit option

FIGURE 7-8   The Edit option is available when viewing images from My Photo Stream.

FIGURE 7-9   Once you tap the Edit option, all of the Photo app's photo editing and image enhancement tools are available.

As you're looking at a single image from My Photo Stream, a Share icon is also accessible in the lower-left corner of the screen. Tap it to select the image, select additional images from My Photo Stream if you like, and then share the selected image(s). The options offered by the newly expanded Share menu are shown in Figure 7-10.

In addition to allowing images to be shared via AirDrop, Messages, Mail, iCloud, Twitter, Facebook, and Flickr, this Share menu offers a handful of options for managing an image, including Copy, Save to Camera Roll, Assign to Contact, Use as Wallpaper, and Print.

To delete a single image from My Photo Stream as you're viewing it, tap the Trash icon and then confirm your deletion decision by tapping the Delete Photo option. Keep in mind, this deletes the image from My Photo Stream (stored in your iCloud account). The deleted image will no longer be available on any of your computers or iOS mobile devices, and the deletion decision is not reversible.

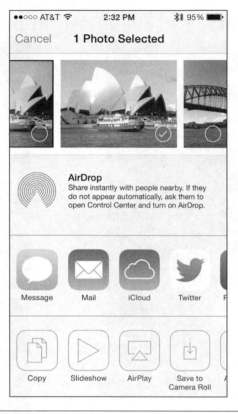

FIGURE 7-10 Thanks to iOS 7, the Photo app has a newly expanded Share menu. You can now share selected images via AirDrop, Messages, Mail, iCloud, Twitter, Facebook, or Flickr.

View or Delete Photo Stream Images on Your PC

On a PC, access the subdirectory where My Photo Stream images are stored, and use your photo management/editing software to view, edit, or delete them.

View Photo Stream Images on Your HD Television

To view your My Photo Stream images on your HD television set, the optional $99 Apple TV device must be connected to your television or monitor, and also connected to a high-speed Wi-Fi or Ethernet Internet connection.

From Apple TV's main menu, select the Photo Stream option, which is displayed as a Channel icon on the main menu screen. Thumbnails representing images from My Photo Stream will be displayed on your television screen. Use Apple TV's remote control to select the Slideshow option or to highlight and select one image at a time to view it in full-screen mode.

How to... Save an Image to the Photo App's Camera Roll

When you're viewing images from the My Photo Stream feed on your iOS mobile device, it's possible to save one or more of those images to the Camera Roll album in the Photos app, where it can be stored indefinitely, edited, enhanced, shared, printed, or moved to another album.

To save an image to the Camera Roll, first view that image in full-size mode. Next, tap the Share icon and select the Save to Camera Roll option from the Share menu. Alternatively, you can tap the Edit option while viewing an image, and use any of the photo editing or enhancement tools on the image that are normally available using the Photos app (including Rotate, Enhance, Red-Eye, or Crop). When you tap the Save command, the image will be saved to the default Camera Roll album in the Photos app—not the My Photo Stream album. The image will, however, be treated as a new image and ultimately be synced with My Photo Stream.

Save to Camera Roll option

Image Resolution Is Maintained on a Computer, but Not on an iOS Mobile Device

When uploaded to iCloud, your digital images are always kept at their existing resolution, and they're kept at that resolution when they are downloaded to your Mac or PC for viewing. However, when you view photo stream images on your Apple TV, iPhone, iPad, or iPod touch, the images are automatically optimized for those devices when they are downloaded from iCloud. In most cases, an optimized photo will have a 2048×1536 resolution when it's downloaded from iCloud to your Apple TV or iOS device.

Tip While viewing photo stream images on your television via Apple TV, select the Slideshow Settings option to add music to the slideshow and to choose a slideshow theme, for example.

Apple TV integrates with iCloud in a handful of different ways—not just to display photos but to showcase content acquired from the iTunes Store. You'll learn all about how Apple TV can be used in conjunction with iCloud in Chapter 13.

Manually Add Images to Your My Photo Stream from Your Computer

Once you've activated My Photo Stream on one or more of your computers or iOS mobile devices that are linked to the same iCloud account, you can begin manually adding digital photos to the My Photo Stream collection.

By default, whenever you import any new photos to your Mac or PC, they'll automatically be uploaded to iCloud and added to My Photo Stream, assuming this is how you set up the iPhoto or Aperture app. Likewise, when you snap photos using the camera that's built into your iPhone, iPad, or iPod touch, or import photos into your iOS device, those images will also automatically be uploaded to iCloud and included in My Photo Stream.

However, on your Mac, if other images are stored on your computer (in iPhoto or Aperture) that you want to add to My Photo Stream, drag the thumbnails representing those images from their current album or event to the My Photo Stream album (listed on the Source list on the left side of the iPhoto screen).

On a PC, you can drag and drop or copy images you want to add manually to your photo stream into the My Photo Stream subdirectory on your computer. By default (unless you change it), this subdirectory can be found at C:\Users\Apple\Pictures\ Photo Stream\My Photo Stream.

Note   If images are stored on your iPhone, iPad, or iPod touch that you want to add to your photo stream, you'll need to edit those images manually first using the Photos app (or optional iPhoto app). Your iOS device considers the edited images to be newly created images and will then automatically add them to the My Photo Stream collection.

Note   By default, if you use the My Photo Stream feature with a primary computer and iOS mobile devices, every image that's added to My Photo Stream automatically gets stored in the Photo Library on your primary computer's hard drive. This includes images shot using your digital camera or that were imported to your computer, as well as images shot using your iOS mobile device's built-in camera, for example. All images will remain in the Photo Library on your primary computer indefinitely, until they are manually deleted (even if they're automatically removed and archived from My Photo Stream after 30 days or the 1,000 image limit of My Photo Stream is reached).

Turn Off Photo Stream Without Deleting Photos on Your Mac

On your Mac, you can turn off the My Photo Stream feature without deleting any images stored on your computer (or from your My Photo Stream). However, when you turn off the My Photo Stream feature in iPhoto or Aperture, for example, the My Photo Stream album will no longer be accessible.

Meanwhile, any new photos you take on other devices or computers, and that are added to My Photo Stream, will not be sent (downloaded) on the Macs on which the Photo Stream feature has been turned off. And any images you add to your Mac on which the Photo Stream feature is turned off will not automatically be uploaded to iCloud and added to your photo stream.

Caution   Remember that images stored in My Photo Stream remain there for up to 30 days, after which time they're automatically deleted from all devices connected to your iCloud account and archived only on your primary computer. However, once the My Photo Stream collection grows to 1,000 images, as new images are added, the oldest ones are automatically removed from My Photo Stream, even if it's before the 30-day period ends.

To turn off the My Photo Stream option in iPhoto on your Mac, from the iPhoto pull-down menu, select the Preferences option, and then click the iCloud option displayed near the top-center of the window. From the iCloud menu, remove the checkmark from the My Photo Stream option.

A pop-up window displays containing the message, "Turning off Photo Stream will remove photos from the Photo Stream View. You can import photos into your library before turning off Photo Stream." Click the Import Photos and Turn Off button to transfer images from My Photo Stream and store them on your Mac in their own album. Alternatively, click the Turn Off button to simply turn off the feature without first downloading and storing the images on your Mac.

 If you turn off photo stream functionality on your Mac (from within System Preferences) or on any of your iOS mobile devices, the My Photo Stream album that's storing your collection of My Photo Stream images on that computer or device will be deleted.

Share Images Among Computers and Devices

All of the steps described in this chapter are required if you want to activate the iCloud My Photo Stream feature, and then use it with your Macs, PCs, Apple TV, and iOS mobile devices that are linked to the same iCloud account. Once you set up My Photo Stream just once and turn it on, all the My Photo Stream images become accessible on each of your computers and iOS mobile devices.

On your iOS mobile devices, for example, if you don't see the My Photo Stream images at all, or the image collection is not being updated with images added to your My Photo Stream from other devices, this is probably because your iPhone, iPad, or iPod touch is not currently connected to the Internet via a Wi-Fi connection. As soon as you connect to a Wi-Fi hotspot (or your home wireless network) and then launch the Photos app (or the optional iPhoto app), your My Photo Stream images will synchronize with the iOS mobile device you're using.

When using Apple TV, if you have trouble accessing My Photo Stream from iCloud, make sure your Apple TV is connected to the Internet and that you're signed in using the same Apple ID and password you used to create your iCloud account. Plus, make sure you have the most recent version of the Apple TV operating system installed.

In addition to or instead of using My Photo Stream to automatically share images between computers, Apple TV, and iOS mobile devices linked to the same iCloud account, it's possible to utilize iCloud's separate Shared Photo Stream feature in order to share selected groups of images with specific people using online galleries which are stored online as part of your iCloud account.

When you use a Shared Photo Stream (which is the focus of Chapter 8), you decide who can see your images, as well as which images you want to share. Everything else that's stored in your iCloud account remains secure and inaccessible from the people you invite to enjoy your Shared Photo Streams.

8

Share Your Digital Images with Others Using Shared Photo Streams

HOW TO...

- Set up and manage Shared Photo Streams using iPhoto on a Mac.
- Set up and manage Shared Photo Streams using an iOS mobile device and the Photos app.
- Access Shared Photo Streams on an HD television using Apple TV.

If you want to share groups of digital photos with other people via the Internet, you have a variety of options. For example, you can send images using email, text/instant messages, or wirelessly using AirDrop. You can also post digital photos on Facebook, Twitter, Google+, Instagram, Pinterest, or on many other popular social networking sites.

Yet another option is to create one or more online galleries using an online photo-sharing service, such as Flickr, Google's Picasa, Snapfish, Shutterfly, or SmugMug, and then invite your friends and family to view those online galleries using the web browser that's installed on their computer or mobile device.

Meanwhile, in addition to the My Photo Stream feature that's integrated into iCloud (which allows you to sync and share up to 1,000 of your most recent digital images between your Macs, PCs, iOS mobile devices, and televisions equipped with Apple TV, as long as all of your computers and devices are linked to the same iCloud account), the service also offers Shared Photo Streams.

A Shared Photo Stream allows you to select multiple digital images, publish them as an online-based gallery (each with its own unique website URL), and then invite specific people to access and view each gallery. These galleries can also be viewed as albums in other people's iPhoto or Aperture software (Mac), or Photos or iPhoto app (on iOS mobile devices).

As an iCloud user, you can create as many separate Shared Photo Streams as you desire, each can include as few or as many photos as you'd like, and each can have a separate group of invitees who are allowed to view them.

Note All of the online storage space that's required to maintain an iCloud user's Shared Photo Streams is provided free of charge by Apple. This is separate from the 5GB of online storage space that Apple provides with each iCloud account to store personal files and data.

You can create and manage Shared Photo Streams from your Mac (using the iPhoto or Aperture software), or from an iPhone, iPad, or iPod touch (using the Photos or optional iPhoto app). As you'd expect, once a Shared Photo Stream is created, it can be accessed and managed using any computer or device that's linked to your iCloud account.

Thus, you can create a Shared Photo Stream using iPhoto on your Mac, include 10 images in it, for example, and then invite 15 of your friends and family members to view it. Later, you can access the Shared Photo Stream from your iPad, add five additional photos to it that were taken using that tablet, and then invite five additional friends to view all of that Shared Photo Stream's images. On a subsequent occasion, from your iPhone, you might access the same Shared Photo Stream to delete two of the images and add six more.

Note Using an Apple TV device that's connected to an HD television, it's possible to view Shared Photo Streams, create animated slideshows from the images in a Shared Photo Stream, but not edit or manage the Shared Photo Streams.

In essence, Shared Photo Streams offer a quick, easy, and practical way to share groups of high-resolution images with other people, yet maintain control over who can see the images and where they're stored. Sure, some online photo-sharing services offer the ability to create customized online galleries, and then share them with others, but the majority of these online photo-sharing services don't work seamlessly with the photo management software that's running on a Mac (in this case iPhoto or Aperture) or on an iOS mobile device. You either need to use a web browser to access the service and manually upload images, or install a special app on your iPhone or iPad to help handle this task.

Keep in mind, to keep file sizes manageable, the Mail app that's integrated with iOS 7 only allows up to five digital photos to be sent in one email as attachments. Most email accounts limit the maximum file size of an email message (including attachments) to between 5MB and 10MB, which limits how many high-resolution images can be attached to an outgoing (or incoming) email message. One reason why Shared Photo Streams are so practical is because you can easily share many high-resolution images with one or more people, from directly within the iPhoto software or the Photos app.

Did You Know?

Creating Shared Photo Streams Is a Quick and Easy Process

iCloud's Shared Photo Streams offer a free alternative to storing and sharing groups of digital photos using online social networking services (like Facebook). The main reason why Apple users often prefer to share photos using Shared Photo Streams is because the ability to create and manage these online galleries is built right into the iPhoto and Aperture software on the Mac, as well as the Photos and iPhoto apps running on an iPhone, iPad, or iPod touch. There's no need to manually copy, sync, or transfer images out of these Mac or iOS apps in order to share them with other people.

Note   Shared Photo Streams created by an iCloud user can easily be accessed by any Mac, iPhone, iPad, or iPod touch user who has iPhoto or Aperture installed on their Mac, or the Photos or iPhoto app installed on their iOS mobile device. Windows-based PC users and others can also view a Shared Photo Stream (as an online gallery) using any web browser. No special software or apps are required.

Create and Manage a Shared Photo Stream from a Mac

Because iCloud functionality has been fully integrated into iPhoto, creating a Shared Photo Stream while working in iPhoto is a quick and easy process. Before you can create Shared Photo Streams, you must activate this feature on the Mac you're using.

To activate the Shared Photo Stream feature, launch System Preferences, click the iCloud icon, add a checkmark to the Photos option of the iCloud menu, and then click the Options button that's associated with the Photos option. Next, add a checkmark to the checkbox associated with Shared Photo Stream and click OK.

Alternatively, from within iPhoto, access the iPhoto pull-down menu (displayed near the top-left corner of the screen) and select the Preferences option. Near the top of the Preferences window, click the iCloud icon. Then add a checkmark to the checkbox that's associated with the Shared Photo Streams option.

Note   If you're using Apple's Aperture software on the Mac instead of iPhoto to manage your photo library, you can also create and manage Shared Photo Streams using this software. However, you first need to activate this feature with the software on each of your Macs. For information on how to do this, as well as how to create and manage Shared Photo Streams using Aperture, visit Apple's website at http://support.apple.com/kb/PH11962 and http://support.apple.com/kb/PH11961.

Create a New Photo Stream Using iPhoto on a Mac

To create a new Shared Photo Stream, follow these steps:

1. Launch iPhoto on your Mac.
2. Open an event, or click the Photos, Faces, or Places option.
3. When viewing thumbnails of images, highlight and select the specific images you want to include in a Shared Photo Stream (shown in Figure 8-1).

 If you want to upload an entire album or event to iCloud in order to create a Shared Photo Stream, highlight and select the album or event thumbnail (instead of opening it). Then click the Share command icon that's located near the bottom-right corner of the iPhoto screen.

4. Once two or more images are selected and highlighted (or you've selected and highlighted the thumbnail that represents an entire album or event), click the Share command icon that's located near the bottom-right corner of the screen. (You know when a thumbnail has been selected because it will have a yellow frame around it.)
5. From iPhoto's Share menu, click the iCloud option (shown in Figure 8-2.)

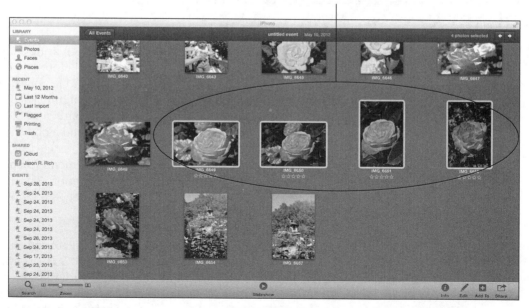

FIGURE 8-1 Select the images in iPhoto that you want to include in the Shared Photo Stream you're about to create.

iCloud option

FIGURE 8-2   Click on the iCloud option to access Shared Photo Stream options from the Share menu.

6. In the Share window, click on the iCloud option, followed by the New Photo Stream (+) option to create a new Shared Photo Stream from scratch. Alternatively, you can add the selected images to an already existing Shared Photo Stream by clicking on its album thumbnail that's displayed in the Share window.

7. The New Shared Photo Stream window that appears has two empty text fields (shown in Figure 8-3). In the To field, enter the email address for each person you'd like to invite to view the Shared Photo Stream (online gallery) you're creating.

Tip   For people who already have an entry in your Contacts database, instead of entering their email address into the To field, you can type their name and let iPhoto automatically access the database to acquire their email address.

8. In the Name field of the New Shared Photo Stream window, by default the date is displayed. You have the option, however, to manually enter a title for the Shared Photo Stream, such as "Nick's Birthday Party," "Christmas Vacation 2013," or "My Day at the Zoo."

FIGURE 8-3 Determine who will be invited to view your Shared Photo Stream.

9. If you want your Shared Photo Stream to be accessible by anyone, regardless of whether or not they use a Mac (running iPhoto or Aperture) or an iPhone or iPad (running the Photos or iPhoto app), be sure to add a checkmark to the checkbox that's associated with the Public Website option in the New Shared Photo Stream window.

10. Click the Share button to create the Shared Photo Stream. At this point, iPhoto will automatically send an email inviting each of the people you listed in the To field to view your Shared Photo Stream. At the same time the emails are sent, your images will be uploaded to your iCloud account and a new Shared Photo Stream will be created with the title you entered into the Name field of the New Shared Photo Stream window.

As soon as the new Shared Photo Stream is created, it will become accessible on your Mac from within iPhoto. Click the Photo Stream option that's listed on the left side of the screen (in the Source List). The Shared Photo Stream will be listed along with an album thumbnail for My Photo Stream and each of your other Shared Photo Streams (shown in Figure 8-4).

At this point, you can open the Shared Photo Stream album at any time from within iPhoto in order to view the images. It's also possible to later add or delete

FIGURE 8-4   As you create Shared Photo Streams, you can view and manage them using the iPhoto software on your Mac.

individual images from the Shared Photo Stream or delete the entire Shared Photo Stream altogether. When you delete images (or the entire Shared Photo Stream), the people you invited to view it will no longer have access to the deleted photos.

Using iPhoto (or Aperture), you can create as many separate Shared Photo Streams as you desire. Each should be given a different name (or showcase a different creation date) to avoid confusion. Plus, each Shared Photo Stream can have a separate list of invitees associated with it.

Edit a Shared Photo Stream Using iPhoto

After you've created and published a Shared Photo Stream, and it's being stored online in your iCloud account, you can access it anytime from iPhoto or Aperture (running on any Mac that's linked to the same iCloud account) or from your iOS mobile device that's running the Photos app (or iPhoto app), and that's also linked to your iCloud account.

As you're viewing one of your Shared Photo Streams, you can delete it altogether, delete individual images, or add images. Keep in mind, any changes you make to a Shared Photo Stream become almost immediately visible to all of the people who have previously been granted access to it.

Did You Know?

People You Invite to View a Shared Photo Stream Receive a Special Email

The email each person receives as an invitation to view your Shared Photo Stream includes a unique website URL. If they're using a Mac (and the Mail app) or an iPhone, iPad, or iPod touch (with the Mail app), when they click on the embedded link to the Shared Photo Stream, it will open in the iPhoto software on their Mac or in the Photos app on their iOS mobile device. They can then view and manage the images in your Shared Photo Stream using the tools available in their photo management software or app.

However, if they're not using an Apple computer or iOS mobile device to access your Shared Photo Stream, it can be accessible to them as an online gallery using their web browser software. (Be sure to turn on the Public Website option when creating the Shared Photo Stream.)

Any Changes to Your Shared Photo Stream Have an Immediate Impact

As soon as you create a new Shared Photo Stream or later edit it, any additions or changes you make from iPhoto on your Mac will immediately be uploaded to your iCloud account and impact the Shared Photo Stream that you've invited other people to see. For this to happen, your Mac needs access to the Internet. If no Internet connection is present, the changes will be synced with the iCloud-based Shared Photo Stream as soon as the Mac reconnects to the Internet.

Thus, almost immediately after you delete one or more images from a Shared Photo Stream, those images will no longer be visible or accessible to those you've invited to view it. Likewise, images you add to the Shared Photo Stream will almost immediately become visible to those people who have already been granted access. This is also true if you edit or delete a Shared Photo Stream using an iOS mobile device.

Delete One or More Images from a Shared Photo Stream

To delete one or more individual images from a Shared Photo Stream from within iPhoto, click the Photo Stream option (on the left side of the screen, in the Source List), open the Shared Photo Stream album by clicking on its thumbnail, and then select and highlight one or more images that you want to delete. Once the thumbnails are selected, press DELETE on your keyboard. When the Remove Photos from This Photo Stream window appears (shown in Figure 8-5), click the Delete Photos button.

FIGURE 8-5 You can manually delete one or more images from a Shared Photo Stream any time you want.

Add One or More Images to a Shared Photo Stream

To add one or more images to an existing Shared Photo Stream from within iPhoto, open the album or event that contains the images you want to add. Select and highlight each image's thumbnail. When all of the images are selected, drag and drop them over the Photo Stream option that's displayed on the left side of the iPhoto screen (in the Source List), or click the Add To (+) command icon that's displayed near the bottom-right corner of the screen.

When the Share window appears (shown in Figure 8-6), click on the album thumbnail for the Shared Photo Stream you want to add the selected images to. Those images will then be uploaded to that Shared Photo Stream and become visible to everyone who already has access to that Shared Photo Stream.

Edit Who Has Access to a Shared Photo Stream

When you initially create a Shared Photo Stream, the people who will ultimately be able to view it are the people you list in the To field of the New Photo Stream window. At any time later, however, you can modify who has permission to access the Shared Photo Stream. In other words, you can invite additional people or revoke further access to people you've already invited.

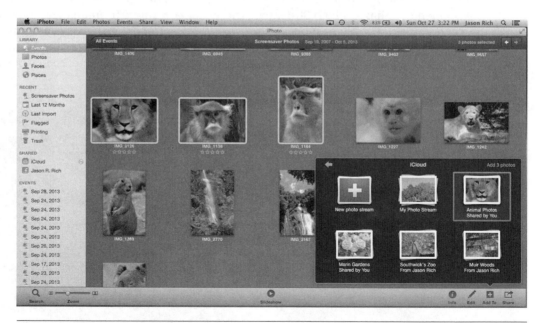

FIGURE 8-6 When adding images to a Shared Photo Stream from iPhoto, you need to decide which preexisting Shared Photo Stream album the additional images will be added to.

To edit the list of people who can access a Shared Photo Stream (in addition to yourself, from any of your own Macs, Apple TV devices, or iOS mobile devices that are linked to the same iCloud account), follow these steps:

1. Launch iPhoto.
2. Click the Photo Stream option in the Source List (on the left side of the screen).
3. Select and highlight the album thumbnail for the Shared Photo Stream you want to work with.
4. Once the album thumbnail is selected and has a yellow frame around it, click the Info command icon that's displayed near the bottom-right corner of the iPhoto screen. Along the right side of the screen, the Info pane will be displayed (shown in Figure 8-7).
5. In the Info pane, you'll see a field that's labeled Shared With. In this field are the names or email address of the people you've already invited to access that Shared Photo Stream.

   To revoke someone's permission, click on their name or email address to highlight it, and then press DELETE on your keyboard. A variety of other options related to that person are displayed if you click on the downward-pointing arrow icon that appears to the immediate right of the person's name or email address.

Shared With box

FIGURE 8-7   From the Info pane in iPhoto that relates to a Shared Photo Stream, you can edit the list of people who can access it.

These options include Copy Address, Add to Contacts, and Remove Subscriber. The Remove Subscriber option does the same thing as pressing DELETE when the person's name or email address is highlighted.

To invite additional people to access the Shared Photo Stream, enter each person's name or email address in the Shared With field, one at a time. Those people will automatically receive an email inviting them to access and view your Shared Photo Stream.

Delete an Entire Shared Photo Stream

To delete an entire Shared Photo Stream (and revoke everyone's permission to view its contents) from within iPhoto, click the Photo Stream option that's displayed in the Source List. Next, highlight and select the thumbnail for the Shared Photo Stream album.

When you see the yellow frame around the thumbnail, press and hold down the COMMAND key on your keyboard while simultaneously pressing the DELETE key. Confirm your deletion decision by clicking the Delete Photos button when the Delete pop-up window (shown in Figure 8-8) appears. If you change your mind, click the Cancel button. Keep in mind, there is no "undo" command once you delete a Shared Photo Stream. You would need to re-create it and then re-invite people to access it.

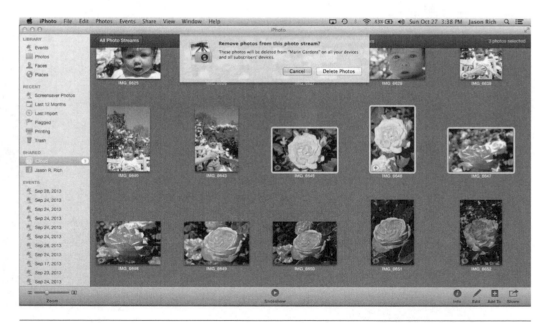

FIGURE 8-8   Confirm your decision to delete an entire Shared Photo Stream.

> **Did You Know?**
>
> ## People Viewing Your Shared Photo Streams Can Leave Comments and "Like" Images
>
> When someone you've invited to view your Shared Photo Stream is looking at your individual images using their Mac (running iPhoto or Aperture) or their iOS mobile device (running the Photos or iPhoto app), they have the option to add text-based comments to individual images.
>
> When comments are added, they immediately become viewable by everyone who has access to that Shared Photo Stream. It's also possible for people to click the "Like" button that's associated with each photo to show their admiration for it (a feature that was made popular on Facebook.)
>
> Yet another option people have when viewing your images (regardless of how they're accessing the Shared Photo Stream) is to download your individual images to their own computer or mobile device. When this is done, images actually get stored in their computer or device's internal storage, and the images can then be edited, printed, and potentially shared with other people.

Create and Manage a Shared Photo Stream from an iPhone or iPad

Shared Photo Streams work much the same way on an iPhone, iPad, or iPod touch as they do when working with them on a Mac. On an iOS mobile device, you'll be using the Photos app that comes preinstalled with iOS 7 (or the optional iPhoto app) to create and manage your Shared Photo Streams.

As always, you'll be using the same iCloud account as you use for everything else that's iCloud-related, including managing your My Photo Stream. Be sure to turn on the Shared Photo Stream feature on your iOS mobile device.

To turn on the Shared Photo Stream feature on your iOS mobile device, launch Settings, tap the iCloud option, and then tap the Photos option. From the Photos menu screen in Settings, turn on the virtual switch that's associated with Photo Sharing. Alternatively, from within Settings, select the Photos & Camera option and then turn on the virtual switch associated with Photo Sharing from the Photos & Camera menu. Either option only needs to be done once on each of your iOS mobile devices.

Create a Shared Photo Stream from Scratch Using the Photos App

To create a Shared Photo Stream from the Photos app, follow these steps:

1. Launch the Photos app from the Home screen.
2. Tap the Photos or Albums option displayed near the bottom of the screen (shown in Figure 8-9).

FIGURE 8-9 Select the photos you want to include in a new Shared Photo Stream by accessing the images from within iPhoto.

3. Open the album that contains the images you want to include in a Shared Photo Stream.

 Tip If you want to upload an entire album or event to iCloud in order to create a Shared Photo Stream, highlight and select the album or event thumbnail (instead of opening it). Then click the Share command icon that's located near the bottom-right corner of the screen.

4. As you're looking at the thumbnails that represent the images in the album, tap the Select option that's displayed near the top-right corner of the screen.

5. One at a time, tap on individual thumbnails that represent the images you want to include in your Shared Photo Stream. As you select each image, a checkmark icon will appear in the lower-right corner of the image thumbnail (shown in Figure 8-10).

6. When all of the images you want to include in your Shared Photo Stream are selected, tap the Share icon that can be found near the top-left corner of the Photo app's screen.

Selected images showcase
a checkmark icon

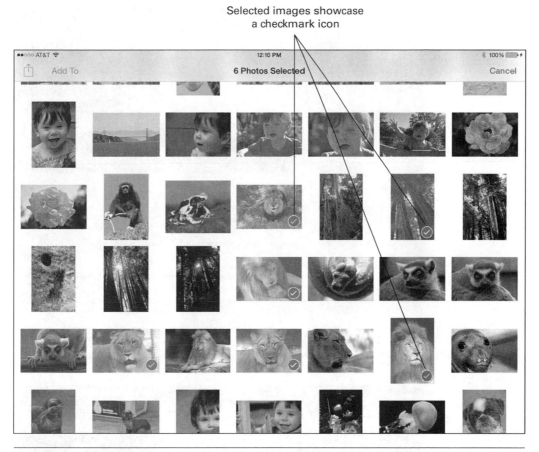

FIGURE 8-10   One at a time, select the images you want to include in the Shared Photo Stream. Choose from the images already stored in the Photos app on your iOS mobile device.

7. From the Share menu, tap the iCloud option.
8. When the iCloud window appears, fill in the Comment section with optional text, and then tap the Stream option that's displayed near the bottom of the window (shown in Figure 8-11).
9. The Add to Shared Photo Stream window will replace the iCloud window on the screen. Tap the New Shared Stream option that's displayed near the top of the window.
10. In the New Stream window that appears next, fill in the Stream Name. Create a unique name for the Shared Photo Stream, such as "Nick's Birthday Party," "Christmas Vacation 2013," or "My Day At The Zoo." Tap the Next option (found in the upper-right corner of the window) to continue.
11. Fill in the To field (shown in Figure 8-12).

FIGURE 8-11 From the iCloud window, fill in the optional Comment section and then tap the Stream option to select the New Shared Stream option.

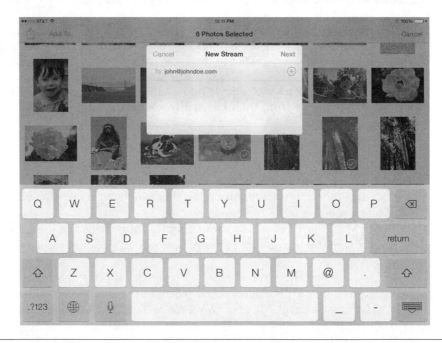

FIGURE 8-12 The names or email addresses you enter in the To field represent the people who will be granted access to view the Shared Photo Stream you are currently creating.

12. In the To field, enter the email address for each person whom you'd like to invite to view the Shared Photo Stream you're creating. Use a comma in between multiple email addresses, if necessary, or tap the plus-sign icon after entering each email address. Tap the Next option (found in the upper-right corner of the window) to continue.

 For people who already have an entry in your Contacts database, instead of entering their email address into the To field, you can type their name and let iPhoto automatically access the database to acquire their email address.

13. Once again, the iCloud window will be displayed. This time, tap the Post option (found near the top-right corner of the window) to publish your Shared Photo Stream and upload it to your iCloud account.

As soon as the new Shared Photo Stream is created, it will become accessible from your iOS mobile device via the Photos app. Click the Shared option that's displayed near the bottom-center of the Photos app's screen. An album for the newly created Shared Photo Stream will be displayed.

At this point, you can open the Shared Photo Stream album at any time from within the Photos app in order to view the images. It's also possible to later add or delete individual images from the Shared Photo Stream, or delete the entire Shared Photo Stream altogether. When you delete images (or the entire Shared Photo Stream), the people you invited to view it will no longer have access to the deleted photos.

Note Shared Photo Streams created using an iOS mobile device can be viewed and managed using your Mac or another iOS mobile device that's linked to the same iCloud account. Likewise, Shared Photo Streams created using a Mac can be viewed and managed using any of your iOS mobile devices that are linked to the same iCloud account. The people you invite to view your Shared Photo Streams can access them from a Mac, iPhone, iPad, iPod touch, or if you turn on the Public Website feature, using a Windows-based PC or any computer or mobile device that has a web browser and Internet connection.

Did You Know?

Each Shared Photo Stream Has a Unique and Separate List of Invitees

Keep in mind, when filling in the To field, you are deciding who will have access to that specific Shared Photo Stream. If you want a particular person to have access to several of your separate Shared Photo Streams, you'll need to invite them to access each Shared Photo Stream separately, as each has its own list of invitees. You can always add or remove access to a specific Shared Photo Stream for individuals at a later time using the steps outlined elsewhere in this chapter.

Edit a Shared Photo Stream Using the Photos App on Your iOS Mobile Device

After you've created and published a Shared Photo Stream from your iPhone, iPad, or iPod touch, and it's being stored online in your iCloud account, you can access it anytime from the Photos app (or the optional iPhoto app), from an Apple TV, or from a Mac that's also linked to your iCloud account.

As you're viewing one of your Shared Photo Streams, it's possible to delete it altogether, delete individual images, or add images. You can also manage the list of people who have been granted access to view the Shared Photo Stream.

To begin managing or editing a Shared Photo Stream from your iOS mobile device, launch the Photos app, tap the Shared option (displayed near the bottom-center of the screen), and then tap on the listing that represents the Shared Photo Stream you want to work with from the Shared Streams screen (shown in Figure 8-13).

Thumbnails representing each of the images already included in that Shared Photo Stream are displayed, and the name of the Shared Photo Stream is displayed near the top-center of the screen.

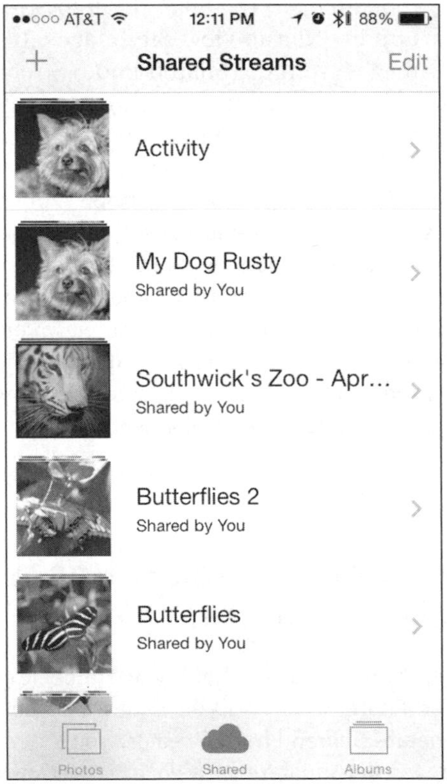

FIGURE 8-13 The Shared Streams screen (shown here on the iPhone 5) displays listings for each of the Shared Photo Streams that you've created or that you've been invited to view.

Many of the Same Tools for Creating and Managing Shared Photo Streams Are Also Available Using the Optional iPhoto for iOS App

Apple's iPhoto for iOS app is available from the App Store. It is designed to more closely resemble the iPhoto software on a Mac, and offers much of the same functionality as its Mac counterpart. This includes full integration with iCloud.

When you launch the iPhoto app and tap the Albums option (displayed near the top of the screen), thumbnails that represent all of the albums being stored in the app are displayed. The album thumbnails that also display an iCloud icon to the left of the album name are Shared Photo Streams that you've already created or have access to.

Using the iPhoto app, instead of creating Shared Photo Streams, you can create online-based journals, which are also online photo galleries. For information on how to do this, visit http://support.apple.com/kb/PH3156.

Delete One or More Images from a Shared Photo Stream

After opening the Shared Photo Stream using the Photos app on your iOS mobile device, tap the Select option that's displayed near the top-right corner of the screen. One at a time, tap on each of the image thumbnails that represent the photos you want to delete from the Shared Photo Stream. As you select each image, a checkmark icon will be displayed near the lower-right corner of the image's thumbnail.

Once all of the images you want to delete have been selected, tap the Trash icon that's found near the bottom-right corner of the screen. Then, when the pop-up window appears that says, "These photos will be deleted from [Shared Photo Stream name] on all your devices and all subscribers' devices," click the Delete Selected Photos option (shown in Figure 8-14) to confirm your deletion decision.

Add One or More Images to a Shared Photo Stream

After opening the Shared Photo Stream using the Photos app on your iOS mobile device, to add images to it, tap on the thumbnail image that displays a plus-sign icon. Then access the album or event that contains the images (which are stored in the Photos app) that you want to add to the Shared Photo Stream. Select those images and tap the Done option to continue.

When the iCloud window appears, enter an optional comment, or tap the Stream option and select the Shared Photo Stream you want to add the selected images to. The name of the Shared Photo Stream you've already selected should be displayed. Tap the Post option (found near the top-right corner of the iCloud window) to publish those images to the Shared Photo Stream. As soon as they're done uploading from your iOS mobile device to your iCloud account, those images will be viewable by everyone who has access to that Shared Photo Stream.

FIGURE 8-14 Think carefully before deleting images from a Shared Photo Stream. There's no "undo" option.

Edit Who Has Access to a Shared Photo Stream

After opening the Shared Photo Stream using the Photos app on your iOS mobile device, tap the People tab that's displayed near the bottom of the screen. Displayed on the screen now will be a listing of the people who already have been granted access to the Shared Photo Stream (shown in Figure 8-15). Tap on the listing for any of those people to either resend the invitation or remove them as a subscriber to the Shared Photo Stream and revoke their permission to view your images.

To invite additional people to view the Shared Photo Stream, tap the Invite People option. Then, from the Invite People screen, fill in the To field with the names or email addresses of the people you want to invite to view this particular Shared Photo Stream. Tap the Add option (found near the top-right corner of the screen) to have the Photos app email invitations to those people.

In this Shared Photo Stream management screen, you'll also see an option labeled Subscribers Can Post. It's associated with a virtual on/off switch. When turned on, this feature allows the people you've invited to view your Shared Photo Stream to also be able to add (upload) their own photos or video clips to it. When turned off, the invitees will only be able to view your images, as well as "Like" and post comments about the images.

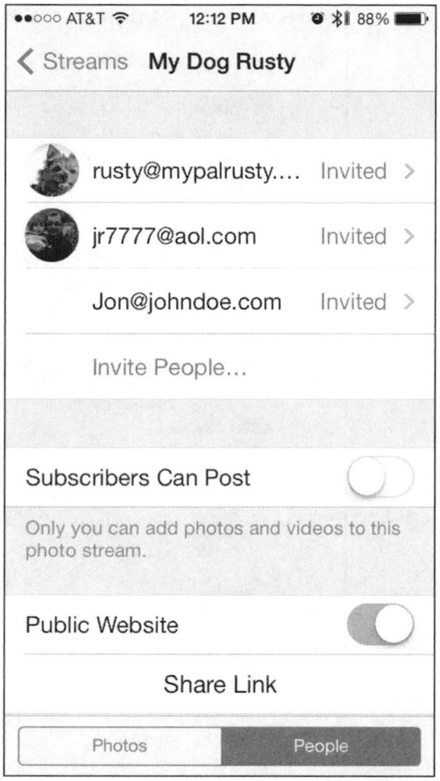

FIGURE 8-15   From this screen, you can manage who will have access to your Shared Photo Stream by adding or deleting names and email addresses from the list of invitees.

Tip   If you know you're inviting people to view your Shared Photo Stream who are not using a Mac or iOS mobile device, be sure to turn on the virtual switch that's associated with the Public Website option. This allows anyone who is invited to view your Shared Photo Stream to see it as an online gallery, using any web browser, on any type of computer or mobile device that has Internet access. Below this option is a Share Link option. Tap it to send the Shared Photo Stream's link to individuals via AirDrop, the Messages or Mail app, Facebook, or Twitter.

Delete an Entire Shared Photo Stream

To delete an entire Shared Photo Stream using your iOS mobile device, launch the Photos app and tap the Shared option. As you're looking at the listing of Shared Streams, tap the Edit option (located near the top-right corner of the screen). Next, tap the red and white minus-sign icon that's displayed to the immediate left of the listing for the Shared Photo Stream you want to delete (shown in Figure 8-16). Tap the Delete button to confirm your decision, keeping in mind there is no "undo" option. Tap the Done option (located near the top-right corner of the screen) to return to the normal Shared Streams menu screen.

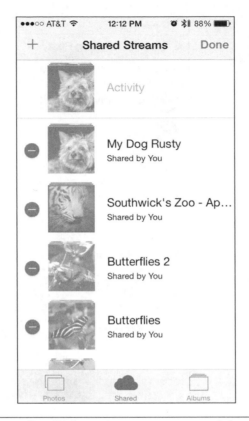

FIGURE 8-16 Tap the red and white minus-sign icon to delete an entire Shared Photo Stream.

Caution When you delete a Shared Photo Stream, it is almost instantly deleted from your iCloud account and will no longer be accessible by you (on any of your computers or iOS mobile devices) or anyone you've previously invited to view it.

 How to... Accept an Invitation to View Someone Else's Shared Photo Stream

As a Mac or iOS mobile device user, if someone emails you an invitation to access the Shared Photo Stream they've created, accept the invitation by clicking on the Join this Photo Stream button that's embedded in the email. Upon doing this, you will be able to access that Shared Photo Stream from within iPhoto (Mac) or the Photos app (iOS mobile device), for example.

(Continued)

As you're viewing someone else's Shared Photo Stream, you have the option to add comments or "Like" individual images, or to download images and store them in an album you create and store on your Mac or iOS mobile device.

To leave a comment or "Like" an image, select an image's thumbnail or open that single image in the Shared Photo Stream and click the Info icon that's displayed in iPhoto. Or from your iOS mobile device, tap the Add a Comment option or the Like icon that's displayed below the image.

Once you download or transfer an image from a Shared Photo Stream to your own album, you can edit, print, view, manage, or share that image just as you would any other image that's stored in the iPhoto software or Photos app.

Access a Shared Photo Stream via Apple TV

In addition to being able to enjoy iTunes Store–purchased content on your HD television, including music, TV shows, movies, audiobooks, and music videos, using the Apple TV device, you can view your own Shared Photo Streams, as well as Shared Photo Streams you've been invited by others to access.

From the main Apple TV menu screen, scroll down to the iCloud Photos channel icon and click on it using the remote control. A listing of your Photo Streams will be displayed. Again, using the remote control, highlight and select a Shared Photo Stream album by clicking on its thumbnail.

Using Apple TV, you can then view thumbnails for each of the images in that Shared Photo Stream, or you can view each image in full-screen mode on your HD television. Another option is to use the Slideshow feature of Apple TV to display all of the images in the Shared Photo Stream as a customized animated slideshow.

While it's not possible to manage Shared Photo Streams using Apple TV, this is a great way to enjoy viewing images in all of their high-definition glory on your television, and to share those images with everyone in the room.

Note Images from a Shared Photo Stream can also be used as Apple TV screensaver images, which will be displayed in a customized animated format when the Apple TV device is not being used for other purposes but remains turned on (and the television it's connected to is also turned on).

For more information about how you can utilize Apple TV in conjunction with your iCloud account, be sure to read Chapter 13. Keep in mind, for Apple TV to be able to utilize iCloud-related features, it's necessary to have the latest version of the Apple TV operating system (version 6.0.1 or later) installed on the device.

PART III

Share Documents, Music, Data, and More via iCloud

9

Manage and Sync Your Safari Bookmarks, Reading List, and Passwords

HOW TO...

- Use the Safari web browser in conjunction with iCloud.
- Sync your bookmarks, Favorites bar, Reading List, and other information using iCloud.
- Let Safari remember your website usernames, passwords, and credit card information with iCloud Keychain.

The Safari web browser that comes bundled with OS X Mavericks on the Mac, and with iOS 7 on the iPhone, iPad, and iPod touch, has been redesigned to utilize iCloud in a handful of ways that will make your web surfing experience more efficient. Once you turn on iCloud functionality to work in conjunction with Safari (and turn on the iCloud Keychain feature) on each of your Macs and iOS mobile devices, you'll discover a lot of information will automatically sync in almost real time, allowing for a seamless web surfing experience as you move between computers and devices.

When used in conjunction with iCloud, Safari will keep track of and sync the following information:

- **Your bookmarks**   This is a customized list of your favorite or most frequented websites. Now, on all of your Macs and iOS mobile devices, you'll be able to access one centralized Bookmarks menu that contains bookmarks you created when surfing the Web on any of your computers or mobile devices that are linked to the same iCloud account.

- **Your Favorites bar** If you choose to display it within Safari, the Favorites bar offers a continuously displayed alternative to your Bookmarks list. It's displayed along the top of the web browser screen, directly below the toolbar. When Safari utilizes iCloud, the websites listed on your Favorites bar get synced continuously and are displayed on your Mac and iOS mobile devices.

> **Note** On the iPhone, Safari allows users to create a Favorites bar, but instead of taking up valuable onscreen real estate to continuously display it, the contents of the Favorites bar is displayed as a separate Bookmark folder when you tap the Bookmarks icon. The contents of this listing, however, will include the same websites that are available from the Favorites bar on your Mac or iPad, for example.

- **iCloud tabs** If you opt to use the Tabbed Browsing feature of Safari, you can open multiple browser windows at once and quickly switch between them. This allows you to access several websites simultaneously. When turned on, iCloud Tabs keeps track of all the tabbed browser windows you have open on each of your Macs and iOS mobile devices that are linked to the same iCloud account, and allows you to access any of those open browser windows (and the web pages they're associated with) from any of your computers or devices. In other words, if you open a web page using Safari on your Mac, you can then open and access that same browser window content from Safari running on your iPhone or iPad (or vice versa).

- **Reading List** Instead of saving just a website's address (URL) in your Bookmarks listing, you can store the entire contents of a web page for later (offline) viewing using Safari's Reading List. Normally, when you save a web page to your Reading List, the contents of that page are stored within Safari on the Mac or iOS mobile device it was initially accessed on. When this feature is used in conjunction with iCloud, all of the content you save in your Reading List on any of your Macs or iOS mobile devices that are linked to the same iCloud account will automatically synchronize. Thus, an article you saved on your Mac while surfing the Web almost instantly becomes accessible from the Reading List feature within Safari on your iPad or iPhone (or vice versa).

- **iCloud Keychain content** The latest version of Safari for OS X Mavericks and iOS 7 can now automatically remember every website username and password you create, as well as any credit card information you use when shopping online from a particular website. Thanks to iCloud, this information also now remains synced in real time with Safari running on your Macs and iOS mobile devices. So, regardless of which computer or device you use to log in to a particular website, you will only need to enter your username and related password once. Safari will automatically log you in when you revisit that website in the future from any Mac or iOS mobile device that's linked to the same iCloud account.

Turn On iCloud Functionality in Safari

On each of your Macs and iOS mobile devices, you'll need to set up iCloud to work with Safari and also with iCloud Keychain, which is a related but separate feature. This initial setup only needs to be done once on each computer and iOS mobile device. Then Safari will automatically sync information as you're surfing the Web, regardless of which computer or iOS mobile device you're using.

Note Keep in mind, iCloud functionality is designed to work exclusively with the Safari web browser for the Mac and iOS mobile devices. While you can download, install, and use other web browsers, such as Google Chrome, the Opera Browser, or Firefox, for example, these third-party browsers do not work with iCloud, although some have the ability to sync bookmarks.

Turn On Web Surfing iCloud Functionality on a Mac

To turn on web surfing iCloud functionality on each of your Macs that are linked to the same iCloud account, follow these steps:

1. Launch System Preferences on the Mac.
2. Click the iCloud option from the System Preferences window.
3. If you haven't already done so, log in to your iCloud account by entering your iCloud username and password when prompted.
4. On the right side of the iCloud window within System Preferences, add a checkmark to the checkbox that's associated with Safari (shown in Figure 9-1).

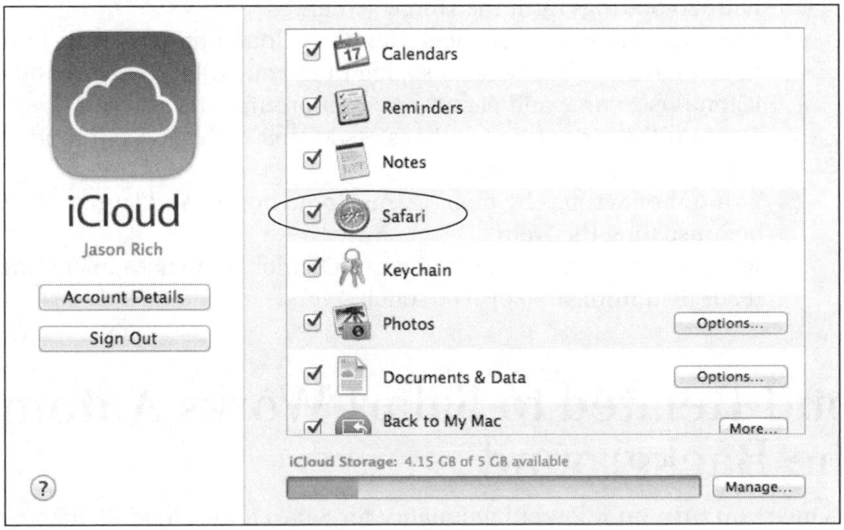

FIGURE 9-1   Turn on Safari functionality associated with iCloud from within System Preferences on your Mac.

5. Also on the right side of the iCloud window within System Preferences, add a checkmark to the checkbox that's associated with iCloud Keychain.
6. Exit out of System Preferences and then launch Safari to begin surfing the Web.
7. Repeat these steps on each of your Macs that are linked to the same iCloud account.

Tip For security purposes and to help protect your database of website usernames, passwords, and credit card information, after you turn on the iCloud Keychain feature on one of your Macs or iOS mobile devices, when you attempt to turn on this feature on your other computers or iOS mobile devices, you will be prompted to reenter your Apple ID (iCloud) password. For security purposes, you may be given a four-digit PIN code from the original computer or device the feature was activated on, which will need to be entered on the additional devices you want to use with iCloud Keychain. Or, from one of your other computers or devices that have already been set up to work with iCloud Keychain, you may be prompted to manually approve each new computer or device. As you'll discover, several different security features have been implemented to insure your iCloud Keychain data remains safe.

Turn On Web Surfing iCloud Functionality on an iOS Mobile Device

To turn on web surfing iCloud functionality on each of your iOS mobile devices that are linked to the same iCloud account, follow these steps:

1. Launch Settings from the Home screen.
2. From the main Settings menu, tap the iCloud option.
3. If you haven't already done so, log in to your iCloud account by entering your iCloud username and password when prompted.
4. Turn on the virtual switch that's associated with the Safari option and the separate Keychain option.
5. Exit out of Settings by tapping the Home button and launch the Safari app to begin surfing the Web.
6. Repeat these steps on each of your iOS mobile devices, including your iPhone, iPad, iPad mini, and/or iPod touch.

iCloud Related to Safari Works Automatically in the Background

Once you turn on iCloud functionality for Safari and iCloud Keychain on each of your Macs and iOS mobile devices, all of the iCloud-related features and functions will begin working immediately and continuously, automatically, and in the background.

You'll notice that when you create a new bookmark, for example, within a few seconds that same bookmark will be accessible from the Bookmarks menu of Safari on all of your Macs and iOS mobile devices that are linked to the same iCloud account.

Likewise, if you make a change to your Favorites bar, that information will also be updated within seconds on each of your Macs and iOS mobile devices. For this syncing functionality to work, however, each computer and mobile device needs access to the Internet.

Caution If you delete a bookmark from your Bookmarks menu, that bookmark will be deleted from the Bookmarks menu on all of your Macs and iOS mobile devices almost immediately. This is also the case with all other information that Safari syncs with iCloud (which was outlined at the beginning of the chapter).

Create New Bookmarks Using Safari

When surfing the Web using Safari on the Mac, to create a new bookmark for the web page you're currently visiting, access the Bookmarks pull-down menu from the top of the Safari screen and select the Add Bookmark option.

The Add This Page To pop-up window will appear. From this window (shown in Figure 9-2), click the pull-down menu to choose where you want to save the bookmark. Your options include your Top Sites, Favorites bar, Bookmarks menu, or within a custom-created subfolder of your Bookmarks menu.

FIGURE 9-2   From the Add This Page To window, enter details about the bookmark you want to save.

In the field displayed below the pull-down menu, enter the title for the bookmark you want to create. The default will be the web page's title, but you may want to shorten this, especially if it will be displayed as part of your Favorites bar.

Another option for quickly creating a bookmark for the web page you're visiting is to click the Share icon that's displayed on the toolbar. When the Share menu appears, click the Add Bookmark option, and then provide the information requested from the Add This Page To pop-up window.

Assuming you have iCloud functionality already turned on for Safari, as soon as you create or edit a bookmark, that information will automatically be uploaded to your iCloud account and sync with your other Macs and iOS mobile devices that are running Safari.

On your iOS mobile device, to create a new bookmark, tap the Share icon to access the Share menu (shown in Figure 9-3), and then tap the Bookmark option. The Add Bookmark screen (iPhone) or window (iPad) will appear (shown in Figure 9-4). If you choose, edit the title for the bookmark and tap the Location option to determine where it will be saved. Tap the Save option (near the top-right corner of the screen/window) to save the bookmark in Safari and have it sync with iCloud.

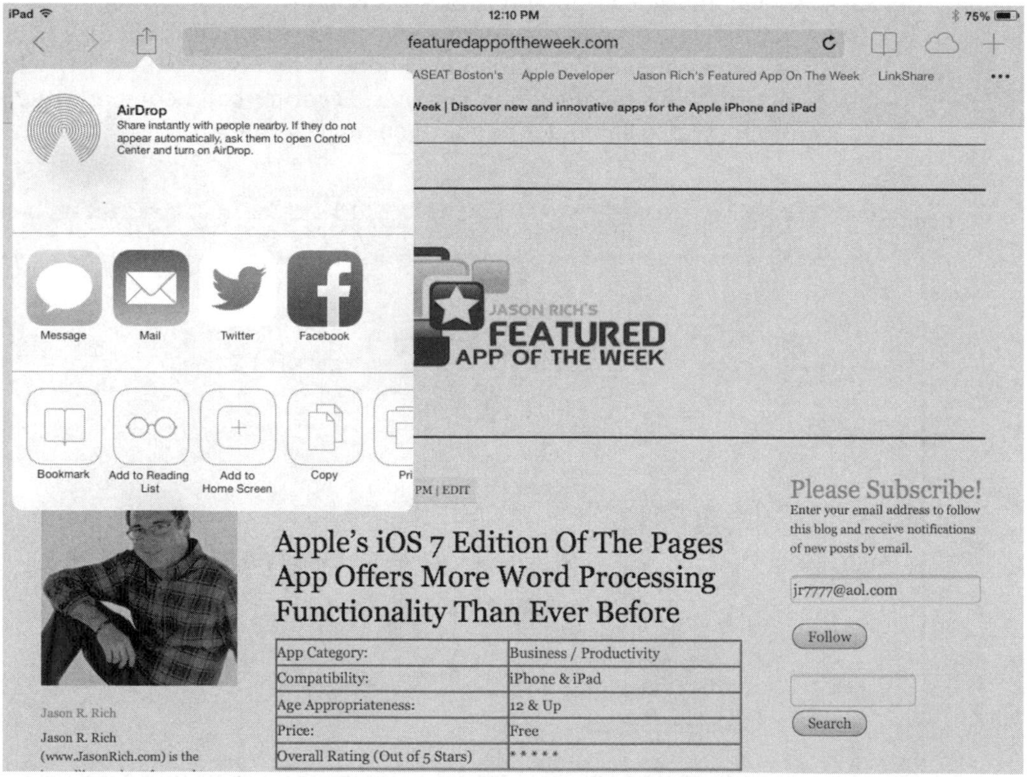

FIGURE 9-3 From the Share menu of Safari, tap the Bookmark option (shown here on the iPad).

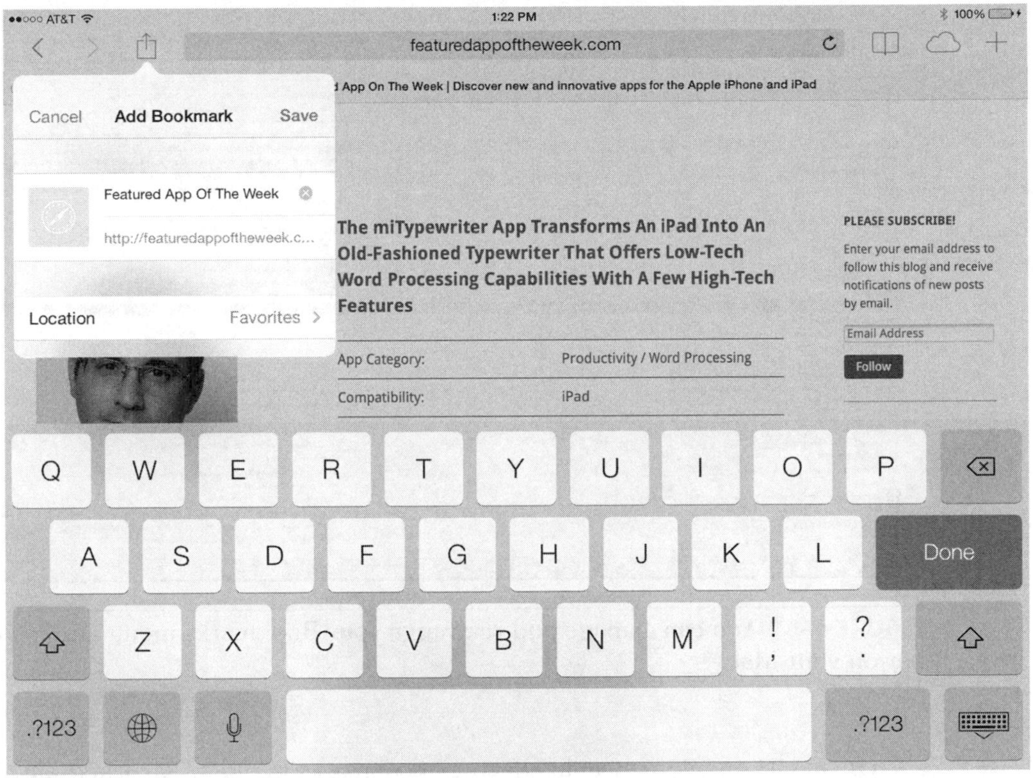

FIGURE 9-4   From the Add Bookmark screen/window (shown here on the iPad), edit the bookmark title and choose a location where it will be stored.

Create and Manage Your Favorites Bar

Creating new web page listings to appear on your Favorites bar is done exactly the same way as creating a new bookmark. However, from the Add This Page To pop-up window, click on the pull-down menu and select the Favorites Bar option.

Edit Your Bookmarks Menu or Favorites Bar Listings

From any of your Macs or iOS mobile devices, you can edit your Bookmarks menu or the listings on your Favorites bar at any time. To do this on a Mac, access the Bookmarks pull-down menu and select the Show Bookmarks option. When the listing of websites stored in your Bookmarks menu and your Favorites bar is displayed (shown in Figure 9-5), it's possible to drag and drop entries to rearrange the listing, or highlight an entry and press DELETE on the keyboard to delete it.

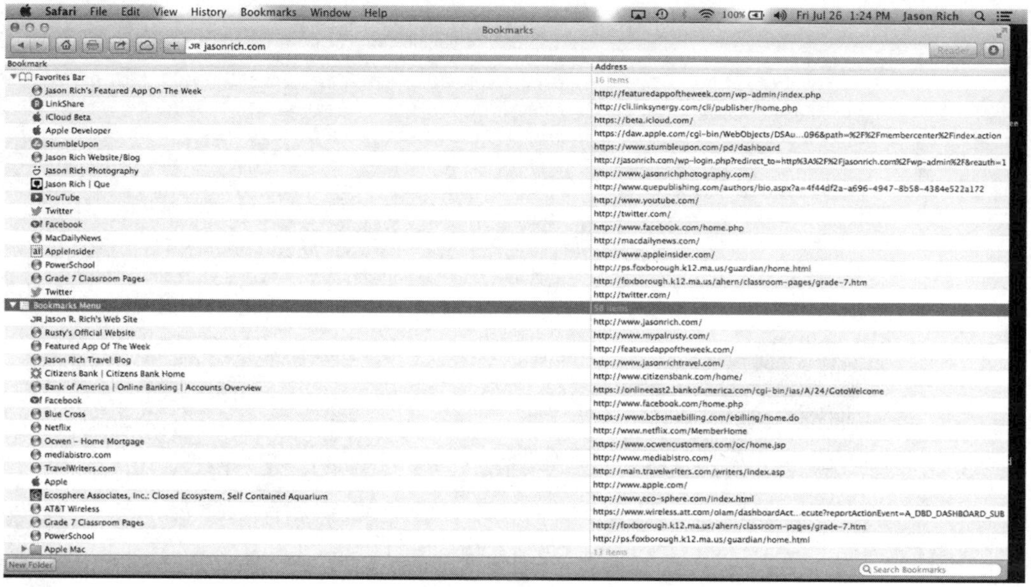

FIGURE 9-5 You can manage and rearrange your Bookmarks menu and Favorites bar on your Mac.

On an iOS mobile device, to edit your Bookmarks menu or Favorites bar, tap the Bookmarks icon on the right side of the toolbar (near the top of the screen). The Favorites screen (iPhone) or window (iPad) will be displayed. Near the top of this window are three tabs. They're labeled Bookmarks, Reading List, and Shared Links (shown in Figure 9-6).

To edit your Bookmarks menu, tap the Bookmarks tab and then tap the Edit option that's displayed near the bottom-right corner of the screen. Then tap the red and white minus sign icon to delete any of the bookmark listings. To rearrange the order of the list, place your finger on any listing's Move icon (it looks like three horizontal lines that are displayed on the right of the website's name) and drag the listing up or down to the desired location.

As you're editing the Bookmarks menu, you can add a new subfolder by tapping the New Folder option that's displayed near the bottom-left corner of the screen. Name the folder by filling in the Title field, and then tap the Location pull-down menu to determine where the folder will be stored. When you're finished editing the Bookmarks menu, tap the Done option.

Note Remember, as you make changes to your Bookmarks menu or Favorites bar listings, the changes will be uploaded to iCloud and almost immediately sync with the other versions of Safari running on your other Macs or iOS mobile devices.

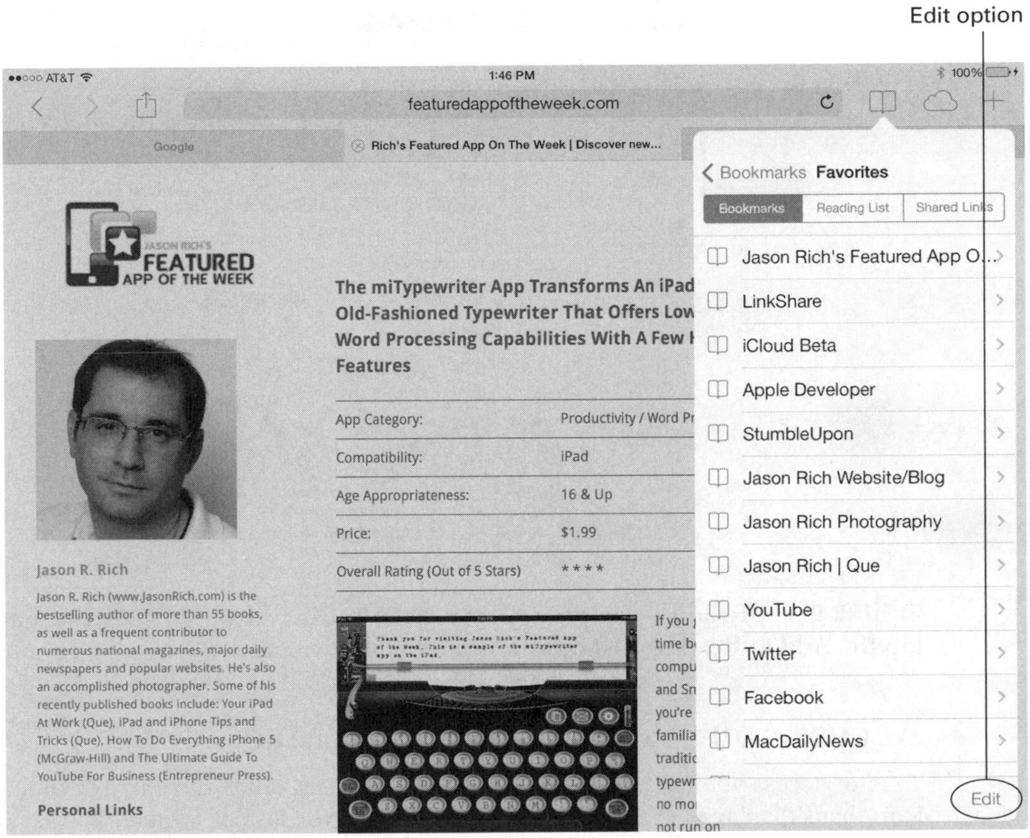

FIGURE 9-6   Safari on your iOS mobile device (shown here on an iPad) allows you to manage and rearrange your Bookmarks menu and Favorites bar.

Create and Manage Your Reading List

The Reading List feature that's built into Safari allows you to store the entire contents of a web page for later viewing (as opposed to just the website's URL within the Bookmarks menu or Favorites bar, for example). When you save a web page to your Reading List, any multimedia content associated with that page will not be saved. However, the majority of the content from that page, including all text, will be available to you for offline reading.

As you're surfing the Web, when you come across an article or a web page you want to add to your Reading List for later viewing, tap the Share icon (found on Safari's toolbar) and select the Add to Reading List option (shown in Figure 9-7). This works on both the Mac and iOS versions of Safari.

FIGURE 9-7 To add a web page or an article from a website to your Reading List, tap the Add to Reading List option from the Share menu.

Access Your Reading List on a Mac

To later access your Reading List from Safari on a Mac, click the small Bookmarks icon that's displayed to the extreme left of your Favorites bar to make the Reading List sidebar menu appear. Alternative, from the View pull-down menu, click the Show Reading List Sidebar option.

As you're viewing the Reading List sidebar, click the All or Unread tab to sort the listings. The All tab reveals all content stored in your Reading List, while the Unread option displays only articles you haven't yet accessed or read. Click the "X" icon to the right of each listing to delete it from your Reading List. Click on a listing to open and read the content or article. To quickly find content stored in your Reading List, use the Search field, which is displayed near the top of the Reading List sidebar.

Access Your Reading List on an iOS Mobile Device

To access your Reading List on your iOS mobile device, tap the Bookmarks icon that's displayed on the right side of the toolbar, and then tap the Reading List tab that's displayed near the top of the screen (iPhone) or window (iPad). By default, all of the content stored within the Reading List is displayed. However, if you want to view only unread articles, tap the Show Unread option that's displayed near the bottom-right corner of the screen/window.

As you're reviewing the Reading List screen/window, swipe your finger from right to left across a listing to delete it from the Reading List, or tap on the listing itself to open and read the content within Safari.

Remember, as you make changes to your Reading List, the changes will be uploaded to iCloud and almost immediately sync with the other versions of Safari running on your other Macs or iOS mobile devices.

Utilize Tabbed Browsing in Safari

As you know, the tabbed web browsing feature of Safari allows you to open multiple browser windows at once and quickly switch between them. On the Mac, to open a new tabbed browser window, click the plus sign icon that's displayed to the extreme right of the Favorites bar, or from the File pull-down menu, select the New Tab option. You can also use the Command (⌘) + T keyboard shortcut to open a new browser window.

Once multiple browser windows are open (shown in Figure 9-8), click the tab for any of them to switch between browser windows.

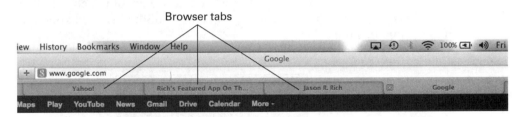

FIGURE 9-8 This is what having multiple browser tabs open in Safari for the Mac looks like.

On an iPad, to open a tabbed browser window, tap the plus sign icon that's displayed to the right of the toolbar. On the iPhone (shown in Figure 9-9), tap the Multi Browser icon (found near the bottom-right corner of the main Safari screen) to switch between open browser windows (tap the browser window thumbnail), close an open browser windows (tap the "X" icon), or open a new browser window (tap the plus sign icon).

When you use tabbed web browsing in Safari and have iCloud functionality turned on, you can access open browser windows on your other computers or devices from whichever computer or device you're currently using. To do this on a Mac, click the iCloud Tabs icon that can be found to the left of Safari's Smart Search field. The iCloud Tabs window will appear listing the open browser windows on each of your other computers and iOS mobile devices that are linked to your iCloud account. Tap on any listing to open that browser window on the version of Safari you're currently using.

On the iPad, the iCloud Tabs icon can be found to the right of the Smart Search field (shown in Figure 9-10). On the iPhone, tap the Multi Browser icon and then scroll toward the bottom of the screen to view iCloud tabs, each of which will be listed under a separate computer or device heading. Tap on any of the listings to open that browser window on your iPhone.

FIGURE 9-9 The iPhone version of Safari offers a new way to view open, switch between, and view browser windows.

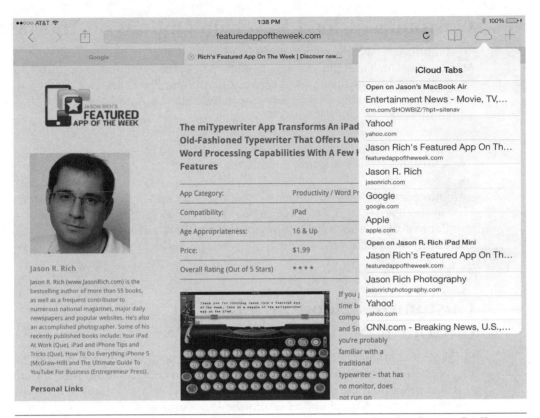

FIGURE 9-10   The iCloud Tabs window, shown here on Safari for the iPad, allows you to view browser windows that are open on other iOS mobile devices linked to the same iCloud account.

Tips for Using iCloud Keychain

After you turn on the iCloud Keychain feature, it automatically stores and syncs usernames, passwords, and related credit card information for each website you visit, and then stores this information securely in an encrypted format within your iCloud account. The information then automatically gets shared with all of your other computers and iOS mobile devices that are linked to the same iCloud account.

Caution   If you know other people will be using your Mac, iPhone, or iPad, for example, be careful about turning on and using the iCloud Keychain option. Someone could easily launch Safari, access one of your bookmarked websites, and log in using your username and password that are stored in iCloud Keychain. To prevent this on a Mac, set up multiple user accounts and be sure to sign off from your account when you're done using the computer. On an iPhone or iPad, you can set up the Passcode Lock Option to prevent unauthorized people from getting past the Lock screen on your device.

Customize iCloud Keychain Options on Your Mac

To customize what information iCloud Keychain will gather, store, and sync on the Mac, access the Safari pull-down menu and select the Preferences option. When the Preferences window opens, click the Autofill option. You then have the option to add checkmarks to the four checkboxes associated with the Autofill Web Forms options, which include:

- Using Info from My Contact Card
- Usernames and Passwords
- Credit Cards
- Other Forms

Each of these options is accompanied by an Edit button which you can click to customize the functionality of each of these options and specifically which websites they'll work with.

Customize iCloud Keychain on Your iOS Mobile Devices

On your iOS mobile device, launch Settings and tap iCloud option. Be sure the virtual switch that's associated with Keychain is turned on. Then, return to the main Settings menu and tap on the Safari option. From the Safari menu within Settings, tap the Passwords & Autofill option. From the Passwords & AutoFill menu, turn on or off (or customize) the Names and Passwords feature, as well as the Credit Cards feature. If you want Safari to autofill your name, address, phone number, and email address as you complete online forms, turn on the Use Contact Info option, and then tap the My Info option to link your own entry from the Contacts app with this option.

Website operators, such as those operated by banks or financial institutions, can opt out of being compatible with iCloud Keychain for security reasons. As a result, your username and password for your online banking account may not be stored. When this is the case, Safari will alert you that your account information is not automatically being stored.

10

Working with iWork for iCloud

HOW TO...

- Access the iWork for iCloud apps from a popular web browser.
- Use the online edition of Pages for word processing, Numbers for spreadsheet management, and Keynote for digital slide presentations.
- Sync iWork for iCloud files with your Macs and iOS mobile devices.

In conjunction with Apple's release of OS X Mavericks for the Mac and iOS 7 for its iPhone, iPad, and iPod touch mobile devices in October 2013, Apple also dramatically enhanced its iCloud service. In the past, iCloud allowed iWork for Mac and iWork for iOS users to sync files between computers and devices via iCloud.

Note
The iWork for iCloud applications include Pages for word processing, Numbers for spreadsheet management, and Keynote for digital slide presentations. Each of these online-based apps is compatible with their Mac or iOS counterparts. All three online-based apps also allow you to easily import Microsoft Office files or export files into Microsoft Office format.

For example, if you created a Pages document on your Mac, it would automatically be synced with your iPad, and you could continue working with that document on your tablet, as long as both devices were connected to the Internet.

This functionality is still available. However, instead of iCloud just storing and syncing Pages, Numbers, and Keynote documents and files, the service now offers fully functional online-based versions of the three iWork applications. Thus, from a compatible web browser on a Mac or Windows-based PC, it's now possible to access the iWork for iCloud apps in order to create new documents or files, or work with your existing documents and files that are already stored in your iCloud account.

In addition, when you're using iWork for iCloud, you can simply drag existing Word, Excel, or PowerPoint files into Pages, Numbers, or Keynote respectively, and the online-based app will import and convert those Microsoft Office files. As always, you have the option to export the document or file you're working with to a Microsoft Office–compatible file. Thus, the online versions of the iWork apps are fully compatible with Macs and Windows-based PCs.

The thing to understand about iWork for iCloud is that the three apps—Pages, Numbers, and Keynote—as well as your files, documents, and data, are all stored online and accessible from iCloud's servers via a web browser. No software or files are actually stored on your computer. The iWork for iCloud apps can all work entirely on their own, but they can also work in conjunction with the iWork for Mac and iWork for iOS apps, which do actually get stored on your computer or mobile device.

Use the iWork for iCloud Apps from Any Compatible Web Browser

Once you set up your free iCloud account, access any of the iWork for iCloud apps by launching a compatible web browser, such as Safari (Mac), Internet Explorer (Windows-based PC), or Chrome (PC/Mac), and then visit www.iCloud.com. When prompted, enter your Apple/iCloud ID and password (shown in Figure 10-1). In the future, the iWork for iCloud apps will support additional web browsers.

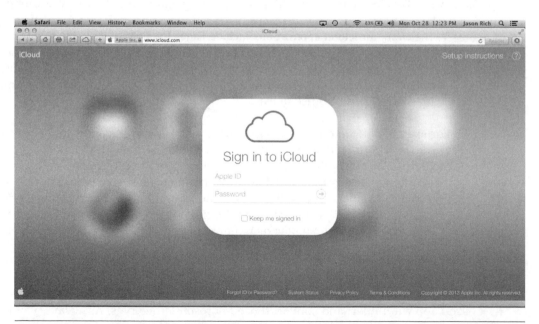

FIGURE 10-1 Enter your Apple/iCloud ID and password when prompted in order to access the iWork for iCloud apps.

Tip When signing in to your iCloud account, add a checkmark to the checkbox that says "Keep Me Signed In." This will prevent you having to log in again each time you revisit this website from the same computer. Only use this feature, however, if you're the only person who uses your computer and you're not concerned about unauthorized people being able to access your documents and files by freely logging into iCloud.

When the iCloud main menu screen appears, click on the app you want to work with. In other words, click the Pages, Numbers, or Keynote icon.

Even if you don't already use the iWork apps for your Mac, or the iWork for iOS apps, you can use the online versions of these apps, for free, via your iCloud account. However, if you do use the iWork apps on your Macs or iOS mobile devices, and you set up these apps to sync documents and files with iCloud, all of your work will constantly be accessible from any computer or device that's linked to the same iCloud account.

Thus, if you start working on a spreadsheet using Numbers on the iPad, you can then access www.iCloud.com from any computer's web browser and continue working on that same spreadsheet using the online edition of Numbers.

Caution When working with an iPhone or iPad, you can't access www.iCloud.com from Safari and then access the online-based Pages, Numbers, or Keynote apps. Instead, you'll need to have one or more of these apps already installed on your iOS mobile device. All of the iWork for iOS apps can then sync your work, in real time, with your iCloud account.

Tip If you're using a Windows-based PC, you can access and work with any of the iWork for iCloud apps using the Microsoft Internet Explorer or Chrome web browser. When you do this, it's then possible to drag and drop Microsoft Office documents or files that are stored on your PC into a compatible iWork for iCloud app in order to work with them.

Get Started Using Pages via iCloud

The first time you access Pages via iCloud, a Welcome screen (shown in Figure 10-2) will be displayed. To discover more about what this iWork for iCloud app can do, click the Learn More link. To begin using the online edition of the app, click the Get Started with Pages button.

Next, the Library screen of Pages will be displayed (shown in Figure 10-3). This screen is almost identical to the Library screen of Pages that is displayed when using the Mac or iOS edition of the app.

Displayed on this Library screen are thumbnails that represent each of the Pages documents you already have stored in your iCloud account. These include documents that were created on your Macs, iOS mobile devices, or other computers you signed in to your iCloud account with when using iWork for iCloud.

To start using Pages, click
on the Continue button.

FIGURE 10-2 Click the Get Started with Pages button in the Welcome window to begin using the online edition of Pages.

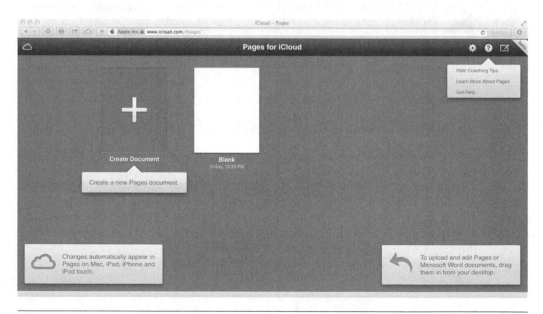

FIGURE 10-3 The Library screen of the Pages app displays your existing documents stored in your iCloud account.

Click on any of the existing document thumbnails to open and begin working with that document. To create a new document from scratch, click the Create Document thumbnail that displays a plus sign within it.

Navigate Your Way Around the Pages Library Screen

As you're viewing the Library screen of Pages from your web browser, click the cloud icon that's displayed near the upper-left corner of the screen to return to the main iCloud menu and exit out of Pages. You can also leave Pages by closing the browser window you're working in.

The Pages File Management Menu

To access the Pages menu for managing files, click the gear-shaped icon that's displayed near the top-right corner of the screen. From the drop-down menu that appears (shown in Figure 10-4), you can choose from the following options:

- **Create Document** To start a new document from scratch, either click the Create Document thumbnail or click the Create Document menu option.
- **Upload Document** To upload a document that's stored on your computer but not yet in your online-based iCloud account, use this menu option. When the Finder window appears, select the document you want to upload in order to use it with the online version of Pages. This document will then also be stored in your iCloud account.
- **Download Document** Transfer a document that's stored in your iCloud account and save it on the computer you're currently working with. This feature is useful if you want to save a copy of your file to work with later when an Internet connection may not be available (such as when you're on an airplane), or to store a copy of the file on a USB thumb drive, for example.

FIGURE 10-4 Manage documents from this pull-down menu displayed near the top-right corner of the Library screen.

- **Duplicate Document** If you want to keep a copy of the document you're working with as is but then make edits to it, using this option allows you to keep the original version of the document intact and create a copy of the document which you can then modify. The end result is that two versions of the document—the original and the newly revised document—will be stored using different filenames in your iCloud account.
- **Delete Document** Use this command to delete a document from your iCloud account. Remember, your iCloud account automatically syncs with the Macs and iOS mobile devices you have linked to the same Apple ID/iCloud account. So when you delete a document or file from iCloud, it will automatically be deleted (almost instantly) from your other computers and mobile devices.

Tip Another way to delete a document stored in your iCloud account and displayed within the Library screen is to click its thumbnail to highlight it. This will cause a yellow frame to appear around the thumbnail that indicates it's been selected. Next, press DELETE on your computer's keyboard. Confirm your deletion request when prompted.

- **Share Document** Use this command to share a particular document with someone else. This will grant them access to just the selected document or file, not to everything stored in your iCloud account. The person you want to share the document with will receive an email that contains a URL link that leads them directly to the selected file in your iCloud account.
- **Send a Copy** This command allows you to send a copy of a selected file to someone else via email. The recipient will not need to access your iCloud account to retrieve the file since it will be included as an attachment with the email message.
- **Sort by Date** Use this command to sort the document thumbnails displayed on the Pages Library screen based on the date each was created or last modified.
- **Sort by Name** Use this command to sort the document thumbnails displayed on the Pages Library screen alphabetically, based on its filename.

Discover What Else You Can Do from the Library Screen

If you want to learn more about the online edition of Pages, click the Help icon that's displayed near the top-right corner of the Library screen. The Help icon is circular and has a question mark displayed within it.

To provide feedback to Apple about Pages, click the Feedback icon that's also displayed near the top-right corner of the screen. When the iWork for iCloud apps are officially released and no longer in their beta testing phase, this option may be removed.

As you're looking at the Library screen within Pages, to import a Microsoft Word document or another compatible text document that's currently stored on your computer (or on a storage device, such as a USB thumb drive, that's connected to your computer), simply drag and drop the document thumbnail from the Finder window to this Library screen. This will allow Pages for iCloud to automatically import the document and convert it to the Pages format so you can view and edit it using this online-based app.

Rename Documents or Files Displayed in the Library Screen

Displayed immediately below each document thumbnail when you're viewing the Pages Library screen is the filename for that document, as well as the date and time it was created or last modified. To manually change the filename, click on the filename once (not the thumbnail). You will then be able to type over the existing filename and replace it with a new filename.

 Note When you change a filename using Pages via iCloud, this will impact the document's name on all computers and devices that are linked to your Apple ID/iCloud account.

Work with Documents Using Pages for iCloud

Once you open a Pages document from the app's Library screen, you'll be able to view, edit, and share the document just as you would if you were using Pages running on your Mac or iOS mobile device.

Tip To open an existing document and begin working with it, from the Library screen, double-click on the document's thumbnail.

If you opt to create a document from scratch, the Choose a Template screen (shown in Figure 10-5) will appear. Pages, Numbers, and Keynote all have a handful of document or file templates that you can customize and work with, which will save you time when it comes to formatting your work.

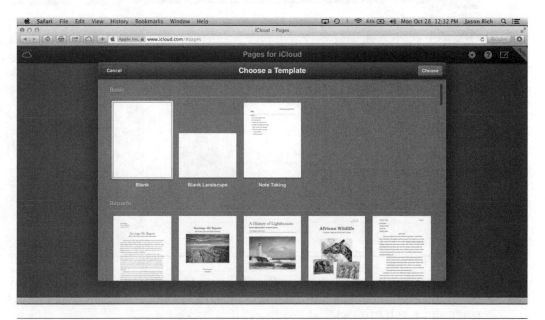

FIGURE 10-5 The Choose a Template screen within Pages for iCloud

Select the Blank template if you want to truly create a document from scratch and handle all of your own formatting. Otherwise, select one of the other templates based on the type of document you'd like to create. Your new document will be displayed on the screen in a separate browser window.

Next, when looking at an open document (shown in Figure 10-6), all of your available commands will be displayed as icons or menu options along the top of the screen, as well as within a sidebar that's displayed along the right side of the screen. This sidebar is called the format panel.

Displayed near the top-left corner of the main Pages screen is the Magnification menu. Click it to change the view of the document being displayed. You can adjust the magnification from between 25 percent and 400 percent, or choose the Fit Width or Fit Page options displayed near the bottom of this pull-down menu.

To the right of the Magnification menu are the Undo and Redo icons. Click the Undo icon to go back one step and undo the last thing you just did when using Pages. Likewise, click the Redo command to repeat the last thing you just did when using Pages.

When you look along the top-center of the main Pages display, you'll see three command icons: Text, Shape, and Image. Click the Text icon to add a text box to the document you're working with. When the box appears within the main editing window, you can adjust its size and placement using the mouse. To add a shape to your document, click the Shape icon. From the menu that appears, choose the shape you want to import. It's then possible to customize the appearance, size, and placement of the shape.

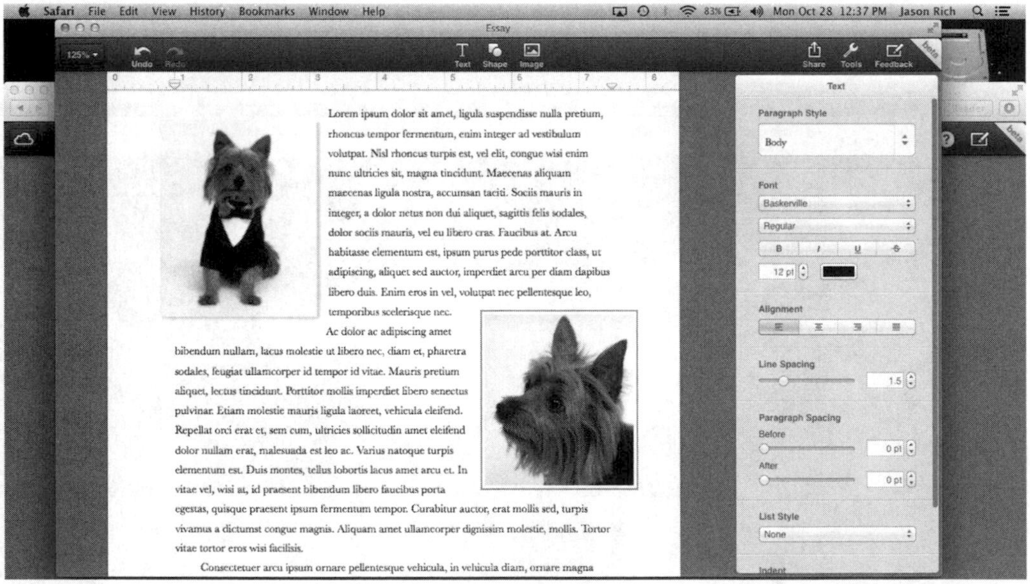

FIGURE 10-6 Pages for iCloud offers full word processing capabilities via any computer that's connected to the Internet. This version of Pages works through a computer's web browser.

Click the Image command icon to import an image, such as a digital photo, that's stored on the computer you're working on into the Pages document you're currently working with. First, you'll be prompted to select the image. Then you'll have the option to resize the image, adjust its placement, and customize its appearance.

Tip   As you're working with any of the iWork for iCloud apps, if there's a digital photo or graphic that's stored on the computer you're using that you want to import into the document or file, simply drag and drop that image or graphic into the browser window that contains your document or file. The content you drag and drop will automatically be imported into your work. Once imported into your document or file, you can resize or reposition it, and alter its appearance using the tools built into the app. To do this, simply select the image or graphic and then access the format panel.

Displayed near the top-right corner of the main Pages screen are three additional command icons: Share, Tools, and Feedback. When you click the Share icon, you'll be given the option to export the document you're working with to a Pages, PDF, or Word formatted file (shown in Figure 10-7). Click on your selection.

After you select an export file format for the document or file you're working with, it will be automatically formatted. Click the Email button to send the document to its intended recipients.

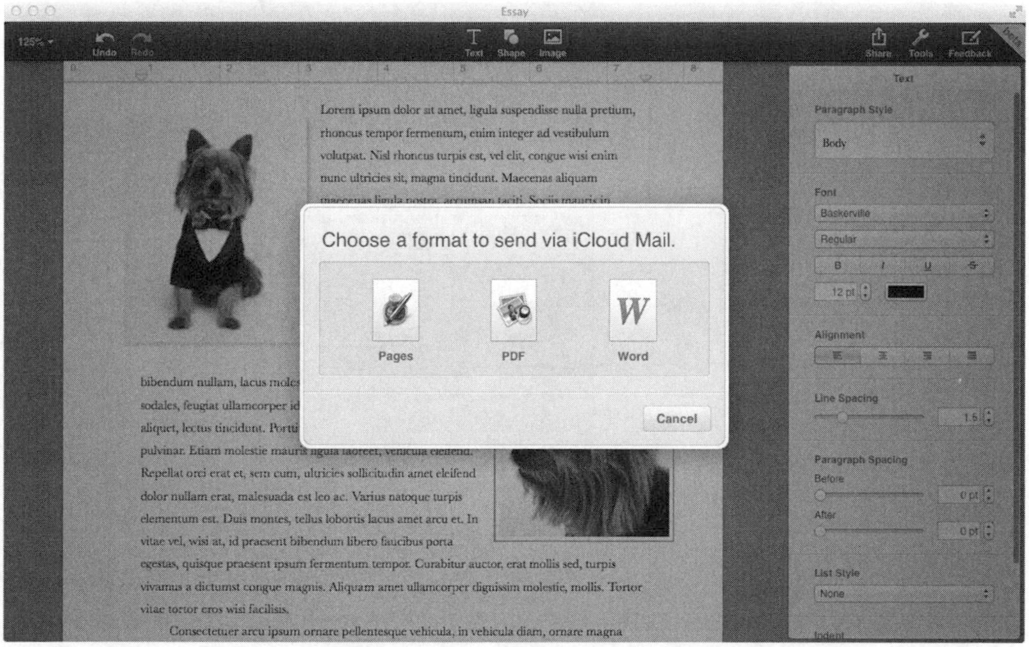

FIGURE 10-7   When you opt to share a document, you must select a file format. When using Pages, your options include Pages format, PDF format, or Microsoft Word format.

Format a Document as You Work

As you're working with a Pages document, you can control the formatting in that document by clicking on the Text icon (displayed near the top-center of the browser window), and then adjusting the formatting-related options that are displayed along the right margin of the document you're working with.

Clicking on the Tools icon (displayed near the top-right corner of the document window) reveals the new Tools menu. From here, you can access a variety of options, including the online app's Settings menu.

 As you're entering text into a Pages document (or working with a Numbers or Keynote file), instead of using the tools displayed with the format panel, it's possible to use a wide range of keyboard shortcuts, such as COMMAND-B for bold text or COMMAND-I for italic text. These are the same keyboard shortcuts available when using Pages for Mac or Pages for iOS.

In the format panel displayed along the right side of the screen (shown in Figure 10-8), the options available to you change based on what you're doing in Pages.

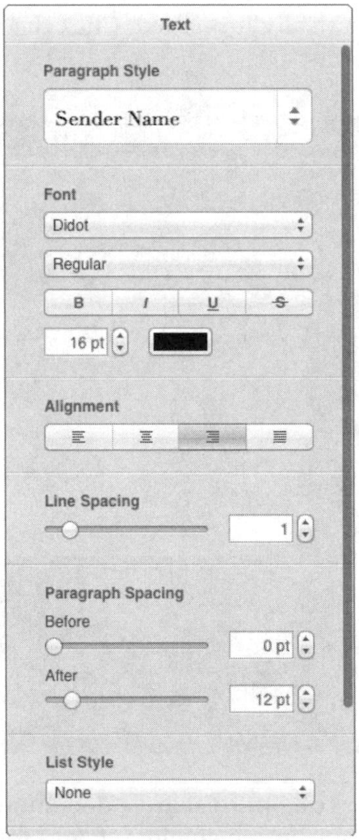

FIGURE 10-8 The format panel in Pages allows you to custom format your text as you work.

If you're working with text, for example, the options related to paragraph style, font selection, typestyles selection (including font size and color), text alignment, line spacing, paragraph spacing, list style, and indent spacing are all displayed. However, if you're working with an image you've imported into the document, the format panel will display an entirely different selection of options (shown in Figure 10-9).

When you're done working with a document in Pages for iCloud, either click the Share icon to send the document to someone else or click the Tools icon, followed by the Send a Copy option icon, to email your work to others. To save your work, return to the Library screen and select the Go to My Documents option.

Keep in mind, your work is continuously being saved. So if you close the browser window you're working with, the document or file you're working with will be saved automatically. When you reopen Pages for iWork, Pages for Mac, or Pages for iOS, you will be able to reopen that document and continue working where you left off.

Note The Feedback icon that's also displayed near the top-right corner of the screen allows users to contact Apple and provide feedback about the app. Once the iWork for iCloud apps are officially launched, this feature may or may not continue to remain available.

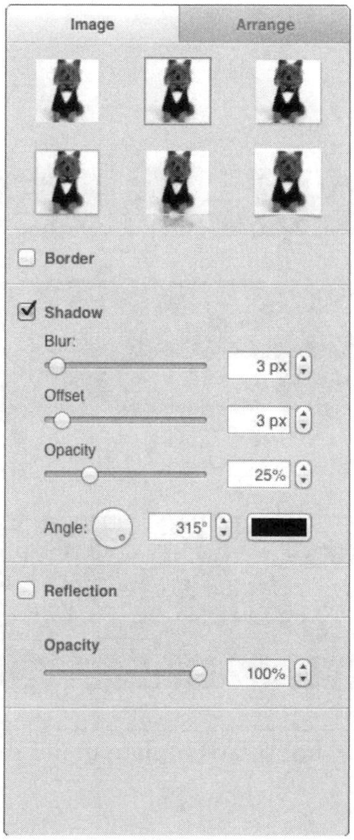

FIGURE 10-9   Here, the format panel shows options available when working with a digital image within a document.

The Interface for Numbers and Keynote Is Very Similar to Pages

You'll quickly discover that the interface when using Numbers or Keynote via iCloud is very similar to Pages. When you launch one of these apps from the main iCloud.com menu screen, the app's Library screen will appear and all of the same functionality will be available to you.

For example, when working with Numbers, you can drag and drop an Excel file to the Library screen and then automatically import that file. Likewise, you can import a PowerPoint digital slide presentation into Keynote from that app's Library screen.

The Library screens for Pages, Numbers, and Keynote all work basically the same way when it comes to creating new documents/files, as well as renaming, deleting, or sharing documents or files. Likewise, if you opt to create a new file, a handful of templates within Numbers or Keynote will be displayed. Figure 10-10 shows the Choose a Template menu in Numbers.

When you actually begin working with Numbers or Keynote, the basic interface is the same as Pages, but once again, the menu commands and what's available from the format panel will be different. How you go about sharing documents and files, however, remains the same.

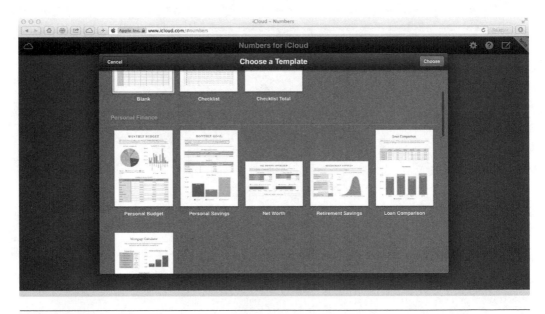

FIGURE 10-10   The Choose a Template menu in Numbers

What's Not Yet Possible Using the iWork for iCloud Apps

At the time *How to Do Everything iCloud: 2nd Edition* was being written, the ability to print documents, spreadsheets, and presentations directly from the iWork for iCloud apps was not yet possible. This is functionality that Apple promises will become available in the near future. By the time you read this, a Print menu option will most likely be available from the Tools menu.

 Until the Print feature is incorporated into the iWork for iCloud apps, if you want to print your work, you'll need to download the document or file to the appropriate iWork app on your Mac or iOS mobile device, and then print it from within the app.

In addition, the ability to edit and format tables within a document or file was not yet made available, although this too is a feature Apple plans to implement. Another feature that will be added to the iWork for iCloud apps is the ability to automatically track and maintain multiple versions of the same document or file, without having to manually create and then rename them. In other words, in the future, the iWork for iCloud apps will maintain a Version History for each document or file.

Manage Numbers Spreadsheets via iCloud

The Library menu window displayed when using the Numbers app offers the same basic functionality as the Library screen of the Pages and Keynote apps. However, once you start working with the Numbers online app to do some number crunching or spreadsheet management, some of the command icons and menu options are different.

Displayed on the main Numbers screen (shown in Figure 10-11) are a handful of command icons and menu options. You can also opt to display the format panel related to the app along the right margin of the browser window.

Located near the top-left corner is the Magnification menu icon, along with the Undo and Redo command icons. These all work the same way as in Pages. Displayed near the top-center of the browser window are four command icons: Table, Text, Shape, and Image.

Click the Table command icon to insert and format a new table within the Numbers file you're working with. Next, choose a table format. Once the new table has been imported into the file, you have the ability to adjust its size and position, and then use the various format panel commands to fully customize the tablet itself, as well as the content to be included within it.

By clicking the Text icon, it's possible to format the text that's being incorporated into a spreadsheet or Numbers file. This includes the ability to add a text box and then fully format, resize, and reposition the box, as well as determine the appearance of text that will be displayed within the box.

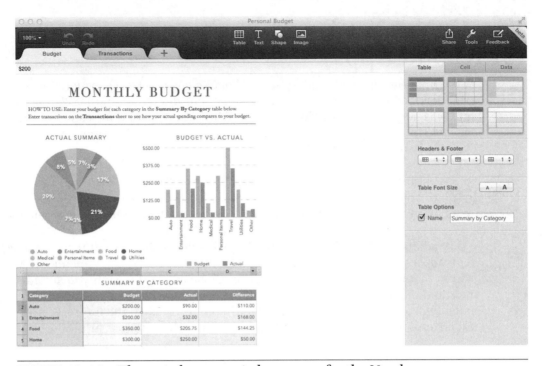

FIGURE 10-11 The main browser window screen for the Numbers app

Just as with Pages, clicking the Shape icon allows you to import and customize a shape. Once you click on a shape option, you can resize and reposition it using the mouse, and customize its appearance using the commands displayed within the format panel.

The Image command works just like it does in Pages. It's used to import a graphic or digital photo that's already stored on your computer. Now, look to the upper-right corner of the Numbers window. Here, you'll discover the Share, Tools, and Feedback icons.

Once again, when you click the Share icon, you will have the option to export your work using the Numbers, Excel, or PDF file format. Then, once the file has been processed, you can email it by clicking the Email button.

The options available from the Tools menu are very similar to what you found in Pages for iCloud. To exit out of the file you're working with, save your work, and return to the Library screen in Numbers, click the Spreadsheets menu option.

When you display the format panel within Numbers, the formatting options available to you will vary based on the type of content that is selected and that you're currently working with. For example, if you click on a numeric cell within a spreadsheet (shown in Figure 10-12), the Functions options are displayed in the format panel. Chart editing, text formatting, and other functions will all vary, based on what you have selected in the Numbers file you're currently working with. The functions that become available, however, are virtually identical to what's offered by the Numbers for Mac and Numbers for iOS apps.

FIGURE 10-12   When crunching numbers, use the Functions menu that's displayed in the format panel in Numbers for iCloud.

Work with Keynote Presentations via iCloud

From the main iWork for iCloud menu, which is accessible by visiting www.icloud .com and signing in with your Apple ID/iCloud username and password, click the Keynote icon to launch the Keynote for iCloud app. Using this app, you can create, edit, share, or present digital slide presentations.

From the Library screen of Keynote, it's possible to drag and drop Microsoft PowerPoint presentations directly into the Keynote app and begin working with them. When you do this, however, keep in mind that you may encounter minor incompatibilities with fonts, slide transitions, and slide animations. When an incompatibility arises, the app will notify you and do its best to replace the incompatible content with something similar.

 After importing a PowerPoint presentation into Keynote, before you present it to an audience using Keynote for iCloud, be sure to review the presentation carefully. You may need to fix minor formatting issues, for example.

The Library screen of the Keynote for iCloud app is very similar to the Library screen of the Pages for iCloud and Numbers for iCloud apps in terms of appearance and file management capabilities. Likewise, if you opt to create a new presentation from scratch, the Choose a Template menu screen that's specific to Keynote will be displayed.

Once you select a template for a new presentation or load an existing presentation, the main Keynote screen will be displayed in a separate browser window (shown in Figure 10-13). Once again, the now familiar Magnification menu icon, as well as the Undo and Redo command icons, will be displayed near the top-left corner of the screen.

To the immediate right of the Redo icon, however, you'll find the Play command icon, which is specific to Keynote. Click the Play icon to switch from presentation editing mode to presentation mode in order to showcase your presentation to an audience.

As you're editing a presentation, displayed near the top-center of the screen are the Text, Shape, and Image icons. Near the upper-right corner of the screen, you'll see the Share, Tools, and Feedback icons—all of which work the same as in Pages for iCloud or Numbers for iCloud.

Also displayed within the main Keynote for iCloud app screen, along the left margin, are thumbnails for each of the slides in your presentation. Click once on a slide thumbnail to access various animation and transition options. You can also double-click on the thumbnail to edit the content of a specific slide.

To create a new slide within a presentation, click the Add Slide icon (which looks like a plus sign) that's displayed near the bottom-left corner of the app window. Once again, based on what content you have selected at any given time, the options available to you from the format panel (displayed along the right margin of the screen) will vary.

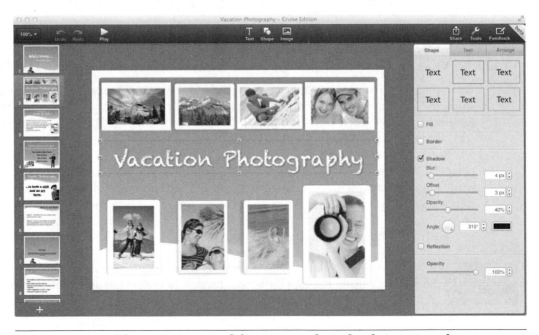

FIGURE 10-13 The main screen of the Keynote for iCloud app. From here, you can create or edit a digital slide presentation.

For example, if you click on an image, image customization options will be displayed in the format panel. However, if you click on an entire slide, Transition Effect and Advance Slide options are displayed. If you have text within a slide selected, text formatting options will be available in the format panel.

To exit out of the Keynote app as you're editing a slide presentation, click the Share icon to save and email your presentation to someone else, or click the Tools icon, followed by the Presentations option, to save your work and return to Keynote's Library screen. Next, click the cloud-shaped icon (it's displayed near the top-left corner of the screen) to return to the main iCloud menu. At any time, you also have the option to simply close the browser window. All of your work will automatically be saved in your iCloud account.

To save the presentation you're working with on your computer, in addition to in your iCloud account, from the Library screen within the app, click the gear-shaped icon and then choose the Download Presentation option.

As you're using Keynote for iCloud, keep in mind you always have the option to manually connect your computer to an LCD projector to showcase your presentation to an audience. Simply click the Play icon to begin playing the presentation in full-screen mode on your computer or via a projector.

One of the great things about the iWork for iCloud apps is that each operates within a separate web browser window. Thus, by opening multiple browser windows at the same time (using the Tabbed Browsing feature of Safari, for example), you can work with two or more apps or multiple documents or files simultaneously, simply by switching between active browser windows. This makes it easy to drag and drop or copy and paste content between documents or files, or easily switch between several files and multitask.

The iWork for iCloud Apps Can Utilize Full-Screen Mode

If you're working with any of the iWork for iCloud apps via Safari on a Mac, you can make full use of the computer's online real estate by switching Safari into full-screen mode. To do this, click the Full Screen mode icon that's displayed in the extreme upper-right corner of the browser window. Then, to exit out of Full Screen mode, press the Escape (ESC) key on the keyboard.

All of the pull-down menu options that are specific to the web browser you're working with, which are displayed along the app's menu bar and toolbar, continue to be fully operational. However, if you try using the Print command from your browser's main menu or toolbar, what will be printed is the entire iWork for iCloud window or screen you're looking at, not the document or file you're working with.

Collaboration with Others Is Now Possible Using iWork Apps

One of the new features added to the latest versions of Pages, Numbers, and Keynote for the Mac and iOS mobile devices, as well as the online versions of these apps, is the ability to collaborate in real time with others. When you turn on this feature for a specific document or file you're working with, you can decide exactly which people you want to collaborate with, and then grant only those people access to a specific document or file via iCloud.

When you use the new collaboration feature, you are not granting people access to all of your documents and files stored within iCloud. Collaborators will only have access to a specific document or file. As you're composing, editing, or reviewing a document or file, you can turn on the Collaboration option within the iWork app you're using. Then, decide who you'd like to collaborate with. A special website URL will be created for that document or file, and you'll have the ability to contact the people you'd like to collaborate with (via email, for example). The email or text message will automatically include a specific link to one document or file (that's stored within iCloud).

Your invited collaborators can then use any version of Pages, Numbers, or Keynote (on their own Mac, iOS mobile device, or on a Windows PC using an online edition of the app) to access your document or file and begin viewing and/or editing it. As changes are made by any collaborator, those changes are synced in real time, so everyone is always working with the latest version of the document or file. Later, if you opt to revoke someone's access to a document or file, this can be done as well, or you can turn off the collaboration feature associated with a document or file altogether.

From a Mac that's running one of the iWork apps, to turn on Collaboration functionality, click on the Share icon that's displayed near the top of the screen, and then click on the Share Link via iCloud option. Next, choose your Share method, which can include Email, Messages, Twitter, or Facebook. Depending on how you have the app set up, you may be promoted to manually save your document or file to iCloud. However, this can be set up to be done automatically. Next, click on the Share icon again and select the View Share Settings option. Click on the Share Document button (if you're using Pages, for example). Then, click on the Send Link button to invite collaborators to have access to your document or file.

From an iPhone that's running one of the iWork apps, from the Library screen, tap the Share icon and select the Share Link via iCloud option. Next, from the Library screen, tap on the thumbnail for the document or file you want to share. Then, from the Share menu, choose how you want to invite collaborators. (Based on how your iPhone is set up, options may include AirDrop, Message, Mail, Twitter, or Facebook.) If you choose Mail, when the Compose email screen appears, fill in the To field with the names or email addresses of your intended collaborators, and tap the Send option. The thumbnail for the document or file you chose to share will now display a Share icon in the upper-right corner when you're viewing the Library screen.

From an iPad that's running one of the iWork apps, to begin collaborating with others on the document or file you're working with, as you're composing, editing, or reviewing the document or file, tap on the Share icon (displayed near the top-right corner of the app screen). Tap on the Share Link via iCloud option. Choose how you want to share the document or file. (Based on how your iPad is set up, options may include AirDrop, Message, Mail, Twitter, or Facebook.) When the Compose Mail screen appears, fill in the To field with the names or email addresses of your intended collaborators, and tap the Send option.

If you're an iWork for iCloud user who wants to collaborate with others when working with a Pages document or a Numbers or Keynote file, simply click on the Share icon that's displayed near the top-right corner of the app window, and then click on the Share Document, Share Spreadsheet, or Share Presentation button. A pop-up window will display the unique link (IRL) for that document or file. Click on the Email Link button to invite other people to work with you on that document or file. When the Compose email window appears, fill in the To field for your intended collaborators, and then click on the Send option.

When using iWork for iCloud, as you're working with a document or file that's being shared, a new Share icon will be displayed near the top-right corner of the screen. Click on it at any time to turn off the Sharing feature to invite additional collaborators to work with you, or to revoke access to someone you're already collaborating with.

Once you opt to collaborate with one or more people on a document or file, from the iWork app you're using, be sure to tap or click on the Tools icon (which is shaped like a wrench) and then turn on the Change Tracking option. Also, from the Tools menu, tap on the Settings option. From the Settings submenu, turn on the virtual switch associated with Comments, and also tap on the Author Name option and enter your full name, first name, or initials. This way, when you include a new comment or edit, all of your collaborators will know who made the change to the document or file you're all working on.

For iWork file or document collaboration to work, you will need to have an active iCloud account and your computer or mobile device will need continuous access to the Internet while you're working in real time with others. With no Internet access, you can still view and edit a document or file, but your edits or changes will not be visible to your collaborators, and you will not see their edits or changes in real time. The document or file will automatically synchronize with iCloud and update once your computer or device reconnects to the Internet.

Instead of collaborating on a document or file, when using any version of any iWork app, it's possible to simply send a copy of your document or file to someone else from within the app you're working with. To do this, access the Tools menu within the app you're working with and select the Send A Copy option. Next, select what file format you want to use as you export the file or document out of the iWork app you're using in order to send it to someone else.

When working with the online version of Pages, you can export the document in Pages, Word, or PDF format. When working with the Mac or iOS version, you can also export a document in ePub format.

When working with the online version of Numbers, it's possible to export a file in the Numbers, Excel, or PDF file format. However, when working with the Mac or iOS version of Numbers, it's also possible to export the spreadsheet in CSV format.

Meanwhile, if you're working with the online, Mac, or iOS version of Keynote, a presentation file can be exported and sent in Keynote, PowerPoint, or PDF format. Using the Send A Copy option does not activate the collaboration functionality of the iWork app. You're simply able to send a copy of a document or file to someone else.

Note The iWork for iCloud apps are continuously being upgraded with new features, functions and menu options. Thus, by the time you read this chapter, and in the months to come, the screens may look different as Apple updates these online-based applications. Compatibly with the Mac and iOS versions of these apps, as well as Microsoft Office document and file compatibility will remain available.

PART **IV**

Discover More Uses for iCloud When Used with Your Mac and iOS Mobile Devices

11

Manage Apps, App-Related Data, and Ebooks with iCloud

HOW TO...

- Synchronize Contacts, Calendar, Reminders, Notes, and your iCloud email data.
- Set up iCloud to synchronize ebooks and other app-specific data.
- Keep all of your mobile devices and computers up to date with the latest information.

Setting up your free iCloud account is your first step toward being able to use the features of Apple's cloud-based service from your computers and iOS mobile devices. However, each device you'll be using with iCloud needs to be set up separately so that many of the specific iCloud-related features you want to use will ultimately work automatically and behind the scenes.

This chapter explains how to set up the Contacts, Calendar, Reminders, and Notes apps on your Mac, iPhone, or iPad so that they synchronize their app-specific data with iCloud (and ultimately with your other computers and iOS mobile devices that are linked to the same iCloud account).

When you're using your iPhone, for example, if you add or update a contact entry using the Contacts app, add or change an appointment using Calendar, create or change a to-do list item with the Reminders app, or create or edit a note with the Notes app, those additions or changes can almost instantly and automatically be uploaded to iCloud, and then shared with your other computers and iOS mobile devices.

Thus, after you make those additions or changes on your iPhone, you should be able to access your primary computer or iPad, for example, and see up-to-date information. Likewise, any additions or changes made on your computer or iPad will be reflected almost instantly on your iPhone.

Did You Know?

Syncing App-Specific Data Serves Several Purposes

The ability for iCloud to sync app-specific data is particularly beneficial if, in addition to an iPhone or iPad, you use the Mac version of the Contacts, Calendar, Notes, or Reminders app, and want to keep app-specific data synced between all of your computers and mobile devices.

It's also particularly helpful if you utilize the online editions of the Contacts, Calendar, Reminders, or Notes apps to access your data remotely. It's possible to do this by pointing any web browser to www.icloud.com and logging in with your Apple ID/iCloud username and password.

In addition, this feature is useful if you own both an iPhone and an iPad, and want app-specific data for Contacts, Calendar, Reminders, and Notes to remain synchronized among your mobile devices in almost real time.

However, if you only use one Apple product, whether it's a Mac, iPhone, iPad, or iPod touch, iCloud's app-specific data-syncing functionality can be used to simply and automatically maintain a backup of this important data in the cloud. If necessary, your app-specific data backup can then be restored to your computer or iOS mobile device from anywhere there's an Internet connection.

For iCloud to synchronize app-specific data between your computers and iOS mobile devices automatically, each must be connected to the Internet. Your iPhone or iPad will be able to use either a cellular (3G/4G LTE) data connection or a Wi-Fi connection for this purpose.

If no Internet connection is available, the additions or changes you make when using Contacts, Calendar, Reminders, or Notes, for example, will not immediately upload to iCloud and will not be downloaded by your other computers or devices from iCloud. The necessary uploads or downloads will automatically occur when an Internet connection is reestablished.

Remember that the iCloud functionality for the Contacts, Calendar, Reminders, and Notes apps needs to be activated and set up by you just once, on each of your iOS mobile devices and computers, in order for them to synchronize app-related data. Once set up, the data synchronization happens in almost real time in the background. You don't have to take any further actions to ensure that all of your most up-to-date data for the relevant apps is stored on iCloud, and thus made available to your other computers and iOS mobile devices that are linked to the same iCloud account.

Note On each computer or iOS mobile device, make sure that when you activate iCloud, you enter the same account-related information that was used to create your iCloud account (such as your Apple ID and password). This is essential if you want all of your computers and iOS mobile devices to be able to share and synchronize data.

How to... **Download the Free iCloud Control Panel Software (PC Users)**

For Windows PC users, multiple references are made to the iCloud Control Panel throughout this chapter. This is a free software download available from Apple. You can download it by pointing your web browser to http://support.apple.com/kb/DL1455. On a Mac, the iCloud Control Panel is built into OS X Mavericks' System Preferences, and on an iOS mobile device, it's part of Settings.

Configure Your iOS Device's Contacts, Calendar, Notes, and Reminders Apps to Work with iCloud

The Contacts, Calendar, Reminders, and Notes apps that come preinstalled with iOS 7 on the iPhone, iPad, and iPod touch are powerful organizational tools that can be used on their own. However, these four apps also offer integrated and automatic data synchronization functionality via iCloud, so you can share app-specific data with other iOS devices and your computers.

Note If you're a Mac user, fully compatible versions of Contacts, Calendar, Reminders, and Notes come bundled with OS X Mavericks, and they function very much like their iOS counterparts.

Use the Contacts App with iCloud

Contacts is a contact manager that allows you to create and maintain a comprehensive and personalized database of people and companies you know and do business with (shown in Figure 11-1). On your iOS mobile device, the information stored in your Contacts database is constantly used by a wide range of other apps, including Phone, Safari, Mail, Messages, Facebook, Twitter, and Maps.

When you turn on iCloud functionality for the Contacts app, the Contacts database you maintain on your iPhone, iPad, or iPod touch will automatically remain synchronized not just with the Contacts app on your other iOS mobile devices, but with the Contacts app that's running on your Macs and/or the Outlook software that's running on your PC. It's also accessible using the online-based Contacts app available from the iCloud website (www.icloud.com).

Note Remember that this iCloud-related, app-specific data-syncing feature needs to be turned on separately on each of your iOS mobile devices and computers, and that only app-specific data is backed up and synced. This is not a comprehensive solution for maintaining a complete backup of your Mac or iOS mobile devices.

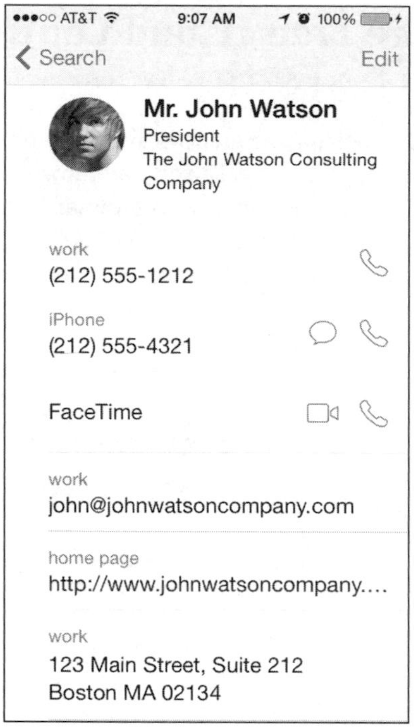

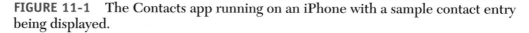

FIGURE 11-1 The Contacts app running on an iPhone with a sample contact entry being displayed.

As changes are made to your Contacts database, for example, from your computer or any iOS mobile device that's linked to the same iCloud account, they'll be reflected almost immediately in the Contacts app (on your iPhone, iPad, or iPod touch), the Contacts app on your Mac (or Outlook on your PC), and on the iCloud website.

To turn on iCloud functionality in relation to Contacts on your iPhone, iPad, or iPod touch, launch Settings from the Home screen, and from the main Settings menu, tap the iCloud option. When the iCloud Control Panel menu appears in Settings, tap the virtual on/off switch associated with the Contacts option to turn it on. Do this on each of your iOS mobile devices and make sure they're logged in to the same iCloud account.

Caution Once Contacts data is being synchronized among your computers and mobile devices, if you delete a contact from your iPhone, iPad, Mac, or PC, for example, that contact will almost instantly be deleted from all of the contacts-related databases with which iCloud is syncing. There's no "undo" option.

How to...

View Your Contacts, Calendar, Reminders, and Notes Data on the Web

Once you sync your Contacts, Calendar, Reminders, and Notes app data (on your Mac/iPhone/iPad/iPod touch) with iCloud (and potentially your Outlook database on your Windows PC), you can view your app-specific data from any computer, tablet, or mobile device that's connected to the Internet by pointing your web browser to www.iCloud.com.

After signing in using your Apple ID and password, click on one of the app icons in the iCloud browser window to launch an online edition of the Contacts, Calendar, Reminders, or Notes app, which will be populated with the most current version of your app-specific data. These online apps look and function almost exactly like their counterparts running on your Mac or iOS mobile device. All data displayed remains perfectly synchronized with your computer and mobile devices, even if changes are made online.

If you use the online version of Contacts, Calendar, Reminders, or Notes from a public computer at an Internet café, or use someone else's computer or mobile device to access your account, be sure to log off from the iCloud.com website when you're done to prevent unauthorized people from accessing your personal data. To log off, click the Sign Out option that's displayed near the top-right corner of the screen.

Use the Calendar, Reminders, and Notes Apps with iCloud

The Calendar app on the iPhone, iPod touch, and iPad is used to manage your schedule. On your Mac or iOS mobile device's screen, you can display your personalized calendar in a variety of formats, including a daily, weekly, monthly, yearly, and list-based format, plus associate alarms with each event or appointment added to your schedule.

Reminders is an advanced to-do list management app (shown in Figure 11-2). Using this app, you can simultaneously create and maintain an unlimited number of separate to-do lists. Each item on each to-do list can have its own alarms and notes associated with it. A version of the Reminders app also runs on the Mac and through the iCloud website.

The Notes app (shown in Figure 11-3) offers basic note-taking capabilities. It resembles a virtual pad, and allows you to type freeform notes that can be shared or synced. A version of the Notes app also runs on the Mac and through the iCloud website.

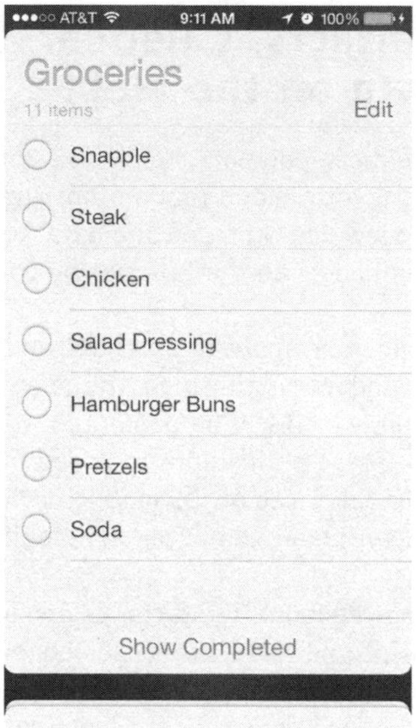

FIGURE 11-2 The Reminders app allows you to manage detailed to-do lists on your iPhone, iPad, or iPod touch, as well as on your Mac. It's shown here on the iPhone.

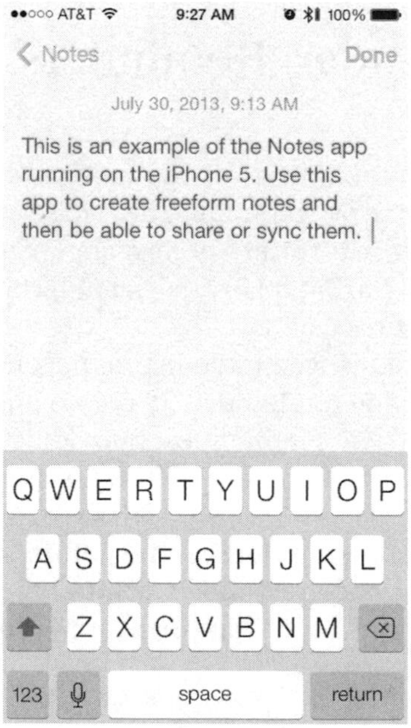

FIGURE 11-3 The Notes app, shown here on an iPhone 5, can sync app-specific data (your notes) with other iOS mobile devices and computers that are linked to the same iCloud account.

To set up the Calendar, Reminders, or Notes app to work with iCloud, from the iPhone, iPod touch, or iPad's Home screen, launch Settings. Then, from the main Settings menu, tap the iCloud option. When the iCloud Control Panel menu appears in Settings, turn on the virtual on/off switches that are associated with the Calendar, Reminders, and/or Notes apps (shown in Figure 11-4). By turning these switches on, each app will automatically begin to sync data with iCloud, starting immediately.

Be sure to turn on iCloud functionality for each app separately. In other words, when you're looking at the iCloud Control Panel menu, the switches associated with Contacts, Calendar, Reminders, and Notes should all be turned on if you want the mobile device you're using to sync app-specific data from these four apps with iCloud. Repeat these steps on each of your iOS mobile devices.

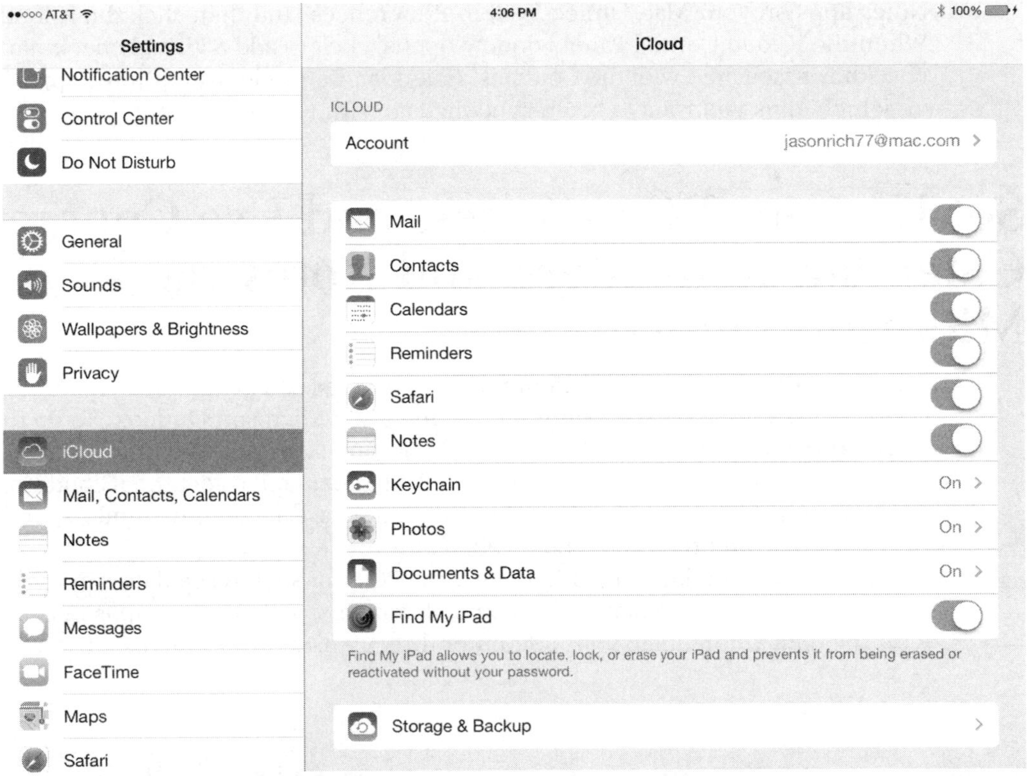

FIGURE 11-4 The iCloud Control Panel, shown here on the iPad

Caution App-specific data from Contacts, Calendar, Reminders, Notes, and Safari that's backed up and synced to your iCloud account and stored on iCloud's servers will use up some of your 5GB of free online storage space included with your iCloud account.

Configure the Contacts, Calendar, Reminders, and Notes Apps on the Mac to Work with iCloud

To turn on iCloud functionality in relation to the Contacts, Calendar, Reminders, and Notes apps on your Mac, launch System Preferences, and then click the iCloud icon. When the iCloud Control Panel window opens, click to add a virtual checkmark to the checkbox associated with the Contacts, Calendar, Reminders, and Notes apps, based on which apps you want to begin syncing data with iCloud.

Set Up Your PC to Access and Use Contacts, Calendar, Reminders, and Notes via Microsoft Outlook

Data from Contacts, Calendar, Reminders, and Notes can be also be synchronized (via iCloud) with a PC that's running Windows and Microsoft Outlook. To do this, you'll first need to download and install the iCloud Control Panel onto your PC.

Once installed, open the Windows Control Panel, and select the iCloud Control Panel option. Add a checkmark next to the Contacts, Calendar, Reminders, and/or Notes options, and then click the Apply icon.

Now when you launch Outlook on your PC, you should see data from your Mac, iPhone, and/or iPad's Contacts, Calendars, Reminders, and/or Notes apps in conjunction with the data entered into your computer directly using the Outlook software.

How to... **Ensure that the iCloud Outlook Add-in Is Active**

Depending on which version of Microsoft Outlook you're using on your PC, to ensure that the iCloud Outlook add-in is active, launch the Outlook software from your PC and access the Tools pull-down menu. From this menu, select the Trust Center option. Click the Add-Ins option. Now look at the list of add-ins displayed under the Active Application Add-Ins heading, and make sure you see a listing for the iCloud Outlook Add-In.

Configure iCloud to Synchronize Apps and Ebooks Among Your Computers and iOS Mobile Devices

Regardless of when or with which computer or device you purchase content from the iTunes Store, App Store, iBookstore, or Newsstand, once you set up an iCloud account, as you know by now, all of your past and present purchases become available on all of your Macs and iOS mobile devices. You'll never need to repurchase that content.

Manually Install Purchased Apps from the App Store

At any time, you can manually install past app purchases onto your iOS mobile devices by launching the App Store app from your iPhone or iPad's Home screen, tapping the Purchased command icon, tapping the Not on This iPhone/iPad option, and then tapping the iCloud icon that's associated with the already purchased app you want to install or reinstall on the iOS mobile device you're currently using.

However, you can set up iCloud functionality so that new apps you purchase (from your iPhone, iPad, or from the iTunes Software on your Mac) automatically install on all of your iOS mobile devices, assuming the app is compatible with the devices. To do this, launch Settings, tap the iTunes & App Stores menu option, and then under the Automatic Downloads heading, turn on the virtual switches associated with Apps.

At the same time, it's possible to turn on the automatic download and install option associated with music and ebook purchases, and turn on the Automatic App Update feature. This feature allows your iOS mobile device to automatically download and install app updates for apps already installed on your device, as they're made available by their respective developers, as long as your iOS mobile device has Internet access.

By turning on the Use Cellular Data option, you give permission for your iPhone or iPad to use its 3G/4G LTE cellular data connection to download and install purchased content automatically. When turned off, only a Wi-Fi Internet connection (which has no monthly usage allocation associated with it) will be used for this purpose.

Manually Access Past iTunes Store Purchases via iTunes

If you have purchased music, TV show episodes, or movies through the iTunes Store, and want to load any of those purchases on another computer or iOS device that's linked to your iCloud account, launch the iTunes Store app, tap the Purchased icon, select what type of content you're looking for, tap the Not on This iPhone/iPad command tab (on your iOS mobile device), and then tap the iCloud icon that's related

How to... **Access Mac App Store Purchases**

Just as iCloud keeps a detailed record of your App Store purchases for your iOS mobile devices, it also maintains information about all of the software you purchase for your Mac via the Mac App Store. To download or redownload and install software you've already purchased from the Mac App Store, launch the Mac App Store app from your Mac. Click the Purchased icon, located near the top-center of the Mac App Store screen. If prompted, sign in to your Apple ID account by typing your password.

Displayed on the screen will then be listings for each Mac app (software application) you've acquired from the Mac App Store. Click the Download button that's associated with a listing to redownload and install that software on the Mac you're currently using. If you see an inactive Installed button, this means the software is already installed on your Mac and ready to use. You can launch it from the Applications folder in Finder or from the Dock, for example.

to the already purchased content you want to download and enjoy on the iOS mobile device you're currently using.

Keep in mind, for content that has a large file size associated with it, such as a TV show episode or a movie, a Wi-Fi Internet connection is required when using an iOS mobile device.

To access past content purchases from your Mac or PC that's running the iTunes software, launch iTunes. Below the Store heading on the left side of the iTunes screen, click the iTunes Store option. Now, from the right side of the iTunes Store screen (under the Quick Links heading), click the Purchased option.

When the Purchased screen appears, click on the tab associated with the type of previously purchased content you want to view (Music, Movies, TV Shows, Apps, Books, etc.). A listing of the available content you own that's stored in your iCloud account will be listed. Click the iCloud icon that's associated with a listing to download or redownload that content to the computer you're using.

Manually Access Past iBookstore Purchases

If you've already acquired ebooks from Apple's iBookstore, you can read them on any of your iOS mobile devices or Macs using the optional iBooks app. In addition to syncing your ebook library (all ebooks purchased through iBookstore) with each of your Macs and iOS mobile devices, iCloud will automatically sync your virtual ebook bookmarks and ebook-related notes (annotations), so you can begin reading an ebook on one computer or device, and then pick up exactly where you left off reading on another device.

To download or redownload an ebook that you've already purchased from iBookstore, launch the iBooks app. From the main Library screen (which looks like a virtual bookshelf), tap or click the Store icon. Once you've accessed iBookstore, tap or click the Purchased icon.

Select the previously purchased ebook you want to download, install, and read on the computer or device you're using by tapping or clicking the iCloud icon associated with that ebook's listing.

As you learned earlier in this chapter, from an iOS mobile device, you can automatically set up iCloud to sync your personal ebook library among all of your devices by adjusting the Automatic Downloads option from within Settings.

Caution   Although it is convenient to have all of your new music, apps, and ebook purchases automatically download and install on all of your computers and iOS mobile devices, this content will take up internal storage space on the computers and devices on which they're stored. So, if you're running low on storage space, you might want to manually download and install only the content that you want access to on each specific device, as opposed to downloading all past and new purchases automatically.

The Benefits of Syncing App-Related Data via iCloud

Using the iTunes Sync process allows you to sync app-specific data between one iOS mobile device and your primary computer. Then, to sync other iOS mobile devices using that same data, the iTunes Sync process (using the same primary computer) needs to be performed again with the other device. This data synchronization process does not occur in real time, so the data on all of your devices will be up to date only after each manual iTunes Sync process is completed. When you use the now antiquated (but still viable) iTunes Sync process, your app-specific backups are stored on the hard drive of your computer, not in the cloud.

However, when you use iCloud to sync app-specific data, as soon as changes are made to the data within an app, such as Contacts or Calendar, for example, that information is almost immediately uploaded to iCloud, and then downloaded and synced to all of the other computers and iOS mobile devices that are linked to the same iCloud account. This process happens automatically, so all of your app-related data is always up to date, regardless of when or on which computer or device you're viewing it. The app-specific data is also stored in the cloud, and can be accessed from virtually anywhere.

Plus, at any time, you can access your Contacts, Calendar, Reminders, and Notes databases, along with your iCloud-specific email account, from the iCloud website, using any computer or mobile device's web browser, as long as an Internet connection is present.

Keep in mind, when you use the iCloud website to access your data, the computer or device you use does not need to be linked to your iCloud account. You can securely access the information using your Apple ID and password. Thus, if something goes wrong with your Mac, iPhone, or iPad while you're traveling, for example, you still have full access to your personal Contacts database, schedule, to-do lists, notes, and iCloud email account, even if you need to access it from an Internet café or a friend's computer.

12

Back Up Your iPhone and iPad

HOW TO...

- Use iCloud to create a backup of an iOS mobile device, such as your iPhone, iPad, and/or iPod touch.
- Use the iTunes Sync or Wireless iTunes Sync process to back up your iOS device.
- Restore your iOS device from a backup.

Back when Apple first released the original iPhone, users had to connect it to a Mac or PC running the iTunes software using the supplied USB cable in order to create a backup of the iPhone's entire contents, update the iOS, or synchronize other files, data, and iTunes Store content. Today, thanks to iCloud, you no longer need the USB cable connection for syncing and backing up data related to your iOS mobile device (including your iPhone, iPad, or iPod touch).

Note When you back up your iOS mobile device using iCloud, that backup file is available to you from anywhere there's a Wi-Fi Internet hotspot or wireless home network, because the information is stored in the cloud as part of your iCloud account. Should you need to restore data to your iPhone or iPad, you no longer need to connect the device to your primary computer, as long as a current iCloud backup file exists.

Using iCloud, files, data, and content can easily be transferred and synced wirelessly between your iOS mobile devices, Macs, and PCs, as well as with the iCloud .com website. Plus, if you have access to a Wi-Fi Internet connection, you can set up your iPhone, iPad, or iPod touch to back itself up each day automatically and wirelessly, and store the backup information on iCloud (in your password-protected account).

Once you have established an iCloud backup of your iOS mobile device, if something goes wrong with your iPhone, iPad, or iPod touch, and you later need to restore your device from a backup (or import your data to a replacement device), you can do this from virtually anywhere there's a Wi-Fi Internet connection, without having to connect your device to your primary computer manually using the supplied USB cable.

Your iOS Device Can Do an Automatic Backup to iCloud Every Day

Your iOS mobile device an automatically back itself up to iCloud once per day when a Wi-Fi Internet connection is available. However, you can manually initiate a backup at any time. To save time, only new files and data, or revisions to existing files and data, are backed up. The end result is a complete backup of your iOS mobile device stored on iCloud. For this feature to work, it must be turned on. Then, for the automatic backup process to initiate, the iPhone or iPad must be plugged into an external power source and in sleep mode.

Tip To protect your actual iOS device, consider purchasing the AppleCare+ extended warranty and/or third-party insurance from a company such as Worth Avenue Group (www.worthavegroup.com). AppleCare+ covers certain types of hardware problems (but not loss or theft), while third-party insurance protection covers your iPhone or iPad against theft, loss, or any type of damage whatsoever. Having insurance for your device and maintaining a current backup of its data are two strategies that go hand-in-hand with saving yourself a lot of stress should something happen to your device.

In addition, if you want to back up your iOS mobile device wirelessly, but you want that backup data to be stored on your primary computer, as opposed to on the iCloud service, you can use the Wireless iTunes Sync process (assuming your primary computer and iOS mobile device are connected to the same Wi-Fi network).

Thus, when it comes to maintaining a backup of your iPhone, iPad, or iPod touch, you now have three viable options:

- Use the traditional iTunes Sync process, which involves connecting the iOS mobile device to your primary computer using the supplied USB cable, and initiating the sync using the iTunes software that's running on your Mac or PC.
- Wirelessly back up your iOS mobile device to your primary computer using the iTunes Wireless Sync process, as long as both the computer and device have access to the same wireless network.
- Forego connecting your iPhone, iPad, or iPod touch to your primary computer altogether, and back up your iOS mobile device wirelessly from anywhere using iCloud, assuming your iOS mobile device has access to a Wi-Fi Internet connection. For most people, this is the preferred backup method, because it can be set up to work automatically, and if needed, the device can be restored (using the backup files) from almost anywhere.

Back Up Your iOS Mobile Device to iCloud

To create and then maintain a backup of your iOS mobile device on iCloud, your device must have access to a Wi-Fi Internet connection, and you'll need to have a free iCloud account already established. You should also be running iOS 7 on your mobile device. Keep in mind, the backup files from your iPhone, iPad, and iPod touch will use up some of your allocated 5GB of online storage space on iCloud (which is provided free of charge with the iCloud account). Thus, if you wind up maintaining backups of two or three devices, it may become necessary to increase the amount of iCloud online storage space you have available to your account. An annual fee applies to do this.

Once your iCloud account is set up and functional, make sure your iOS mobile device is connected to a Wi-Fi Internet connection, and then launch Settings. You can tell that your iOS mobile device is connected to a Wi-Fi network when the Wi-Fi signal indicator is displayed in the upper-left corner of the screen.

From Settings, tap the iCloud option. When the iCloud Control Pane appears, scroll down to the Storage & Backup option and tap it.

From the Storage & Backup menu screen, tap the virtual switch that's associated with the iCloud Backup option, and set it to the on position. If this is the first time you're creating an iCloud backup, a pop-up window will appear that says, "Start iCloud Backup: Your iPad [iPhone, iPod touch] will no longer back up to your computer automatically when you sync with iTunes." To continue, tap the OK button.

How to...

Keep Tabs on How Your iCloud Online Storage Space Is Being Utilized

To determine how much of your allocated online storage space on iCloud is currently being used, from the Settings app, tap the iCloud option under the main Settings menu, and then tap the Storage & Backup option near the bottom of the iCloud screen within Settings. Near the top of the Storage & Backup screen, look under the Storage heading to see your Total Storage and Available Storage. Tap the Manage Storage option to see exactly how the online storage space is being used.

From the Manage Storage screen within Settings, you can manually delete online files being stored in your iCloud account, such as old iPhone or iPad backup files, or app-specific data files.

If necessary, tap the Change Storage Plan option to expand your iCloud online storage capacity for an annual fee. From the Buy More Storage menu, choose an additional 10GB for $20 per year, 20GB for $40 per year, or 50GB for $100 per year. This is in addition to the 5GB of online storage you're given for free. So, if you upgrade to the 10GB plan, you'll actually have 15GB of online storage space available. Upon purchasing the additional online storage, it becomes available to you immediately, and the annual fee will be auto-recurring until you manually cancel it.

Another pop-up window will briefly appear that says, "Turning on Backup." Below the iCloud Backup option displayed on the Storage & Backup screen within Settings, a new option will now become active: Back Up Now (shown in Figure 12-1). Just below this option, when the last successful backup was created will be displayed. When the option is turned on for the first time, the message will say, "Last Backup: Never."

Tip Once the iCloud Backup feature is turned on, a backup will automatically be made once per day (when your iOS mobile device is not in use but is connected to a Wi-Fi network and plugged into an external power source). At any time, however, you can create an updated backup manually by tapping the Back Up Now option that's displayed near the bottom of the Storage & Backup screen within Settings.

Because this is your first time creating a backup using the iCloud Backup feature, tap the Back Up Now option. Your device will begin the backup process by determining how long it will take. The message "Backing Up..." and a progress bar will be displayed at the bottom of the Storage & Backup screen within Settings (as shown in Figure 12-2).

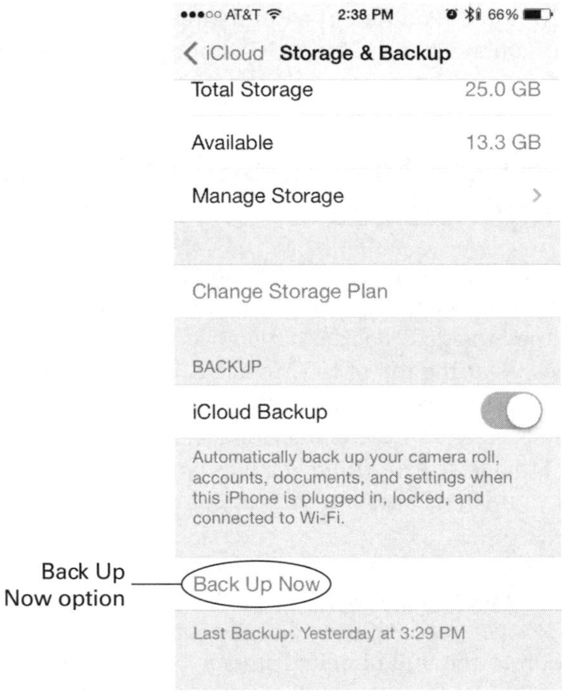

FIGURE 12-1 Look for the Back Up Now option once the iCloud Backup feature is turned on.

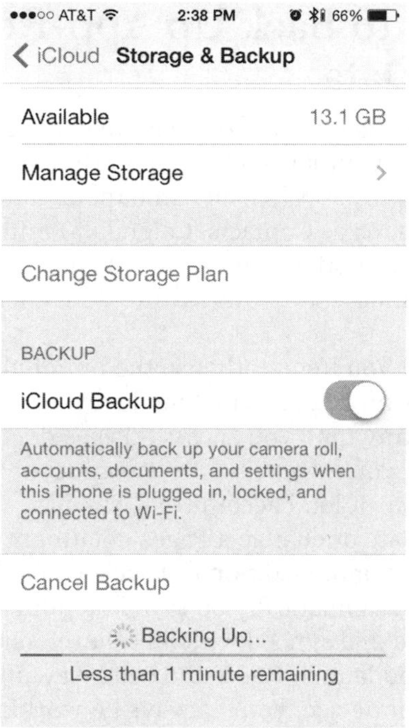

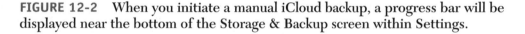

●●●○○ AT&T 📶   2:38 PM   🔋 ⚡📶 66% 🔋

‹ iCloud **Storage & Backup**

Available	13.1 GB
Manage Storage	›

Change Storage Plan

BACKUP

iCloud Backup ⬤

Automatically back up your camera roll, accounts, documents, and settings when this iPhone is plugged in, locked, and connected to Wi-Fi.

Cancel Backup

⟳ Backing Up...

Less than 1 minute remaining

FIGURE 12-2   When you initiate a manual iCloud backup, a progress bar will be displayed near the bottom of the Storage & Backup screen within Settings.

The first time you initiate a backup via iCloud, expect the process to take from 15 to 60 minutes (or longer), depending on how much data, the number of apps, and what content you have stored on your device. Subsequent daily backups, however, will take much less time, as only newly created or revised files, data, and content are backed up.

When the backup process is completed, the Last Backup message displayed near the bottom of the Storage & Backup screen will be updated. As the wireless backup process is under way, you can cancel it at any time by tapping the Cancel Backup option, which replaces the Backup Now option on the Storage & Backup screen within Settings (refer back to Figure 12-2).

Note Once you turn on the iCloud Backup feature, if you opt later to connect your iOS device to your primary computer to initiate an iTunes Sync (either using the supplied USB cable or wirelessly), nothing will happen until you first turn off the iCloud Backup feature from within the Settings app or you adjust the sync settings from the iTunes software on your computer. You can, however, manually initiate an iTunes backup of your mobile device (to your primary computer) by clicking the Back Up Now button in the iTunes software on your Mac/PC once the two devices are linked.

Use iCloud to Back Up App-Related Documents, Files, and Data

In addition to data and information that are backed up using the iCloud Backup feature, you can set your iOS mobile device to use iCloud for specific file/data/ document backup purposes, which can happen automatically and in real time as you're using apps such as Contacts, Calendar, Reminders, Notes, Mail, Safari, Photos, or Camera, as well as optional apps, such as iBooks, Pages, Numbers, Keynote, and many others. You must set up this feature with each compatible app from within Settings.

For example, if you frequently use the optional Pages word processing app, you can access Settings on your iOS mobile device to turn on the iCloud option for Pages. Once you do this, any time you access a Pages document on your iPhone or iPad, it will check to see if you're viewing the most recent version of that document, based on what's stored in your iCloud account.

When you update or change a Pages document in any way (on your iPhone, iPad, or Mac, or using the online edition of Pages available on the iCloud website), not only will those changes automatically be saved on your iOS mobile device, they'll also be uploaded on iCloud and synced with all other versions of iCloud you're using.

Thus, when you launch Pages and start viewing or editing that same document on any computer or device, you'll always be working with the most recent version, but you'll never need to manually back up or transfer the document file.

To turn on this feature on an iOS mobile device, launch Settings and then select Pages, for example, from the main Settings menu. You'll find it listed in the section of the Settings menu where optional apps that you've installed on your iPhone, iPad, or iPod touch are listed.

When the Pages screen appears within Settings, turn on the Use iCloud virtual switch that's found near the top of the screen, below the iCloud heading. You can then exit out of Settings by tapping the Home button. From this point forward, every time you launch Pages from your Home screen, if the device is connected to the Web (using a cellular or Wi-Fi connection), all of your Pages documents will automatically be updated with the latest versions.

Restore Your iOS Device from an iCloud Backup

All of Apple's iOS-based mobile devices are designed to be durable and reliable. However, for a wide range of reasons, things can sometimes go wrong. As long as you have a reliable and current backup of your iPhone, iPad, or iPod touch data, you can restore your device within a matter of minutes. Or, if you wind up having to replace the device, you can use the Restore feature to load all of your apps, data, files, and personalized settings, so the new device will become a duplicate of the old one in terms of what's stored on it.

If you need to restore your iOS mobile device from an iCloud backup, the process is relatively straightforward. However, once again, the device will need access to a Wi-Fi Internet connection.

When you turn on an iPhone or iPad that has been erased, or that's brand new, you'll first need to initialize it before restoring your data. To do this, turn on the iOS mobile device and follow the onscreen prompts.

As soon as the device is turned on, you will see the Apple logo. Within a few seconds, this will be replaced be a Hello screen. Slide your finger from left to right along the Slide to Set Up slider that's displayed near the bottom-center of the screen. Then choose the default language for the device by tapping your selection.

Next, choose the appropriate option from the Select Your Country or Region screen. From the Choose a Wi-Fi Network option, select an available Wi-Fi network, or if applicable, tap the Use Cellular Connection option so your iOS mobile device can access the Internet using a 3G/4G LTE cellular data connection.

Within a few seconds, the Activating Your iPad [iPhone] message will be displayed, and the Location Services setup screen will appear. Here, you have the option to enable or disable your device's Location Services (GPS) functionality. For many of the apps to fully function, you'll need to turn on (Enable) Location Services.

Next, the Set Up Your iPad [iPhone] screen will be displayed. Here, you're given three options: Set Up as New iPad [iPhone], Restore from iCloud Backup, or Restore from iTunes Backup. Assuming you have used the iCloud Backup feature in the past and your iCloud account (stored in the cloud) holds the backup files for your device, select the Restore from iCloud Backup option.

When prompted, enter your Apple ID and password associated with your iCloud account, and than tap the Next option that's found near the upper-right corner of the screen. From the Terms and Conditions screen, tap the Agree option that's displayed near the bottom-right corner, and then tap the Agree button again that appears in the pop-up window.

From the Choose Backup screen, select which iCloud Backup file you want to restore onto the device you're currently using. The most recent backup for the device will be listed first. Tap on the backup file of your choice. The Restore from iCloud screen will be displayed next, and the data restoration process will begin.

Depending on how much information needs to be restored to your iPhone or iPad, this process could take anywhere from a few minutes to an hour or longer. A progress meter is displayed on the screen during this process. Until it's completed, leave the device alone. An Update Completed message will appear on the screen when the Restore process is done.

At this point, you will again be prompted to enter the password that's associated with your Apple ID. Continue through the setup process as prompted. Ultimately, the Welcome to iPad or Welcome to iPhone screen will be displayed. Tap the Get Started option to launch the Home screen and begin using your device. Some apps and content may continue to load from iCloud, but you'll be free to use your device at this point.

When restoring an iPhone or iPad from an iCloud backup, make sure the device is fully charged or that it's plugged into an external power source during the restoration process.

You can restore an iPhone backup to your existing or new iPhone or an iPad backup to your existing or new iPad, but you cannot restore an iPhone using an iPad backup or vice versa.

Create an iTunes Sync Backup from Your iOS Mobile Device

By connecting your iOS mobile device to your primary computer using the supplied USB cable, you can create and maintain a backup of your iPhone, iPad, or iPod touch, as well as transfer any content, apps, or data from your primary computer to your device using the iTunes Sync process. This requires that you run the latest version of the iTunes software on your primary computer.

When you use the traditional iTunes Sync backup process, this in no way uses iCloud. A direct connection is made between your primary computer and your iOS mobile device, and the backup data is stored directly on your primary computer's hard drive. For detailed instructions on how this process works, access this page of Apple's website: http://support.apple.com/kb/HT1386.

If you ultimately need to restore your iPhone, iPad, or iPod touch from an iTunes backup, follow the initial steps outlined previously in the section "Restore Your iOS Device from an iCloud Backup." But when you get to the Set Up screen that has three options, select the Restore from iTunes Backup option, connect your iOS mobile device to your primary computer via the supplied USB cable, and then follow the onscreen prompts.

Create a Wireless iTunes Sync Backup from Your iOS Device

Using the Wireless iTunes Sync option available on the iTunes software on your Mac or PC, it's possible to back up and transfer your iOS mobile device wirelessly, and have the backup files stored on your primary computer's hard drive (just like when you use the traditional iTunes Sync process).

However, when you opt to do this wirelessly, the supplied USB cable is not required. Instead, your iOS mobile device and primary computer (a Mac or PC) must be able to connect to the same Wi-Fi network, which means that depending on the strength of your wireless Internet router, the iPhone, iPad, or iPod touch must be within 150 feet or so of your primary computer.

To use this wireless sync feature, which also bypasses the need to use iCloud altogether, turn on the Sync over Wi-Fi Connection option displayed in the iTunes software on your primary computer after a USB cable connection is made between your iOS mobile device and that computer. Once the feature is turned on, the USB cable connection is no longer required.

Tip For the Wireless iTunes Sync process to work, your iOS mobile device must be connected to an external power source.

When and if you need to restore your iPhone, iPad, or iPod touch from an iTunes backup, follow the initial steps outlined earlier in this chapter in the section "Restore Your iOS Device from an iCloud Backup." When you get to the Set Up screen that has three options, select the Restore from iTunes Backup option, and follow the onscreen prompts.

Use iTunes Sync and iCloud Together

This is where things get a little bit confusing. You can have the iCloud Backup option turned off (which means you'll need to create and maintain primary backups of your iOS mobile device by connecting it to your primary computer, and use the iTunes Sync or Wireless iTunes Sync process), but still be able to use iCloud to back up, sync, or transfer app-specific data (as described in the previous chapters).

For example, the iCloud My Photo Stream feature or the ability to download iTunes Store content you've already purchased to your iOS mobile device from iCloud is separate from the iCloud Backup feature. The feature that allows apps, such as Pages, Numbers, and Keynote, to keep related documents and files up to date on all of your iCloud-connected computers and iOS mobile devices is also separate from the iCloud Backup feature. Also separate is the feature that allows your iOS mobile device to keep your Contacts, Calendar, Reminders, Notes, and Safari data automatically synced between your computers and other iOS mobile devices via iCloud.

If you want to maintain a backup of your iOS mobile device on iCloud *and* on your primary computer, you can do this using a two-step process. After the backup is created on iCloud (either automatically, or by tapping the Back Up Now option from the Storage & Backup screen in Settings), turn off the iCloud Backup feature and connect your iOS mobile device to your primary computer and manually initiate an iTunes Sync or Wireless iTunes Sync. Or, if you typically use iTunes Sync but want to create a one-time iCloud backup, turn on the iCloud Backup feature within Settings, manually create the backup, and then turn off the feature once the backup to iCloud is completed.

13

iCloud and Apple TV: The Perfect Entertainment Combination

HOW TO...

- Enhance your home theater system with an Apple TV device.
- Use Apple TV to experience iTunes Store content (TV shows, movies, music, etc.) retrieved from iCloud.
- Access iCloud's My Photo Stream and Shared Photo Stream to view your photos via Apple TV on your television.

Thus far in *How to Do Everything: iCloud, Second Edition,* you've learned all about how Apple's iCloud service can be used with your Mac, iPhone, iPad, and iPod touch. In conjunction with the release of iOS 7 for its mobile devices and OS X Mavericks for the Mac, the company also updated the operating system used within its popular Apple TV device, and has expanded what it's capable of doing with iCloud.

When an optional Apple TV device is connected to your high-definition television and/or home theater system, as well as to the Internet via your home network, you can access content stored in your iCloud account, including your iTunes Store purchases, past and present. This includes music, music videos, TV episodes, and movies. Now, in addition to experiencing this content through your Mac or iOS mobile device, it can also be experienced through your HD television, so you can take full advantage of your surround-sound audio system that's connected to it.

In addition, Apple TV can access iCloud's My Photo Stream and Shared Photo Stream, allowing you to view digital photos on your television in full HD resolution. It's possible to view individual photos or create animated slideshows that are presented on your television. These same images can also be used as part of an animated screen saver when the Apple TV device isn't otherwise in use, or while music is streaming (playing) and your television remains turned on.

In conjunction with the AirPlay feature that's built into your Mac, iPhone, iPad, or iPod touch, you can stream content directly from your Mac or iOS mobile device to Apple TV in order to experience it through your home entertainment system.

Did You Know?

You Can Use AirPlay to Transfer Audio and Video Content Directly from Your iOS Mobile Device to Apple TV

Any purchased iTunes Store content that you can experience using the Music or Videos app on your iOS mobile device can be streamed directly to your Apple TV and enjoyed on your HD television/home theater system using Apple's AirPlay feature, which is built into iOS 7 and the Apple TV device. This is a wireless system that allows content stored in the internal storage of your iOS mobile device to be sent to your Apple TV in real time. Thus, you can begin watching a television show or movie on your iPad or iPhone (using the Videos app) while you're on the go, and then tap the AirPlay button when you get home and continue watching that content, from where you left off, on your television that's connected to Apple TV.

AirPlay also works with audio content that can be played using the Music app (including music, audiobooks, and iTunes Radio programming). As the audio content is playing on your iOS mobile device, tap the AirPlay icon, and the audio will automatically be sent to your Apple TV and played through your television's speakers or surround-sound system.

AirPlay does not utilize iCloud in any way, because the content that's played on your Apple TV is being sent (wirelessly) from your iOS mobile device to the Apple TV device that's connected to the same wireless network. However, your Apple TV can also access your iCloud account to play your iTunes Store–purchased content.

Note To use Apple TV with AirPlay, and to use some other new Apple TV–related features, the device must be connected to the same home network as your iPhone, iPad, and/or iPod touch.

What Is Apple TV and How Does It Work?

Unlike a TiVo, for example, Apple TV is not a digital video recorder (DVR). It is not designed to record and play back programming from television broadcasts. One of its uses, however, is to grant you access to your iTunes account from your television or home theater system, so you can purchase (or in some cases rent) and stream television show episodes, music videos, or movies to watch whenever you want. Thanks to iCloud, after any compatible content is purchased through the iTunes Store, it becomes accessible any time via your Apple TV device, as well as on your Macs and iOS mobile devices that are linked to your iCloud account.

Note In addition to streaming video content from your iCloud account and from the iTunes Store, Apple TV can stream audio, including your iTunes Store music purchases, iTunes Radio, podcasts, audiobooks, and other programming, all of which can be played through your television's speakers or surround-sound system.

Apple TV ($99, www.apple.com/appletv) is a device that connects to both the Internet (via a Wi-Fi or Ethernet connection) and the High Definition Multimedia Input (HDMI) port of your HDTV or home theater system. Once it's connected, here are some of Apple TV's key features:

- You can watch television shows, music videos, or movies that have been purchased (or in the case of movies, rented) from the iTunes Store.
- You can access and stream movies and TV episodes from Netflix, Hulu +, YouTube, and a growing selection of other Apple TV "channels." (A separate paid subscription is required to access some of these Apple TV–compatible programming services and channels, like Netflix.)
- Using the AirPlay feature that's built into OS X Mavericks, iOS 7, and Apple TV, you can wirelessly stream content that is stored on your iPhone, iPad, or iPod touch, for example, to your HD television or home theater system via Apple TV (if all of the devices are connected to the same wireless home network). So if you want to listen to a song on your iPhone using the speakers of your home theater system, you can stream it with a touch of the iPhone's screen (while running the Music app) using the AirPlay feature, or you can access that music from your Apple TV directly through your iCloud account, if it was purchased from the iTunes Store. (If you're an iTunes Match subscriber, your entire digital music collection becomes available via Apple TV.)
- You can access your My Photo Stream and Shared Photo Streams from your Apple TV device to view your digital images on an HDTV. Select the iCloud Photos "channel" within the main Apple TV menu to do this.
- Thanks to partnerships and deals with professional sports leagues, television and cable networks, and other production companies and producers, a growing lineup of exclusive programming is available via Apple TV by clicking on one of the "channel" icons displayed on the Apple TV main menu.
- As of October 2013, Apple TV also connects directly to the iTunes Store, and allow users to acquire and play back music (in addition to TV shows, movies, and music videos). Plus, Apple TV can stream iTunes Radio programming through your television's speakers or surround-sound system.

When you purchase an Apple TV device from the Apple Store, Apple.com, or any authorized Apple reseller, you'll receive the Apple TV console, a power cord, and a remote control. An HDMI cable is also required to connect your Apple TV to the HDMI port of your television or home theater system. Apple TV can be connected to a television or home theater system via HDMI only. Composite or component cable connections or adapters are not available.

It's also possible to use a digital optical audio cable (sold separately) to connect the Apple TV console directly to your home theater system for an enhanced audio experience, as opposed to experiencing the audio sent to the TV via the HDMI cable.

Note The Apple TV console itself measures about 4 by 4 by 1 inch, and it weighs 0.6 pound. It comes with a handheld remote control device.

Purchasing an Entire Season of a TV Series Saves You Money

TV show episodes can be purchased from iTunes for $1.99 each (Standard definition) or $2.99 each (HD). However, you'll receive a discount if you purchase an entire season's worth of a television series. New, commercial-free versions of TV show episodes are typically made available through the iTunes Store the day after they air on network or cable TV. So, for example, an episode of *Downton Abbey* that airs on PBS on Sunday will be available for purchase from the iTunes Store on Monday.

If you prepurchase an entire new season of *Downton Abbey,* as new episodes air they become accessible through your Apple ID/iCloud account the next day automatically, while all episodes from past seasons (and previously aired episodes) are readily available anytime for purchase through the iTunes Store.

Apple TV must also be connected to the Internet via a high-speed connection. To use any of the AirPlay features, a Wi-Fi connection is necessary. However, Apple TV can also be connected to your home network using a standard Ethernet cable (also sold separately).

To access the iTunes Store or your iCloud account via Apple TV, you must first establish both a free iTunes and iCloud account using your Apple ID, and then link a major credit or debit card to the Apple ID account. When you set up your Apple TV console for the first time, you will be prompted to enter your iTunes Store account and iCloud account information separately, even though, for many people, this information is the same and comprises their Apple ID and password.

In addition to streaming content directly from your iPhone, iPad, or iPod touch to your Apple TV using AirPlay (when the devices are connected to the same home wireless network via Wi-Fi), you can use your Apple mobile device as a feature-packed remote control unit for your Apple TV. To do this, download the free Remote app from the Apple Store.

You Can Use the Apple AV Digital Video Cable to View Content on TV

Although you can circumvent using Apple TV to display everything that appears on your iPhone or iPad's screen on your HDTV by using the optional Apple AV Digital Video Cable ($39), this cable and the "mirroring" feature built into iOS 7 do not work with copyrighted video content, such as TV show episodes, movies, or music videos purchased from the iTunes Store, or with programming that is streamed from a service like Netflix. An Apple TV device is needed to stream this content wirelessly from your iPhone or iPad to your TV using the AirPlay feature.

Make Sure Your Apple TV's OS Is Up to Date

Before attempting to use your Apple TV with iCloud, or use the AirPlay feature in conjunction with your iOS device, make sure your Apple TV has the latest version of its operating system installed. A new update was released in October 2013, in conjunction with the release of OS X Mavericks (Mac) and iOS 7 (for the iPhone and iPad). Here's how to update the operating system, if necessary, for your Apple TV device:

1. From Apple TV's main menu, which you access by pressing the Menu button on the Apple TV's remote control, press the right directional arrow to highlight and select the Settings option.
2. From the Settings menu, select the General option.
3. When the General menu appears, scroll down to the Update Software option, and select it with the remote.
4. If your Apple TV's operating system is up to date, the message "Your Apple TV Is Up to Date" will be displayed. However, if an operating system update is required, follow the onscreen prompts. The update process will take between 5 and 15 minutes.

Use Apple TV to Access iTunes Store Content via iCloud

Once you get your Apple TV connected to your HDTV and/or home theater system, the main menu (accessible by pressing the Menu button on the Apple TV remote control) will display multiple options and unique Apple TV Channels from a wide range of content providers, including:

- **Movies**   From here, you can access any movies stored on your Apple TV that were purchased from the iTunes Store and that you own. You can also shop for movies to rent or purchase directly from the iTunes Store, and these can be watched almost instantly. The Movies menu option reveals a pull-down menu that allows you to shop for top movies, search by movie genre (action/adventure, classics, comedy, drama, horror, and so on), use a general search feature (which allows you to find movies based on any keyword), or access an In Theaters option, for example.
- **TV shows**   From this menu, you can access purchased TV show episodes (via your iCloud account), or shop for new TV show episodes or entire seasons of shows from the iTunes Store. It's also possible to search for TV shows based on what's popular, genre, TV network, or using a general keyword search.
- **Music**   From Apple TV, take control over your digital music collections stored in your iCloud account. You can also access your playlists, complete albums, individual songs, or select music by artist, genre, or a wide range of other criteria. Using Apple TV, it's also now possible to shop for new music from the iTunes Store.

- **Special programming "channels"** By clicking on one of the Apple TV "channel" icons, you can access Apple TV exclusive programming from the National Basketball Association (NBA), the National Hockey League (NHL), Major League Baseball, ESPN, WSL Live, Sky News, HBO, The Weather Channel, The Smithsonian Channel, The Disney Channel, and other networks, plus access Netflix, YouTube, Vimeo, Hulu+, Crunchyroll, Qello, podcasts, your iCloud Photo Streams, or Flickr. Content that is streamed from the Internet does not get saved (or stored) on your Apple TV device.
- **iTunes Radio** Stream iTunes Radio programming, for free, from the Internet to your Apple TV, and hear the audio through your television's speakers or surround-sound system. Any custom iTunes Radio channels you've created on your Mac or iOS mobile device will be accessible through Apple TV, so you can truly customize your listening experience.

Tip By adjusting the Settings related to your iTunes Store account, it's possible to set up parental locks to keep kids from accessing/purchasing content that is not suitable, based on content or lyrics. To do this, from the iTunes software on your Mac/PC, access the iTunes pull-down menu, click the Preferences option, and then click the Parental button that's displayed near the top-center of the Preferences window.

- **Computers** This feature allows you to access iTunes Store content that is stored on your Mac, assuming the computer is connected to the same home network via Wi-Fi as your Apple TV. To use this feature, turn on Home Sharing within the iTunes software on your Mac. From iTunes on your Mac, select the Home Sharing option from the Advanced pull-down menu. When prompted, enter your Apple ID and password, and then click the Create Home Share icon. When a connection with Apple TV is established, the message "Home Sharing Is Now On" will be displayed on your Mac's screen. Click the Done icon and return to using your Apple TV. You will now have access, via Apple TV, to movies, TV show episodes, music videos, music, photos, and other content saved on your Mac. This content will be streamed from your computer to Apple TV but will not be stored on your Apple TV device.
- **Settings** From the Settings menu, you can customize a handful of options relating to the operation of your Apple TV device. For example, in terms of iCloud-related options, you can set the screen saver to access your My Photo Stream or any of your Shared Photo Streams, and display those images as an animated slideshow on your television screen.

Access Movies Rented from the iTunes Store Using Another Computer or Device

In addition to purchasing movies from the iTunes Store to watch on your Apple TV, as well as your Macs, PCs, and iOS mobile devices, using your Apple TV, it's possible to rent movies.

> **Tip**   When using the Search feature to find a TV show or movie, you can enter a show or movie title, part of a title, an actor's name, or any other keyword that will help you find what you're looking for.

However, if you have previously rented a movie from the iTunes Store using your Mac or an iOS mobile device (such as your iPhone or iPad), and you haven't yet watched it, or you're still within the 24-hour viewing period, you can access that movie on your Apple TV from iCloud (via iTunes) and watch it on your TV.

Here's how to do this:

1. From the Apple TV main menu, select the Settings option.
2. From the Settings menu, select the General option.
3. When the General menu appears, select the iTunes Store option.
4. Scroll down toward the bottom of the iTunes Store menu screen and select the Check for Rentals option. If any iTunes Store movie rentals are available to you, listings for them will be displayed, and you will be able to load those rented movies from the iTunes Store to your Apple TV in order to watch them on your television. Rented movies are not stored in your iCloud account.

Use AirPlay to Stream Content from an iOS Mobile Device to Apple TV

If you have rented movies already loaded and saved on your iPhone, iPad, or iPod touch, and the devices are linked to the same home network as your Apple TV console, you can use the AirPlay feature to stream your rented movies or any iTunes Store content from your iOS mobile device to your Apple TV, and then watch that content on your TV or home theater system. (This also applies to music that you can listen to through the speakers of your television or surround-sound system.)

To use AirPlay, connect your iOS mobile device to your home network via a Wi-Fi connection (a 3G or 4G LTE cellular connection will not work), and then follow these steps:

1. Launch the Video app on your iOS mobile device.
2. Select the TV show episode, movie, or music video you want to watch, and begin playing it on your iPhone, iPad, or iPod touch's screen.
3. As soon as the video content begins playing, tap anywhere on the screen to access the onscreen controls.
4. Near the bottom of the screen, to the right of the Rewind, Play/Pause, and Fast Forward icons, the AirPlay icon appears. This icon appears only when your iOS mobile device and Apple TV have a connection established through your wireless home network (or audio from your iOS mobile device can be streamed to AirPlay-compatible speakers). Tap the AirPlay icon.
5. When the AirPlay menu appears on your iOS mobile device's screen, select the Apple TV option.
6. Within a few seconds, the video content will be sent wirelessly (streamed) from your iOS mobile device to your Apple TV, and that content will appear on your television screen.

7. Use the onscreen control options on your iPhone, iPad, or iPod touch to rewind, fast forward, pause, or resume playing the movie. Or you can use the Apple TV's remote control to do this.

Note When you use the AirPlay feature to stream video content between your iOS mobile device and Apple TV, that content will not be stored on your Apple TV. If you want to access other iTunes Store purchases (made from other devices or computers) from your Apple TV, you will need to access it via iCloud from Apple TV's main menu. From the Movies or TV Shows menu options on your Apple TV, select the Purchased option to access content from your iCloud account.

Access Purchased TV Shows from iCloud to Watch via Apple TV

If you've already purchased TV show episodes via the iTunes Store using your Mac, iPhone, iPad, or iPod touch, those purchases (past and present) automatically get stored within your iCloud account. To access TV show episodes you've already purchased using your Apple TV device (so you can watch them on your television), follow these steps:

1. From the Apple TV main menu, select the TV Shows option using the Apple TV remote control.
2. From the TV Shows pull-down menu, select the Purchased option that's found near the top of the screen.
3. The Purchased TV Shows screen will display thumbnail images representing every TV series for which you have previously purchased episodes. Whether you have purchased just one or two episodes of *Homeland* or *Boardwalk Empire,* or an entire season of *Downton Abbey,* for example, each TV series will be represented by a single thumbnail.
4. Using the Apple TV's remote control, highlight, and select a TV series icon.
5. On the TV screen, a listing of all episodes from that TV series will be displayed. Associated with each listing, if you see an iCloud icon, this means the episode is currently stored in your iCloud account and can be viewed using your Apple TV device.
6. Again, using the Apple TV's remote control, highlight and select a specific TV series episode that you currently own and want to watch.
7. When the TV episode's Description screen appears, select the Play option. That TV episode will be accessed from your iCloud account, sent to your Apple TV device, and begin playing on your TV screen or home theater system within a few seconds.

Tip Just as you can with movies, you can also use the AirPlay feature to wirelessly stream iTunes Store–purchased TV show episodes and music videos to your Apple TV that are currently stored on an iOS mobile device. To do this, follow the directions outlined in the earlier section, "Use AirPlay to Stream Content from an iOS Mobile Device to Apple TV."

Did You Know?

You Can Always Purchase More Episodes of Your Favorite TV Series

On the Apple TV screen that lists the specific episodes of a TV series that you own, you'll also see an option to find and purchase additional episodes from the iTunes Store. If you opt to purchase additional episodes, they will be streamed directly to your Apple TV device and will become viewable within seconds after they're purchased. Those newly purchased episodes will simultaneously be stored in your iCloud account, and become accessible from your Mac and iOS mobile devices via iCloud.

Use Apple TV to Access Your iCloud My Photo Stream or Shared Photo Streams

You already know from Chapters 7 and 8 that iCloud offers its My Photo Stream and Shared Photo Stream features. My Photo Stream allows you to synchronize, view, and access up to 1,000 of your most recent digital images on any computer or iOS mobile device that is linked to your iCloud account.

Meanwhile, Shared Photo Streams allow you to showcase selected groups of images and share them with specific people. While your iCloud account only has one My Photo Stream associated with it, you can create and share as many Shared Photo Streams as you desire.

Both My Photo Stream and your Shared Photo Streams can also be accessed from your Apple TV device and displayed on your TV in two ways:

- You can view the images individually or create a slideshow of those images by selecting the appropriate option from the main menu of your Apple TV.
- You can use My Photo Stream or specific Shared Photo Stream images as your Apple TV's screen saver, which can be displayed as you're listening to music or audio content but not watching video supplied by your Apple TV device to your TV or home theater system.

To access your My Photo Stream or Shared Photo Streams, from Apple TV's main menu, scroll down and select the iCloud Photos "channel" option, and then choose the My Photo Stream option or a specific Shared Photo Stream you want to view. Thumbnails for all images in the selected Photo Stream will be displayed on the TV screen.

Also on the screen, you'll see options for Slideshow and Settings. Select Slideshow to view a customizable animated slideshow of your My Photo Stream or Shared Photo Stream images. To customize the appearance of a slideshow, select the Settings option. From the Slideshow Settings screen, you can customize a wide range of options, including the order in which "slides" appear, the music that will accompany the slideshow, the image transitions that'll be displayed in between showcasing your photos, and the overall theme of the slideshow.

Customize Your Slideshows on Apple TV

Your animated slideshow that features your digital images from My Photo Stream or a Shared Photo Stream can be displayed using a variety of animated special effects and transitions. Under the Themes heading, you'll discover many options, such as Origami, Scrapbook, Holiday Mobile, Flip-Up, and Ken Burns. As you use the Apple TV's remote to highlight a theme, it will be previewed on the TV screen so you can see what it will look like before selecting it.

After selecting a theme, customize the theme-specific options, such as how long each slide will be displayed (in seconds), as well as the transition effect that will be used between images. When you're done making your theme and transition selections, press the Menu button on the Apple TV's remote control to return to the Photo Stream menu. Then select the Slideshow option to view your slideshow.

View Individual Photo Stream Images on Your Television via Apple TV

To view individual images in full-screen mode on your television and manually scroll through the images stored as part of My Photo Stream or a Shared Photo Stream (as opposed to viewing the images as part of an animated slideshow), follow these steps:

1. From the Apple TV main menu, select the Photo Stream option using Apple TV's remote control.
2. The Photo Stream screen will be displayed. It will include thumbnails of all individual photo streams stored in your iCloud account. Using the directional arrows of your Apple TV's remote control, select and highlight one image thumbnail.
3. The photo stream will open and thumbnails of each image in that photo stream will be displayed. Select the thumbnail image you want to view in full-screen mode.
4. When the image thumbnail is highlighted and has a blue box around it, press the Select button on the Apple TV's remote control (in the center of the directional arrows). Your selected image will be displayed in full-screen mode on your TV set.
5. Again, using the Apple TV remote control, press the left or right directional arrow to advance or move back and view another image in your photo stream. This allows you to create a manually controlled slideshow, but with no special effects or transitions.

Set Up the Screen Saver to Display Photo Stream Images

Another way to enjoy looking at the digital images stored as part of your iCloud My Photo Stream or Shared Photo Streams is to adjust the Apple TV's Settings to use your photo stream as an animated screen saver.

This screen saver automatically appears when the Apple TV's main menu is dormant for a predetermined amount of time (the default is five minutes), or when music is being played using your Apple TV device.

To set up Apple TV's Screen Saver option to showcase My Photo Stream or Shared Photo Stream digital images, follow these steps:

1. From the Apple TV main menu, use Apple TV's remote control to select the Settings option.
2. When the Settings pull-down menu appears, choose the Screen Saver option.
3. The Screen Saver menu allows you to adjust a handful of options relating to how your Apple TV's screen saver will appear. Start by adjusting the Start After option, which determines how long the Apple TV device will remain dormant before displaying the screen saver. Your options include Never, or 2, 5 (the default), 10, 15, or 30 minutes.
4. Also from the Screen Saver menu screen, you can choose whether or not the screen saver will automatically be displayed while music is being played. Turn on the Show During Music feature by selecting the Yes option.
5. Next, from the Photos option that appears within the Screen Saver menu, select the Photo Stream option and select which photo stream you want to showcase.
6. You can now use the Apple TV's remote control to select the preview option to see how your screen saver will look. Or you can scroll down on the Screen Saver menu screen to select a screen saver theme. You can choose from among a dozen different themes, including Floating, Reflections, Scrapbook, Photo Wall, and Shifting Tiles. Make your selection, and then press the Menu button on the Apple TV's remote control to save your changes and return to the main menu. The Screen Saver option is now programmed and will launch at the designated times.

Apple TV's integration with iCloud and the AirPlay feature that's built into the iOS operating system are just the initial steps in making the programming and content you want to experience available to you whenever and wherever you want it. As this book was being written, rumors were circulating about Apple launching a line of HDTVs in 2014 or 2015 that would have Apple TV–like functionality built in.

At the same time, Apple is in ongoing negotiations with the various broadcast networks, cable TV networks, television and movie studios, and other media content producers and distributors to expand its offering of exclusive and on-demand programming available from the Apple TV device and the iTunes Store.

PART V

Additional iCloud Features and Functions

14

Locate a Lost Mac, iPhone, iPad, or iPod touch with iCloud's Find My... Feature

HOW TO...

- Turn on the Find My... feature on an iOS mobile device.
- Turn on the Find My... feature on a Mac.
- Locate a compatible Apple device using the Find My iPhone app.
- Locate a compatible Apple device using iCloud.com.

The concept behind a smartphone, such as the iPhone, is that you can carry it around with you everywhere, and in addition to serving as a powerful communications tool, it can also provide you with feature-packed organizational, productivity, and entertainment tools that are readily available just about anywhere.

Since your device is being carried with you most of the time, this increases the chances for it to get lost, damaged, or stolen. While AppleCare will help you cover the cost of fixing a broken Apple device, it can't help you find and retrieve a lost or stolen device, and AppleCare does not cover the loss of your personal data. To handle these protection and recovery tasks, you'll want to utilize the enhanced Find My iPhone functionality that's built into iCloud and the iOS 7 operating system.

Using Find My iPhone, if your iPhone gets lost or stolen, it's possible to access the iCloud.com website and use the Find My iPhone online app to determine the location of your device, lock it down, erase its contents, or prevent an unauthorized person from reactivating it as their own.

For all of the most current Find My iPhone features to work on an iPhone, it needs to be running iOS 7. Plus, you need to manually turn on the Find My iPhone feature in advance. This is extremely important! Then, in order for the Find My iPhone feature to work, your iPhone also needs to be turned on and able to connect to the Internet via a 3G, 4G (LTE), or Wi-Fi connection.

Find My iPhone Has Expanded to Work with Macs and Other iOS Mobile Devices

While the Find My iPhone feature still makes reference to the iPhone in its name, Apple has expanded the capabilities of this feature to work with all Macs (including MacBook Air and MacBook Pro notebook computers), as well as the iPad, iPad mini, and iPod touch. Thus, once you turn on the Find My... feature on each of your compatible Apple computers or mobile devices, you can track their whereabouts in real time, plus manage certain security-related features related to each device remotely in order to protect your data.

The Find My... feature can be used from the web browser of any Internet-enabled computer or mobile device. Simply visit www.icloud.com, sign into the website using your Apple ID/iCloud username and password, and then click the Find My iPhone icon from the website's main menu.

However, if you have the Find My iPhone app installed on any of your iOS mobile devices, you can also use it to quickly figure out the exact location of your Macs and all of your other iOS mobile devices. The Find My iPhone app is available for free from the App Store.

Turn On and Set Up the Find My... Feature on an iOS Mobile Device

The best time to turn on and activate the Find My iPhone feature on your iPhone or iPad is when you first purchase and set up a new iOS mobile device or when you upgrade to iOS 7. However, you can turn on this feature at any time from within Settings.

Caution Unless the Find My iPhone feature is turned on in advance, it will not function. If turned off, it will be utterly useless if your iOS mobile device gets lost or stolen.

How to... Turn On and Set Up the Find My... Feature: iOS

If you haven't already done so, on each of your iOS mobile devices (including your iPhone, iPad, and iPod touch), follow these steps to turn on and activate the Find My... feature:

1. Launch Settings from the Home screen.
2. Tap the iCloud option.
3. From the iCloud Control Panel within Settings, tap on the virtual switch that's associated with the Find My... feature.
4. Exit out of Settings and continue using your iOS mobile device.

(Continued)

At this point, as long as your iPhone, iPad, or iPod touch is turned on (it can be in sleep mode) and has access to the Internet, you can use the Find My iPhone app from another iOS mobile device or access the iCloud.com website to determine the location of your missing device and manage certain security-related features remotely.

Keep in mind, to see the real-time location of all of your Macs and iOS mobile devices at the same time, they all need to be linked to the same iCloud account, and you need to turn on the Find My... feature on each device separately and in advance, before you need to actually pinpoint the location of the computer or device and use the Find My... features to lock it down and/or recover it. You only need to turn on and activate the feature once.

Then, when you log in to the iCloud.com website and access the online-based Find My iPhone feature, or when you use the Find My iPhone app, the location of each of your devices and Macs can be displayed.

Turn On and Set Up the Find My... Feature on a Mac

When used on or in conjunction with a Mac, the Find My... feature works exactly the same way as it does with an iOS mobile device. Once you turn on this feature, you can track your Mac's location from the iCloud.com website or using the Find My iPhone app that's running on your iOS mobile device (as long as the Mac and mobile device are linked to the same iCloud account).

How to... ## Turn On and Set Up the Find My... Feature: Mac

If you haven't already done so, on each of your Macs (including your iMac, Mac Pro, MacBook Air, MacBook Pro, or Mac mini), follow these steps to turn on and activate the Find My iPhone feature:

1. Launch System Preferences.
2. Click the iCloud icon.
3. From the iCloud Control Panel within System Preferences, scroll down and add a checkmark to the checkbox associated with the Find My Mac feature (shown in the following illustration).
4. Exit out of System Preferences.

(Continued)

5. Repeat these steps on each of your Macs.

At this point, as long as your Mac is turned on and has access to the Internet, you can use the Find My iPhone app from your iOS mobile device, or access the iCloud .com website, in order to pinpoint the location of your computer and manage certain security-related features remotely.

Locate a Compatible Apple Device Using the Find My iPhone App

The latest version of the Find My iPhone app, which is fully compatible with iOS 7, is available for free from the App Store. This app does not come preinstalled on any iOS mobile device, but it is fully compatible with the iPhone, iPad, iPad mini, or iPod touch.

To find, download, and install this free app, launch the App Store app, and in the Search field, enter the keywords "Find My iPhone." Tap the Free button to download and automatically install the app.

Even with the Find My iPhone app installed on your iOS mobile device, you still must activate the Find My... feature on each of your iOS mobile devices from within Settings, by following the steps outlined earlier in this chapter.

When you want or need to discover the exact location of your compatible Apple equipment using the Find My iPhone app that's running on the iOS mobile device you're currently using and that's in your possession, launch the app from your iOS mobile device's Home screen.

From the main Find My iPhone app screen, log in to your iCloud account using your Apple ID/iCloud username (which should already be filled in) and your password. Tap the Sign In button to continue (shown in Figure 14-1).

A compass will appear on the screen, and within a few seconds, the iOS mobile device on which you're running the Find My iPhone app will display the All Devices screen (shown in Figure 14-2). This will list all of your Macs and iOS mobile devices that you have linked to the same iCloud account and that have the Find My... feature already turned on.

To the left of each listing, if you see a green dot, this indicates that the Find My... feature of iCloud has pinpointed the location of that device. Tap on the listing to view a detailed map that showcases the computer or device's current location and access options to take control of your computer or device remotely. The green dot depicts the device's location on the map.

You now have several options when using the Find My iPhone app. To change the Map view, it's possible to zoom in or zoom out using finger gestures. Or tap on the lower-right corner of the screen to reveal the Map View menu and then switch between Standard, Hybrid, and Satellite modes. This works very much like the Maps app that comes preinstalled with iOS 7.

FIGURE 14-1 When you launch the Find My iPhone app, you must log in to your Apple ID/iCloud account. (Shown here on the iPhone.)

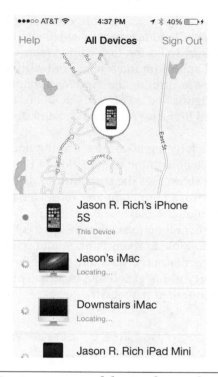

FIGURE 14-2 The All Devices screen of the Find My iPhone app shows you which of your Macs and iOS mobile devices this service is able to track. It's shown here on the iPhone.

To update the map to show the current (real-time) location of your device or computer that you've selected, tap the Refresh icon that's displayed near the top-right corner of the Find My iPhone's Map screen. To return to the All Devices screen, tap the left-pointing Devices icon that's displayed near the top-left corner of the screen.

Take Advantage of the Find My iPhone App's Security Features

As you're looking at the map in the Find My iPhone app, and you see the green dot that's showing the current location of your Mac or another iOS mobile device, tap on that green dot. The name of the device, along with when it was last located by the app, will be displayed in a banner that's positioned just above the green dot on the map.

Once the Find My... service locates your equipment, you will have several options available to help you lock down and/or retrieve your device. Near the bottom of the

Info screen are three command icons. If you're tracking the whereabouts of an iOS mobile device, these command icons include:

- **Play Sound**   Tap this button to take control of your missing iPhone, iPad, or iPod touch and have it emit a sound so as you're searching for the device, you can more easily find and retrieve it.
- **Lost Mode**   Tap this button to display a custom message on the missing iPhone, iPad, or iPod touch's screen that also displays your phone number. You will have the opportunity to enter any phone number where you can be reached (shown in Figure 14-3). After entering a phone number, tap the Next button, and then enter a custom message that will be displayed on your missing device's screen (shown in Figure 14-4). For example, the message could say, "This iPad has been lost. Please call me to receive a reward for its safe return."

As soon as you tap the Done button, your missing iOS mobile device will automatically be locked down remotely. All that someone else will be able to do when they find and turn on your missing device will be to view your custom message and phone number. Otherwise, it will be locked down and passcode-protected (using your custom four-digit passcode).

When you retrieve your lost iOS mobile device, enter your passcode to unlock the device and begin using it.

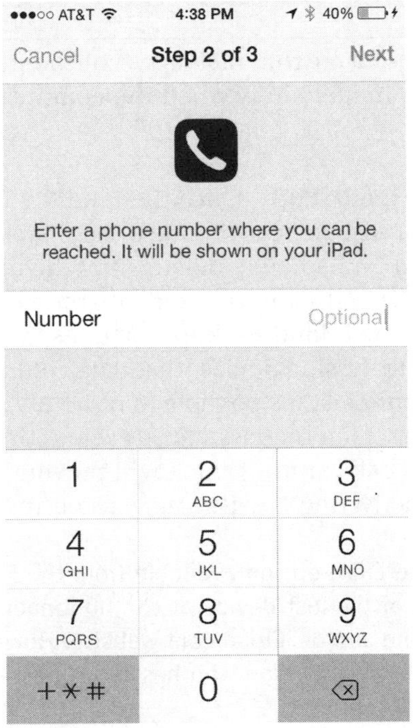

FIGURE 14-3   When prompted, enter a phone number where you can be reached by the person who finds your lost equipment.

FIGURE 14-4 Enter a custom message that the person who finds your lost equipment will see immediately when the computer or device is turned on.

- **Erase iPhone/iPad/iPod** Once the Find My iPhone app has pinpointed the location of your lost device, you have the option to tap the Erase button in order to remotely and immediately delete all of the device's content, including your personal data. Only do this, however, if you know you have a secure backup of your device (using iCloud Backup or iTunes Sync). Otherwise, if you erase the contents of your missing device, that data could be lost forever. In conjunction with erasing your data, it's possible to remotely send a text message to be displayed on the device's screen that asks for its safe return. It's also now possible to turn on the Activation Lock feature, which will prevent a would-be thief from erasing your iPhone and reactivating it with a new account.

 If you use the Erase option available from the Find My iPhone app, once you erase the contents of the lost device, it can no longer be tracked or located using the Find My iPhone app or iCloud.com website. However, all of your data will be kept from the authorized person who has taken possession of your device.

Using the map that's displayed in the Find My iPhone app, as well as the Play Sound, Lost Mode, and Erase options, you now have a handful of tools at your disposal that can assist you in locating and retrieving a lost or stolen iOS mobile device.

When you attempt to use the Find My iPhone app, if your missing device cannot currently be located because it's turned off or in Airplane mode, the Find My iPhone app will allow you to set up the Notify Me When Found feature. When this feature is turned on, iCloud will immediately alert you via email when someone turns on your missing device and attempts to use it (shown in Figure 14-5). At the same time, if you have activated Lost mode, the person who is attempting to use your iOS mobile device will encounter a locked device with your custom message and phone number displayed.

If you're tracking the whereabouts of a Mac, the available command icons include:

- **Play Sound**   Tap this button to take control of your missing Mac and have it emit a sound so as you're searching for the device, you can more easily find and retrieve it. This is particularly useful when trying to locate a missing MacBook Air or MacBook Pro, which is highly portable.

FIGURE 14-5   If you lose your iPad and activate Lost mode using the Find My… feature, but it can't currently be located, use the Notify Me When Found feature to receive an email from iCloud when your device is ultimately located.

- **Lock**   If you opt to lock down your Mac remotely using the Find My iPhone app, the password feature that's built into OS X Mavericks will be activated. Thus anyone who attempts to use your Mac will be locked out of it. Once you turn on this feature, however, you cannot later use the Erase Mac feature.

    After tapping the Lock button, confirm that you understand that the Erase Mac feature will be disabled and tap the OK button. Next, create a four-digit passcode that will be used to unlock the Mac once it's retrieved. Enter the code twice, as prompted. You'll then have the opportunity to create a custom message that will be displayed on the Mac's screen and be visible to the person who finds your Mac and tries to use it. Enter your message and tap the Done button.

- **Erase Mac**   This option allows you to remotely erase all of the content on your Mac, including your personal data and files. Only use this feature if you know you have a secure backup of your device (using Time Machine, for example). Otherwise, if you erase the contents of your missing Mac, all your files and data could be lost forever.

Even with the Find My Mac feature turned on, this functionality only works when your missing Mac has access to the Internet. If you try to locate a missing Mac that's been turned off or that has no Internet access, none of the Find My Mac features offered by the Find My iPhone app or the iCloud.com website will work until someone turns on the Mac and allows it to connect to the Internet.

Did You Know?

You Can Use Someone Else's iOS Mobile Device to Track the Location of Yours

One handy feature of the Find My... feature is that if you don't have another one of your own iOS mobile devices handy, and you're not near a computer with Internet access, you can borrow someone else's iPhone or iPad (as long as it has Internet access), and use the Find My iPhone app on their device to track the whereabouts of your compatible Apple equipment.

To do this, you'll need to launch the Find My iPhone app on their iOS mobile device, log out of their Apple ID/iCloud account, and then log in using your own Apple ID and password (or iCloud account information). When you're done using someone else's iOS mobile device, it's essential that you manually log out of the Find My iPhone app.

To log out of the Find My iPhone app, return to the My Devices screen and tap the Sign Out button that's displayed near the top-right corner of the screen.

Locate a Compatible Apple Device Using iCloud.com

Assuming you've already turned on the Find My... feature of your now missing Mac, iPhone, iPad, or iPod touch, using a computer or Internet-enabled mobile device, access the iCloud website by pointing your web browser to www.iCloud.com. Log in to your iCloud account using your Apple ID (iCloud username) and password, and then click the Find My iPhone icon.

Tip   You can speed up your access to the Find My iPhone feature of the iCloud website by visiting www.icloud.com/#find. You will still need to log in to the service, however.

Upon clicking the Find My iPhone icon when viewing the main iCloud.com menu screen, you'll be required to log in. Within a few seconds, the computer you're using will pinpoint the exact location of your Macs and iOS mobile devices that are turned on, have the Find My... feature activated, and are linked to the same Apple ID/iCloud account.

A series of green dots, each representing one of your Macs or iOS mobile devices that have been located, will be displayed on the Map screen (shown in Figure 14-6).

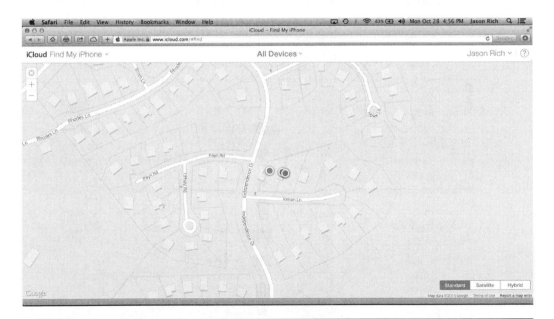

FIGURE 14-6   The map screen of the Find My iPhone feature is shown here. Access it from the iCloud.com website.

Gray dots indicate the device cannot currently be found. As you're viewing the Map screen, you have multiple options. To exit out of the Find My... feature and return to the iCloud.com website's main menu screen, click on the iCloud menu. It's displayed near the top-left corner of the screen.

To view a list of your devices that the Find My iPhone feature is currently tracking, click the All Devices pull-down menu. The My Devices window (which is similar to the My Devices screen when using the Find My iPhone app) will be displayed. Click on one of your device or computer listings (shown in Figure 14-7).

To zoom in or out when viewing the main map, click on the plus-sign or minus-sign icon that's displayed near the top-left corner of the map. Click on the target-shaped icon to re-center the map around the located Mac or iOS mobile devices that the service is tracking.

If you want to switch map views, click the Standard, Satellite, or Hybrid button that's displayed near the bottom-right corner of the screen. To receive help using the Find My iPhone online application, click the Help button that's found near the top-right corner of the map.

Once your missing Mac or iOS mobile device has been located using iCloud.com's Find My iPhone feature, click the on-map listing for your device to remotely take control of your compatible missing Apple equipment, using the same functions that are available from the Find My iPhone app.

As you're looking at the My Devices menu (after clicking the All Devices menu option found near the top-center of the map screen), to the left of each listing, if you

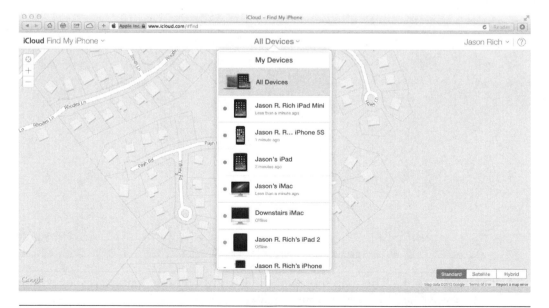

FIGURE 14-7 From the All Devices pull-down menu, see a listing of the computers and iOS mobile devices the Find My... service is able to locate.

see a green dot, this indicates that the Find My... feature of iCloud has figured out the location of that device. Click on a device listing to access the computer or device-specific menu that gives you options to remotely accessing and/or locking down the lost or stolen computer or device (shown in Figure 14-8).

Near the bottom of the Info window are three command icons. If you're tracking the whereabouts of an iOS mobile device, these command icons include:

- **Play Sound**   Tap this button to take control of your missing iPhone, iPad, or iPod touch and have it emit a sound so as you're searching for the device you can more easily find and retrieve it.
- **Lost Mode**   Tap this button to display a custom message on the missing iPhone, iPad, or iPod touch's screen that also displays your phone number. You will have the opportunity to enter any phone number where you can be reached. After entering a phone number, tap the Next button, and then enter a custom message that will be displayed on your missing device's screen. For example, the message could say, "This iPad has been lost. Please call me to receive a reward for its safe return."

  As soon as you tap the Done button, your missing iOS mobile device will automatically be locked down remotely. All that someone else will be able to do when they find and turn on your missing device will be to view your custom message and phone number. Otherwise, it will be locked down and passcode protected (using your custom four-digit passcode). When you retrieve your lost iOS mobile device, enter your passcode to unlock the device and begin using it.

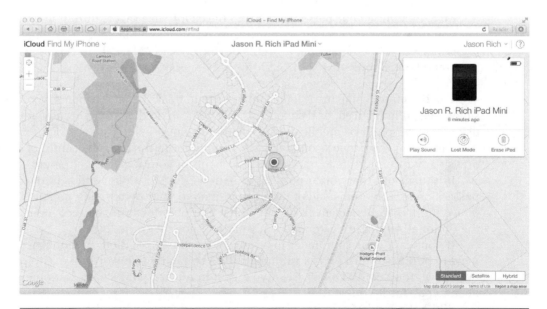

FIGURE 14-8   Take control of a lost Mac or iOS mobile device in order to use the Find My... feature's security, retrieval, lock down, or data deletion options. The device's Info window is displayed near the top-right corner of the map screen.

- **Erase iPhone/iPad/iPod**   Once the Find My iPhone app has pinpointed the location of your lost device, you have the option to tap the Erase button to remotely and immediately delete all of the device's content, including your personal data. Only do this, however, if you know you have a secure backup of your device (using iCloud Backup or iTunes Sync). Otherwise, if you erase the contents of your missing device, that data could be lost forever.

If you're tracking the whereabouts of a Mac, the command icons include:

- **Play Sound**   Tap this button to take control of your missing Mac and have it emit a sound so as you're searching for the device you can more easily find and retrieve it. This is particularly useful when trying to locate a missing MacBook Air or MacBook Pro, which is highly portable.
- **Lock**   If you opt to lock down your Mac remotely using the Find My iPhone app, the password feature that's built into OS X Mavericks will be activated. Thus anyone who attempts to use your Mac will be locked out of it. Once you turn on this feature, however, you cannot later use the Erase Mac feature.

    After tapping the Lock button, confirm that you understand that the Erase Mac feature will be disabled and tap the OK button. Next, create a four-digit passcode that will be used to unlock the Mac once it's retrieved. Enter the code twice, as prompted. You'll then have the opportunity to create a custom message that will be displayed on the Mac's screen and be visible to the person who finds your Mac and tries to use it. Enter your message and tap the Done button.
- **Erase Mac**   This option allows you to remotely erase all of the content on your Mac, including your personal data and files. Only use this feature if you know you have a secure backup of your device (using Time Machine, for example). Otherwise, if you erase the contents of your missing Mac, all your files and data could be lost forever.

The benefit of using the iCloud.com website to track the whereabouts of your lost or stolen Mac, iPhone, iPad, or iPod touch is that you can do this from virtually anywhere, using any computer or mobile device whether or not it belongs to you. For example, you can borrow someone's computer, use a computer in the business center of a hotel, or visit any Internet café to track the whereabouts of your missing equipment.

If it turns out that your Apple equipment was in fact stolen and is in the possession of a thief, instead of taking matters into your own hands, contact the police immediately. However, if your stolen equipment cannot be recovered, the optional AppleCare extended warranty will not cover the loss.

If you want your equipment to be covered against loss, theft, or damage, you will need to purchase third-party insurance from a company like Worth Ave. Group (www .worthavegroup.com). Otherwise, if you want to replace your stolen equipment, you'll need to pay for it yourself.

While the Find My... feature can help you recover lost or stolen equipment, this service is not foolproof. Plus, if you wind up needing to use the Erase command, in order to recover your data, files, and apps, you will need to restore them from a recent backup. Thus, in addition to turning on the Find My... feature on your Mac or iOS mobile device, immediately implement an ongoing, secure, and reliable system backup plan.

For a Mac, this might include using the Time Machine feature that's built into OS X Mavericks, in addition to the app-specific data backup features of iCloud. On an iOS mobile device, this can include using the iCloud Backup feature or iTunes Sync process, in addition to the app-specific data backup features of iCloud.

By taking steps starting immediately to protect your Apple equipment, as well as your data, files, and content, should something go wrong as a result of loss, theft, or damage, you will be able to recover much faster, with a lot less frustration, and with little or no loss of important data. Correctly using the services and features offered for free in conjunction with iCloud make recovering from many problems much easier and more cost effective.

15

Manage Your iCloud Email Account

HOW TO...

- Set your own iCloud email account.
- Manage your email account using the Mail app on your Mac or iOS mobile device.
- Manage your email account using the online edition of the Mail app available through iCloud.com.

In conjunction with your iCloud account, you're given a free email account that you can use instead of or in addition to any of your other preexisting email accounts that have been set up for your personal or work-related use.

Your iCloud email address uses a *[username]@icloud.com* format. If you already have an Apple ID account set up, and it uses the *[username]@mac.com* or *[username]@me.com* format, for example, this email address now automatically has a *[username]@icloud.com* equivalent that will work with your iCloud account.

You can then manage all aspects of your iCloud email account from the Mail app (on your Mac or iOS mobile device), or from the iCloud.com website using the online version of the Mail app.

Keep in mind, while the Mail app that comes bundled with your Mac or iOS mobile device allows you to manage multiple email accounts simultaneously, including all of your personal and work-related email accounts, the online version of the Mail app that's part of the iCloud.com website can be used exclusively to manage your iCloud-related email account.

All emails you compose and send or receive through your iCloud email account are stored in the cloud as part of your iCloud account. This information utilizes some of your allocated 5GB of free online storage space that's provided by Apple. Thus, if you wind up heavily using your iCloud email account, plus store other app-specific data and files in the account, as well as iCloud Backup files for one or more iOS mobile devices, you may need to increase the amount of online storage space associated with your iCloud account, and for this there's an annual fee.

How to... ## Access Your iCloud-Related Email Account

Using the Mail app that's built into OS X Mavericks and iOS 7, you'll be able to manage your iCloud-related email account. However, you can also manage this email account (compose, send, receive, and read incoming emails) from any computer or mobile device that has a web browser and that's connected to the Internet.

To access your iCloud-related email account from any computer or wireless device that's connected to the Internet using iCloud's online-based Mail app, simply point your web browser to www.icloud.com, log in using your Apple ID/iCloud username and password, and then click the Mail app icon to access the online version of the Mail app. It's then possible to manage your iCloud-related email account. Any updates or changes made to this email account (to your Inbox, for example) will be reflected on all of your computers and iOS mobile devices in almost real time.

From iCloud's online version of Mail, you can read incoming emails, compose and send outgoing emails, or organize email messages into various folders, just as you can using the Mail app on your Mac or the Mail app that's installed on your iOS mobile device.

If you opt to use another email app and not Apple's own Mail app to manage your email accounts, including your iCloud email account, you can easily do this. Your iCloud-related email account is compatible with any email software or app that can handle the industry-standard IMAP (Internet Message Access Protocol) format. Beyond the Mail app, to set up other email software or apps to work with your iCloud account, follow the setup process for an IMAP account.

Turn On the iCloud Mail Sync Option on Each of Your Macs and iOS Mobile Devices

Once your main iCloud account is active, your iCloud-related email account will automatically remain synchronized among all of your computers, iOS mobile devices, and the iCloud.com website, as long as everything is linked to the same iCloud account. It's also necessary to turn on iCloud's Mail feature on each computer or device.

 Remember, iCloud's ability to sync email works only with your iCloud-related email account, not with your other preexisting email accounts.

To turn on the iCloud email sync feature on your iOS mobile devices, follow these steps:

1. Launch Settings from the Home screen.
2. From the main Settings menu, tap the iCloud option to open the iCloud Control Panel.
3. Make sure the email address that is displayed in the Account field of the iCloud Control Panel within Settings has the appropriate iCloud account-related information listed.
4. Tap the virtual on/off switch associated with the Mail option.
5. Repeat this process on each of your iOS mobile devices.

On your Mac, you'll also need to turn on the Mail synchronization feature for your iCloud-related email account. To do this, follow these steps:

1. Click the System Preferences icon on your Mac's Dock, or launch it from the Applications folder to open the System Preferences window.
2. From the System Preferences menu, click the iCloud icon to open the iCloud Control Panel.
3. Click to add a checkmark to the checkbox that's displayed next to the Mail option.

Once you set up your iCloud-related email account, the Mail app on your Mac or iOS mobile devices will automatically be configured to manage that account. You'll need to configure your other email accounts to work with the Mail app separately. At any time in the future, you can update your iCloud email account information.

To add or update the Mail app so you can use it to manage your iCloud-related email account on a Mac, follow these steps:

1. Click the System Preferences icon on the Mac's Dock, or launch it from the Applications folder.
2. Click the Internet Accounts option from the System Preferences menu.
3. On the left side of the Internet Accounts window, all of the email accounts your Mac (and the Mail app) are already set up to work with are displayed. To add your iCloud email account, click the plus-sign icon that's found near the bottom-left corner of the Internet Accounts window (shown in Figure 15-1).
4. On the right side of the Internet Accounts window, click the iCloud option.
5. When prompted, enter your existing Apple ID and password, and then click the Sign In icon (shown in Figure 15-2). If you haven't yet set up an Apple ID account, click the Create Apple ID button that's displayed near the lower-left corner of this window.

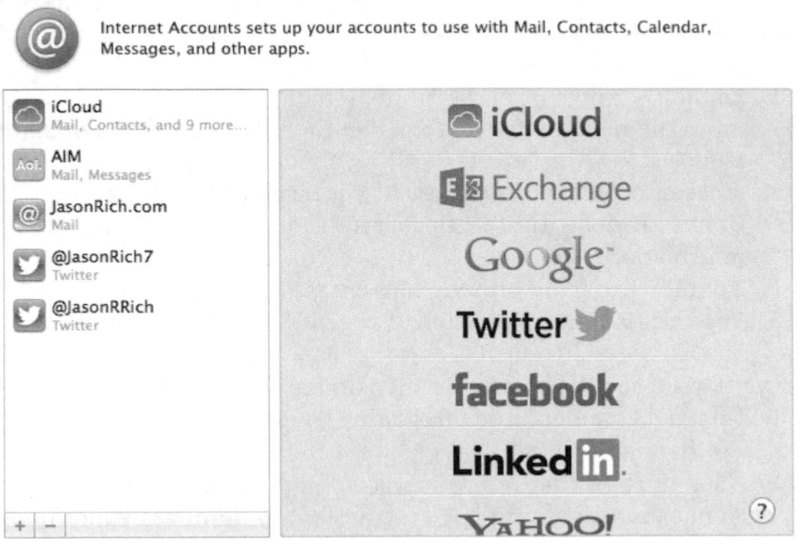

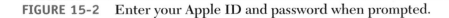

FIGURE 15-1 The Internet Accounts window within System Preferences is where you set up email accounts to work with your Mac (and the Mail app).

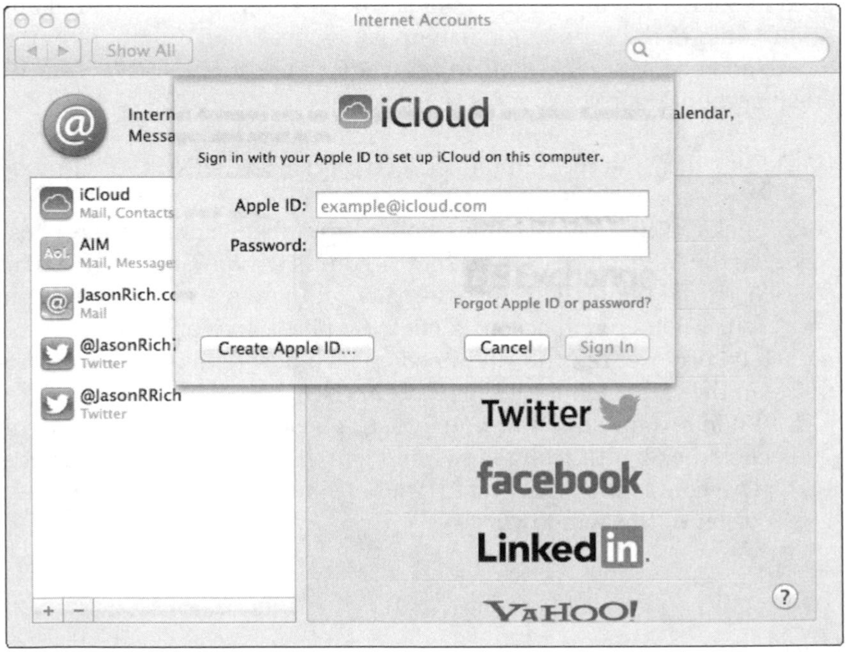

FIGURE 15-2 Enter your Apple ID and password when prompted.

On a PC that's running Windows, set up your iCloud-related email account just as you would any other IMAP email account from within Microsoft Outlook, for example. How to do this will vary based on which version of Outlook or the email software you're running.

Once you turn on iCloud's Mail feature on your computers and iOS mobile devices, everything pertaining to your iCloud-related email account will automatically remain synchronized on all of your computers, the Web, and your iOS mobile devices. Thus, if you delete a message from your Inbox on your iPhone, for example, it will automatically be deleted from your Inbox on all computers and devices.

Caution   Email messages (in your Inbox, for example) that are stored on iCloud's servers use up some of your 5GB of free online storage space that's included with your iCloud account. So if you use this email account a lot, and many emails with large attachments are stored indefinitely, your free allocated online storage space will get used up quickly, even if you're not using iCloud's other features.

Manage Your Email Account Using the Mail App on Your Mac or iOS Mobile Device

The Mail app that comes bundled with your Mac or iOS mobile device is designed to help you manage one or more email accounts, including your iCloud-related email account. This app can be used to retrieve and read incoming email messages from others, compose and send email messages, and organize your messages into folders.

With each new edition of the Mail app that Apple releases, new features are added, such as the ability to create and manage VIP lists (to view and organize incoming emails from people who are important to you) and the ability to flag individual email messages or email conversations that are important.

The Mail app is also designed to work seamlessly with other apps. For example, if you maintain a Contacts database using the Contacts app, as you're composing an outgoing email message and filling in the To field, instead of typing someone's email address, if the intended recipient has an entry in your Contacts database, and that entry already contains their email address, you can simply type the recipient's name. As you begin to type, the Mail app will suggest similar matches from people in your Contacts database, as well as people you've previously corresponded with using the Mail app.

The Mail app can also work in conjunction with the Photos app (iOS) and iPhoto app (Mac or iOS), and makes it easy to add digital photos stored on your Mac or iOS mobile device into email messages as attachments (or embedded within the message).

Tip   To learn more about how to use the Mail app on your Mac, visit www.apple.com/support/osx/mail. To discover how to use the Mail app on your iPhone, visit www.apple.com/support/iphone/mail. You can learn more about the iPad edition of the Mail app by visiting www.apple.com/support/ipad/mail.

Manage Your Email Account Using the Online Edition of the Mail App Available Through iCloud.com

Once your iCloud-related email account is set up, you can access and manage it from any computer or mobile device that has Internet access. Simply point your web browser to the iCloud.com website, log in to your iCloud account, and then click the Mail app icon. This will allow you full access to the online-based Mail app (shown in Figure 15-3).

The online-based Mail app can be used exclusively for managing your iCloud-related email account—not your other preexisting email accounts. You'll discover that as soon as you log in to the Mail app on iCloud.com, all of your emails (incoming and outgoing) are already loaded into the app, because all of this information remains synchronized and stored in the cloud as part of your iCloud account.

 As you're about to discover, managing your iCloud-related email account using the online version of the Mail app is a straightforward process, especially if you're already familiar with how to use email in general, or you know how to use the Mail app that comes with OS X Mavericks (Mac) or iOS 7 (iPhone, iPad, iPod touch).

Mail app menu icon   iCloud icon   Message listings column   Command icons   Folders (+) option   Compose message icon

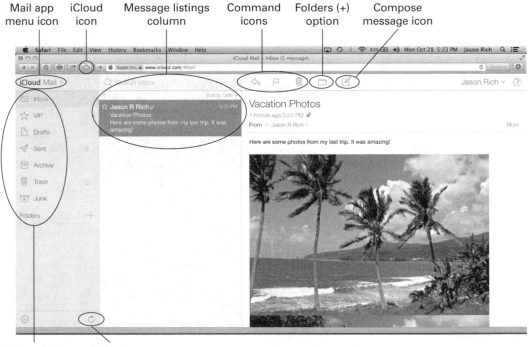

Mailbox folder menu   Refresh icon

FIGURE 15-3 The online edition of the Mail app can be accessed from www.icloud.com.

Explore the Online Edition of the Mail App's Mailbox Folders Menu

On the left side of the Mail app's browser window, you'll see your mailbox folder menu. By default, your iCloud-related email account has the following mailbox folders:

- **Inbox** This is where new incoming email messages are automatically stored and placed for your review.
- **VIP** This is a separate "smart mailbox" that displays only incoming messages from senders whom you have previously placed on your VIP list, meaning that the messages from those people are important to you.
- **Drafts** Here you can store drafts of messages you have composed or you're in the process of composing but have chosen not to send yet. As you're viewing individual messages in the Drafts folder, you can opt to send them to the intended recipients by clicking the Send button.
- **Sent** This mailbox is where all of the messages you compose and actually send from your iCloud-related email account are stored.
- **Archive** Instead of keeping all of your read messages in your Inbox, you have the option to move them to your Archive mailbox to store them for easy retrieval and keep your Inbox clutter-free.
- **Trash** When you delete a message, it gets automatically moved to the Mail app's Trash folder where it will remain until you use the Empty Trash command to permanently delete the contents of this folder.
- **Junk** This email box is where the Mail app will automatically store incoming messages that it determines are spam (unsolicited and unwanted messages). You can also manually move incoming messages from your Inbox into the Junk mailbox folder. Once you do this, all future emails from that sender will also automatically be placed in your Junk mailbox folder.

Keep in mind, any time you take any action within the online Mail app, such as delete a message, respond to a message, compose a new message, or reorganize where specific messages are stored, all of those actions will almost instantly be synced with the Mail app running on your Macs and iOS mobile devices that are linked to the same iCloud account.

Displayed between the mailbox folder menu and where the Mail app displays the contents of individual messages is a middle column that displays the contents of the selected folder, in a message preview listing format. Thus, if you click on the Inbox, for example, the contents of this middle column will be message previews for your new incoming emails that are stored in your Inbox.

Near the top of the message column are the tiny Hide All Mailboxes icon (top-left) and the Sort By option (top-right). Click the Hide All Mailboxes icon to remove the leftmost Mailbox Folder menu column from the browser window in order to free up onscreen real estate. To reorganize how the individual messages are listed within the middle messages column, click the Sort By option.

How to... Create Custom Folders to Organize Email Messages

In addition to the folders that are created by the Mail app to help you manage your iCloud-related email account, you can create your own custom folders and then move email messages into them. For example, you can create folders for work and personal messages, as well as to store messages from specific customers, clients, friends, or family members.

To create a new folder, which will then be available to you when managing your iCloud-related email account using the iCloud.com website, as well as the Mail app on your Macs or iOS mobile devices, click the Folders (+) option that's displayed near the bottom of the Mailboxes menu. When the New Folder field appears, create and enter a name for that folder, such as "Work," "Family," "Book Club," or "Friends," and then press the RETURN key.

Under the Folders (+) heading, your newly created mailbox folder will be displayed and becomes usable. From this point on, you can highlight and select individual or groups of messages from other mailbox folders and move them into the newly created folder by clicking the Move to Folder icon (which will be explained shortly).

Creating and using multiple custom folders can make it easier to organize your individual emails and your overall iCloud-related email account.

The default Sort By option is Date, meaning messages are listed chronologically based on when they were received, keeping in mind that related messages are grouped together into conversations, just as they are when using the Mail app on your Mac or iOS mobile device. However, you can also separate and sort individual emails by clicking the Flagged, From, Size, Subject, or Unread option, or choose to display the message listing in ascending or descending order.

Note When each message is listed in the messages column of the Mail app, each can display the same graphic icons to the left of the listing as in the Mail app running on a Mac or iOS mobile device. This includes the unread message dot, a star for a VIP message, a flag icon, a Reply icon, and a Forward icon. How messages are displayed and managed, in terms of making a sender of an incoming message a VIP, for example, are the same across all versions of the Mail app.

When an individual message from the middle column of the Mail app is clicked on (selected and highlighted), the complete content of that message is displayed on the right side of the Mail app browser window. Keep in mind, because you are accessing the online edition of the Mail app using your web browser (such as Safari), the Mail app is actually running within a web browser window.

Explore the Command Icons Available from the Online Mail App

To help you more efficiently work with the Mail app, near the top of the Mail app browser window are a handful of command icons, which from left to right, include:

- **iCloud Mail Menu**   This pull-down menu is located near the top-left corner of the iCloud browser window when using the online edition of the Mail app. Click on it to return to the main iCloud.com menu screen and exit out of the Mail app. Remember, anything and everything you did while using the Mail app will sync with the other versions of the Mail app you use on your Macs and iOS mobile devices.
- **Reply, Reply All, Forward**   As you're reading an incoming email, click this icon to either reply to the message (compose and send a response), use the Reply All command (compose and send a response to everyone listed in the To and Cc fields), or forward the message (send it to someone else by entering their name or email address in the To field.)
- **Flag**   Click on this icon to Flag an email as being important, mark it as Unread or move it to your email account's Junk folder.
- **Trash**   This is a temporary holding folder for messages you plan to delete. When placed in the Trash folder, a message can still be retrieved, read, or moved to another folder. However, once you use the Empty Trash command, the contents of the Trash folder will be permanently deleted. To use the Empty Trash command (from the online edition of the Mail app), click the Mail app's gear-shaped menu icon and then click the Empty Trash command.
- **Move to Folder**   When one or more email message listings are highlighted and selected, or you're viewing the contents of one email message on the right side of the Mail app's browser window, when you click this Move to Folder icon, you will have the option to move the selected messages from their current mailbox folder into another mailbox folder. For example, you can move a message from your Inbox into your Archive folder.
- **Compose**   Use this command to compose a new email message from scratch, which you will send from your iCloud-related email account. How to do this will be explained shortly.

 Use the Search field that's displayed just above the middle message column to quickly search through all emails stored in your iCloud account. You can perform searches based on any keyword, such as a subject, recipient's name, date, or a word that somehow relates to the content of the messages you're looking for.

Discover What's Available from the Mail App's Menu

By clicking on the gear-shaped menu icon that's displayed near the bottom-left corner of the Mail app's browser window (refer back to Figure 15-3), a pull-down menu with a handful of additional options will be displayed. These menu options provide you with additional functionality when managing your emails, including:

- **Preferences** Access the online Mail app's Preferences menu window and then customize specific features and functions of this app. Near the top of the Preferences window are five submenu command tabs that grant you access to additional customizable options.
- **Rules** Use this option to customize how the Mail app will handle all new incoming email messages related to your iCloud-related email account.
- **Delete Folder** Select and highlight one of the custom folders you created within the Mail app and delete it, along with its contents. Remember, deleting a folder when using the online edition of the Mail app will also result in that folder immediately being deleted from the Mail app running on our Macs or iOS mobile devices, and there's no "undo" command.
- **Empty Trash** Use this command to permanently delete the contents of the Trash folder within the Mail app.
- **Print** If there's a printer connected to the computer you're using to access the online edition of the Mail app, use the Print command to print out the email message you're currently viewing.

 As you're working with the online version of the Mail app, to refresh your Inbox and update your other Mail app-related folders, click the Refresh icon that's displayed near the bottom-left corner of the Mail app browser window. This icon looks like a circular arrow.

Compose an Email from Scratch Using the Online Edition of the Mail App

As you're working in the online edition of the Mail app, you can compose and then send an email message (which will come from your iCloud-related email account). To do this, click the Compose command icon that's displayed near the top-center of the Mail app's browser window.

A New Message window will appear (shown in Figure 15-4). Near the top of this window, you'll see To, Cc, and Subject fields, as well as the From field.

Fill in the To field with one or more recipient names or email addresses. You can separate multiple recipients using a comma, or click the plus-sign icon that's displayed to the right of the To field. The Cc field can also be used to enter the names or email addresses of additional people whom you'd like to receive the email.

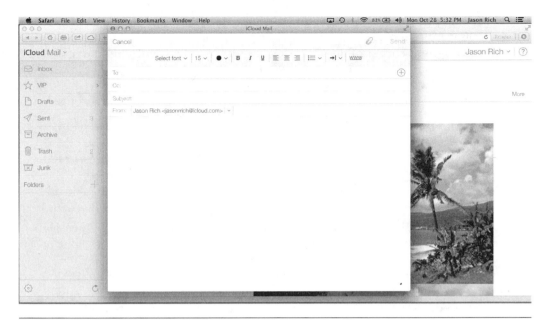

FIGURE 15-4   The New Message window appears after you click the Compose icon in the online edition of the Mail app.

Fill in the Subject field, just as you would when composing any email message. This field is used to briefly tell the recipient what your message is about.

If you have multiple iCloud-related email accounts, the From field will be displayed as a pull-down menu. Otherwise, your single iCloud-related email address will automatically be listed in the From field and it will not be changeable.

Above these empty fields in the New Message window is your formatting toolbar. Click on the paperclip-shaped icon, for example, to add an attachment to your outgoing mail, and use the other formatting options to adjust the font, font size, font color, typestyle, and paragraph justification of the text within the body of your outgoing message. You can also add bulleted or numbered lists, as well as use the Indent option to indent text as needed. Click on the www icon to manage Internet-related hyperlinks that will be part of your email message.

Tip   As you're composing a new email, if you want to save the outgoing message without first sending it, click the Save button. The message will be stored in your Drafts mailbox folder, but will not be sent to the intended recipient until you click the Send button.

Once your message is composed and you've attached whatever files or images you want to include with that message, click the Send button, which is displayed near the top-right corner of the New Message window. This will send the message via your iCloud-related email account to the intended recipients. A copy of that outgoing email message will automatically be saved in the Sent mailbox folder that's associated with this email account.

iCloud Represents an Ongoing Evolution in Cloud-Based Computing

If you read the first edition of *How to Do Everything: iCloud* and are now just about finished reading this all-new second edition of the book as well, you've probably discovered that during the time between the two editions Apple's iCloud service has evolved and improved a lot. This evolution continues.

In the weeks, months, and years ahead, as new versions of the OS X operating system for the Mac and the iOS operating system for the iPhone, iPad, and iPod touch are released by Apple, you'll discover exciting new ways you can use cloud-based computing to allow your computers and mobile devices to work more seamlessly together.

You'll also gain access to cutting-edge new ways to share app-specific data, such as photos and documents, with other people, and be able to more easily collaborate with those people in an online environment. At the same time, Apple will continue to introduce new tools for sharing purchased iTunes Store and related content (including TV shows, movies, music, music videos, ringtones, apps, ebooks, podcasts, audiobooks, etc.) between your computers, mobile devices, and Apple TV using iCloud.

In between and in conjunction with when Apple releases major updates to its operating systems, the iCloud.com website will also continue to undergo improvements, as new features and functions are added that give you greater access and more control over the content, data, and files you have stored in the cloud in your iCloud account. You'll also see third-party app developers adding iCloud functionality into their popular Mac and iOS apps.

So, while iCloud is already a feature-packed and robust cloud-based computing environment, what the future holds for this service is nothing short of exciting. Keep in mind that while iCloud can be used to handle a wide range of different tasks, as a Mac, iPhone, iPad, and/or iPod touch user, you are not obligated to use all of these features and functions. You have the ability to turn on the iCloud-related features and functions you want to utilize, and turn off the ones you don't. Then, as your wants and needs change, or as you acquire new Apple equipment, you can change these settings at any time.

More Ways to Use iCloud Are in the Works

According to rumors, Apple is hard at work developing stand-alone HD televisions that will incorporate Apple TV functionality that's available right now, plus a wide range of other on-demand and live broadcast programming features and functions.

Plus, there are also widespread rumors that Apple will be releasing the iWatch, an iOS mobile device that can be worn around your wrist. Meanwhile, right now, a handful of car manufacturers, including GM, are building iPhone integration into the in-dash infotainment systems of their 2014 and 2015 model-year vehicles. These same car manufacturers have announced plans to incorporate 4G LTE cellular data connectivity directly into new vehicles starting in 2014 or 2015. This will allow vehicles to access the Internet directly, and potentially access content and data directly from your iCloud account in conjunction with the iOS in the Car and Siri Eyes Free functionality that Apple is working with the various car manufacturers to develop and perfect.

As a result of these and other technological developments, in the years ahead, you'll no doubt want and need to access your content and information related to your iCloud account in entirely new ways that will make you more efficient as you handle your everyday computing needs.

At this point in time, the future of computing is "in the cloud." By utilizing your free iCloud account immediately, you're stepping into the future by using a wide range of iCloud-related tools, features, and functions that are available today.

A

Troubleshoot iCloud-Related Problems

Apple's iCloud service is designed to make seamless connectivity between computers and iOS mobile devices easy via the Internet, allowing for data, files, documents, photos, and other content to be synchronized and shared behind the scenes and primarily without user intervention. Like anything else that's technologically complex, when iCloud works, it works well. But when something isn't set up correctly, it doesn't work as expected (or at all).

What to Do if iCloud Doesn't Work as Expected

Perhaps the most common reason why iCloud doesn't function as expected is because the user didn't properly set up iCloud to work on each of his or her computers and iOS mobile devices. Remember that you need to set up an iCloud account, and then turn on iCloud connectivity on each of your computers and mobile devices separately. As you do this, the same Apple ID and password must be used on each computer.

Then, in many cases, you also need to turn on iCloud functionality for specific software or applications, and for specific iCloud features and functions to work. Plus, each of your computers and iOS mobile devices needs access to the Internet. So if you're experiencing problems with iCloud, ask yourself the following questions:

- Did I set up an iCloud account correctly?
- Did I turn on iCloud functionality on each of my Macs and/or PCs using the same Apple ID and password (that is, the same iCloud account information) that I used on my primary computer?
- Did I turn on iCloud functionality on my iPhone, iPad, or iPod touch using the same Apple ID and password (that is, the same iCloud account information) that I used on my primary computer?

- On each computer and iOS mobile device, did I turn on the iCloud features or functions that I want to use from the iCloud Control Panel within Settings (iOS) or System Preferences (Mac)?
- On each computer and iOS mobile device, is the same assortment of iCloud features and functions turned on? (If Contacts or Calendar is activated only on your Mac and not on your iPhone, for example, those two devices will not be able to sync Contacts or Calendar app data via iCloud.)
- On each computer and iOS mobile device, did I turn on iCloud functionality for specific apps? (Remember, in addition to turning on the Documents & Data feature within Settings on your iOS device, for example, you also need to turn on iCloud functionality for Pages, Numbers, and Keynote separately, from within the app-specific menus of Settings. When using the Mac versions of the iWork apps, you also need to turn on iCloud functionality from within each app.)
- Are my computers and iOS mobile devices currently connected to the Internet?
- Am I using a Wi-Fi Internet connection on my iOS devices for iCloud-related tasks that do not work with a 3G or 4G LTE cellular data connection? These include My Photo Stream, Shared Photo Streams, iCloud Backup, or downloading large content files (such as TV show episodes or movies) from iCloud that were iTunes Store purchases. Even if everything is set up correctly, your iPhone or iPad will not handle certain tasks if no Wi-Fi Internet connection is available. Likewise, iCloud Backup will not work unless your iOS mobile device is also plugged in to an external power source.

Chances are, if you're experiencing a problem with iCloud or iCloud's ability to transfer, share, or synchronize data, documents, files, photos, or content among computers and devices via the Web, you answered "no" to at least one of these questions.

However, if after addressing these issues, you're still experiencing a problem, make sure you're running the most recent version of the OS X Mavericks operating system on your Mac; the most recent version of iOS 7 on your iPhone, iPad, or iPod touch; the latest version of the operating system on your Apple TV; version 11.1 or later of the iTunes software on your Mac or PC; the latest version of the iCloud Control Panel on your Windows-based PC; and the latest versions of whatever apps you're trying to use with iCloud (such as Pages, Keynote, or Numbers).

Another "quick fix" to many serious iCloud problems is to remove iCloud from your various computers or devices from within Settings (iPhone/iPad) or System Preferences (Mac), and then reactivate the iCloud account using the same account information. If you're not comfortable doing this yourself, make an appointment at any Apple Store to meet with an Apple Genius or call Apple's toll-free AppleCare support phone number.

Tip If iCloud still isn't functioning as expected, call AppleCare's toll-free phone number for technical support at (800) APL-CARE (800-275-2273), or make an appointment with an Apple Genius at any Apple Store. You might also find the answers you need from Apple's Support website (www.apple.com/support). When making an Apple Genius reservation, a valid Apple ID is required.

Avoid Accidentally Overwriting One File Version with Another

With so much syncing going on among your computers and iOS mobile devices, the goal is for you to have access to the most recent versions of your data, documents, files, photos, and content any time and from any computer or device you're using.

Especially if you're using iCloud's Documents in the Cloud capabilities and iWork for iCloud to sync Pages, Numbers, and Keynote files, as soon as you make any change to any file or document, it will impact that file on all of your computers and devices almost instantly. Or, if you delete a Pages, Numbers, or Keynote file, it will be erased from all of your computers and devices almost instantly (not just from the computer or device you're presently using). This is also true with Contacts and Calendar entries, Reminders lists, and content from the Notes app, as well as with Safari content and ebook bookmarks and annotations, for example.

Note If you're running Time Machine on your Mac, or you've recently performed a backup of your iOS mobile device via iTunes Sync, Wireless iTunes Sync, or iCloud Backup, you can always revert back to an older version of a file from the backup data.

One way to prevent a file from accidentally being modified or deleted is to create a copy of that file on the computer or device you're using before you start working with it. This will result in the original file remaining intact on iCloud and on all of your computers and devices. However, the copy of the file you make and ultimately work with will be synchronized and shared with your other computers and devices as well. You can delete the original version of the file later if you want.

To make a copy, do the following:

1. As you're using Pages, Numbers, or Keynote, from the Document Manager screen of these apps when you're using them on an iPhone, iPad, or iPod touch, tap the Edit icon.
2. When all of the thumbnails (representing your documents or files) start to shake, tap the thumbnail for the document or file you want to edit or work with. A yellow frame will appear around it.
3. Tap the Copy command icon near the upper-left corner of the screen. A duplicate of the original file or document will be created and displayed on the Document Manager screen. It will have the same filename as the original file, but the word "copy" will be added to the filename. (You can always modify the filename from the Document Manager screen.)

Tip If you're concerned about accidentally erasing a file or document, or making changes that you don't want applied to all versions of a file or document that are accessible on all of your computers and iOS mobile devices via iCloud, consider temporarily turning off iCloud functionality for that app or on that device, and then turning it back on when you're ready for the files or documents to synchronize.

What to Do if You Forget Your iCloud Account Information

Apple strongly advises you to use your Apple ID and password when creating and using an iCloud account, and to maintain just one Apple ID account to use all of Apple's services that require your Apple ID information.

 If you've forgotten your Apple ID altogether, visit https://appleid.apple.com. For information about how to manage your Apple ID account (and retrieve your Apple ID and/or password), visit http://support.apple.com/kb/HE34. Once you rediscover your Apple ID, you can use the Reset Your Password option to retrieve or change the related password as well. The My Apple ID web page can also be accessed directly by pointing your web browser to https://iforgot.apple.com.

When prompted, enter your Apple ID, and the website will help you retrieve the related password. Or, if you've forgotten your Apple ID, click the Forgot Your Apple ID option below the Apple ID field. Follow the onscreen prompts to retrieve your Apple ID and/or password.

 You can also access the My Apple ID web page to change your Apple ID password, which is something you should do periodically for security purposes.

From your Mac, if you know your Apple ID but can't remember the password, do the following:

1. Launch System Preferences from the Dock or Applications folder.
2. Click the iCloud option. From the iCloud Control Panel within System Preferences, click the Manage button near the lower-right corner of the window.
3. Click the View Account button near the lower-left corner of the Manage Storage window. Your Apple ID will be displayed, but next to the Password field will be a Forgot? option. Click it to retrieve your forgotten Apple ID or iCloud password.

 If you're a Windows-based PC user, the preceding Apple ID/iCloud password retrieval method also works from the iCloud Control Panel, as long as the computer is connected to the Internet.

Index

Also from author Jason Rich

Print edition ISBN: 978-0-07-180333-5
e-book ISBN: 978-0-07-180334-2

Available from mhprofessional.com
and booksellers everywhere